Law and Philosophy Library

Volume 120

The Law and Philosophy Library, which has been in existence since 1985, aims to publish cutting edge works in the philosophy of law, and has a special history of publishing books that focus on legal reasoning and argumentation, including those that may involve somewhat formal methodologies. The series has published numerous important books on law and logic, law and artificial intelligence, law and language, and law and rhetoric. While continuing to stress these areas, the series has more recently expanded to include books on the intersection between law and the Continental philosophical tradition, consistent with the traditional openness of the series to books in the Continental jurisprudential tradition. The series is proud of the geographic diversity of its authors, and many have come from Latin America, Spain, Italy, the Netherlands, Germany, and Eastern Europe, as well, more obviously for an English-language series, from the United Kingdom, the United States, Australia, and Canada.

More information about this series at http://www.springer.com/series/6210

Bartosz Brożek • Antonino Rotolo • Jerzy Stelmach
Editors

Supervenience and Normativity

Springer

Editors
Bartosz Brożek
Faculty of Law and Administration
Jagiellonian University
Kraków, Poland

Antonino Rotolo
CIRSFID - Faculty of Law
University of Bologna
Bologna, Italy

Jerzy Stelmach
Faculty of Law and Administration
Jagiellonian University
Kraków, Poland

ISSN 1572-4395 ISSN 2215-0315 (electronic)
Law and Philosophy Library
ISBN 978-3-319-61045-0 ISBN 978-3-319-61046-7 (eBook)
DOI 10.1007/978-3-319-61046-7

Library of Congress Control Number: 2017948916

Printed on acid-free paper

This Springer imprint is published by Springer Nature
The registered company is Springer International Publishing AG
The registered company address is: Gewerbestrasse 11, 6330 Cham, Switzerland

Preface

Recently, there has been a renewed interest in the relationship between the concepts of normativity and supervenience. The research on normativity – a term introduced to the philosophical jargon by Edmund Husserl almost one hundred years ago – gained impetus in the 1990s through the works of philosophers such as Robert Audi, Christine Korsgaard, Robert Brandom, Paul Boghossian and Joseph Raz. The problem of the nature and sources of normativity has been investigated not only in morals and in relation to language but also in other domains, e.g. in law or in the context of the theories of rationality. Supervenience, understood as a special kind of relation between properties and weaker than entailment, has become analytic philosophers' formal tool of choice since the 1980s. It features in the theories pertaining to mental properties, but also in aesthetics or the law. It is no surprise that it has also been extensively used to account for the nature of normative properties or normative and evaluative discourse. On the one hand, it may help a moral or a legal philosopher to avoid the Scylla of the "queer" realism and the Charybdis of reductionism. On the other, it is usually claimed that the relation of supervenience is – at least to a certain extent – ontologically neutral; hence, it does not force any particular ontological view. In recent years, the 'marriage' of normativity and supervenience has become an object of many philosophical theories as well as heated debates. It seems that the conceptual apparatus of the supervenience theory makes it possible to state precisely some claims pertaining to normativity, as well as illuminate the problems surrounding it. For example, it seems *prima facie* possible – with the use of the concept of supervenience – to explain how the normative dimension of law and morals is related to physical facts, and avoid the claim that there exists an 'unavoidable gap' between Is and Ought; or to show where normativity, which undoubtedly forms an important part of our experience, fits into a general naturalistic view of the world; or to argue that, as many believe, the law must involve both an ideal and a factual component, without embracing a strange view of the composite ontological nature of legal phenomena. Of course there is no guarantee that the concept of supervenience does indeed constitute the key to the fundamental problems mentioned above. However, given the theoretical promise which comes together with its introduction, it is only reasonable to investigate the possibilities it opens.

This collection represents an attempt to bring together several contributions to the ongoing debate pertaining to normative supervenience. The controversies surrounding the idea of normative supervenience and the philosophical conceptions they generated deserve a recapitulation, as well as a new impulse for further development. The first two essays in the collection are more general, since they concern some logical and epistemological issues. Antonino Rotolo in 'Logics for Normative Supervenience' analyses some formal aspects of the relation of normative supervenience. He argues that normative supervenience can be viewed as a kind of entailment when nonclassical consequence relations are taken into account. Further, he shows that 'counts-as' relations may be treated as an interesting type of normative supervenience. Finally, he argues that modal logics for the Ought change the formal behaviour of standard definitions of weak and strong supervenience. Giorgio Volpe in his 'Propositional and Doxastic Justification: Their Relationship and a Questionable Supervenience Claim' considers the relationship between propositional and doxastic justification. He argues against a recent claim that the propositional justification depends on the doxastic; at the same time, he augments the traditional view by claiming that there is an important sense in which facts concerning epistemic justification supervene not merely on facts concerning the evidential states of agents but on facts concerning their overall doxastic states.

The second part of the volume is centred around the significance of normative supervenience for discussions in ethics, and in particular the relationship between the supervenience thesis and moral realism. Robert Audi in 'Moral Properties: Some Epistemological, Ontological and Normative Dimensions' underscores the 'dual character' of moral properties, which seem perfectly legitimate in everyday discourse but pose a challenge when analysed from a philosophical perspective. He argues, however, that the same applies not only to moral terms but also to psychological discourse and even to (some part of) the physical idiom. This parity leads Audi to formulate an indirect argument for moral realism. Daniel Laurier in 'Reasons and Supervenience' introduces a distinction between a weaker and a stronger sense in which something may be said to be normative, as well as a distinction between conceptual and metaphysical versions of what is known as 'individual' supervenience. He further explains why one should concentrate on the conceptual supervenience claims and discusses the plausibility of various such claims concerning concepts that can be constructed out of the concept of a (normative) reason. Finally, he argues that reasons-concepts of a certain kind conceptually supervene on mental ones and that this is compatible with a form of realism with respect to reasons-propositions. Gerald Harrison in 'The Dubious Moral Supervenience Thesis' argues that the assault on moral realism from the perspective of the proponents of moral supervenience fails. He argues, first, that the three considerations in favour of the global moral supervenience, i.e. the grounding concern, the horrendous deeds concern and the normative authority concern, are all flawed. He then considers the local moral supervenience thesis and claims it is false, which only adds justification to the rejection of the global moral supervenience thesis. In turn, Carla Bagnoli, in her essay 'The Supervenience Dilemma Explained Away', delves into the discussion surrounding normative supervenience in the context of moral realism. She criticises David Enoch's defence of robust moral realism in terms of the explanatory role of moral principles and suggests a constructivist explication of the epistemic and ontological role of normative principles, which proves the notion of supervenience to be redundant.

The final part of the book is concerned with normative supervenience and related concepts in the law. Bartosz Brożek in 'Law, Normativity and Supervenience' argues that the supervenience thesis, i.e. the claim that legal properties supervene on some psychological or sociological facts, has a serious limitation – it cannot explain the normative force of legal rules but rather presupposes it. Considered from a more general philosophical perspective, this result suggests that the relation of supervenience fails to fully account for the existence of the normative sphere – a normative criterion of some sort is logically prior to the establishment of the supervenience relation. In 'The Metaphysics of Law: From Supervenience to Rational Justification', George Pavlakos challenges the view that the metaphysical grounding of the law – in contrast to other domains – requires a special legal grounding relation, which involves the condition of rational determination. He argues that rational determination ought to be extended to all metaphysical grounding, for otherwise general metaphysical grounding would easily deteriorate to supervenience, which has already been rejected as a plausible basis of the grounding relation by many a contemporary metaphysician. What is special about the metaphysics of law is not the general framework of grounding through rational determination, but the engagement in a rational reconstruction of legal facts in terms of their capacity to generate normative reasons for action. Finally, Łukasz Kurek in 'Supervenience and the Normativity of Folk Psychology in the Legal-Philosophical Context' analyses the role of folk psychology – understood as a mechanism of ascribing mental states to others – in the law. He argues that despite criticism, the claim that folk psychological conceptual apparatus supervenes on the physical processes is defendable; hence there is no need to remodel the legal conceptual scheme, which is largely based on folk psychology.

The papers collected in this volume have been prepared within the research project, 'The Limits of Scientific Explanation', carried out by Copernicus Center for Interdisciplinary Studies in Kraków and sponsored by John Templeton Foundation.

Kraków, Poland — Bartosz Brożek
Bologna, Italy — Antonino Rotolo
Kraków, Poland — Jerzy Stelmach

Contents

Logics for Normative Supervenience 1
Antonino Rotolo

Propositional and Doxastic Justification: Their Relationship and a Questionable Supervenience Claim 25
Giorgio Volpe

Moral Properties: Some Epistemological, Ontological, and Normative Dimensions 49
Robert Audi

Reasons and Supervenience 67
Daniel Laurier

The Dubious Moral Supervenience Thesis 89
Gerald K. Harrison

The Supervenience Dilemma Explained Away 105
Carla Bagnoli

Law, Normativity, and Supervenience 123
Bartosz Brożek

The Metaphysics of Law: From Supervenience to Rational Justification 139
George Pavlakos

Supervenience and the Normativity of Folk Psychology in the Legal-Philosophical Context 161
Łukasz Kurek

Logics for Normative Supervenience

Antonino Rotolo

> *One virtue is that the plurality of the consequence relation comes at little or no cost. Another is that pluralism offers a more charitable interpretation of many important (but difficult) debates in philosophical logic than is otherwise available; [...] pluralism does more justice to the mix of insight and perplexity found in many of the debates in logic in the last century.*
>
> (Beall and Restall 2000, 31)

Abstract This essay addresses the problem of logically modelling the concept of normative supervenience. We will argue that alternatives of classical logic can grasp specific aspects of this concept. We will examine two cases: (a) the idea of institutional supervenience corresponding to the counts-as relation, (b) modal logics for jumping or generating the normative dimension of supervenient properties.

1 Introduction: Assumption I – A Plurality of Logics for Normative Supervenience

This essay addresses the problem of modelling forms of normative supervenience (hereafter, NS) from the logical point of view. We will offer in Sect. 2 some clarifications on what we mean by *normative* supervenience.[1] For the moment, let us assume that NS is a special case of the very general idea of supervenience.

[1]More intuitions are of course offered in the other essays in this volume.

A. Rotolo (✉)
CIRSFID, University of Bologna, Bologna, Italy
e-mail: antonino.rotolo@unibo.it

B. Brożek et al. (eds.), *Supervenience and Normativity*, Law and Philosophy Library 120, DOI 10.1007/978-3-319-61046-7_1

With this said, a natural way of logically modelling NS would argue that this relation corresponds to a form of entailment. However, convincing counter-arguments in the literature have been proposed showing that the supervenience relation is in general *different* from entailment (cf. McLaughlin 1995). Indeed, despite the fact that supervenience apparently shares with entailment formal properties, such as reflexivity,[2] transitivity, and non-symmetry, if we take the sets of properties A and B we have that (McLaughlin and Bennett 2014, par. 3.2)

- **entailment does not suffice for supervenience**, since there are cases where B entails A but A does not supervene on B; for example, possessing the property of being a brother entails possessing the property of being a sibling, but being a sibling does not supervene on being a brother;
- **supervenience does not suffice for entailment**, since there are cases where A supervenes on B but B does not imply A; for example, thermal conductivity properties do not entail electrical conductivity properties.

The above approach is apparently irrefutable, but much depends on what we mean by the concept of *entailment*: if it corresponds to the consequence relation of classical logic, we agree with the mainstream literature on the idea that supervenience is not entailment. However, logicians are familiar with the thesis that more logical paradigms can be developed, and that logical pluralism is a suitable option for analysing hard concepts (cf. Beall and Restall 2000):

Definition 1 (Logical pluralism (Informal)) Logical pluralism is the thesis that there is more than one correct logical consequence relation.

From the operational viewpoint, this approach amounts to

1. creating a suitable logical system that is able to capture our philosophical intuitions about the concept of NS, and
2. checking whether conclusions and properties of the system are reasonable in our theory.

This is what we will do in this essay by considering two different philosophical aspects related to the idea of normative supervenience and thus developing two different suitable logical systems.

Our methodological perspective is not new. Humberstone (1993, 2002) offered a route where a non-classical consequence relation does the job.

Definition 2 (Inference-determined vs supervenience-determined consequence relation; Humberstone 1993, 2002) Let $\mathscr{V}$ be a set of valuations.

- **A consequence relation inference-determined by** $\mathscr{V}$ is as follows:

$$\Gamma \models^{I}_{\mathscr{V}} A$$

iff, if for all $v \in \mathscr{V}$ and all $B \in \Gamma$, $v(B) = T$ then $v(A) = T$;

[2] We will discuss later some complexities behind reflexivity.

- **A consequence relation supervenience-determined by $\mathscr{V}$** is as follows:

$$\Gamma \models^{S}_{\mathscr{V}} A$$

iff, for all $v, z \in \mathscr{V}$ and all $B \in \Gamma$, if $v(B) = z(B)$ then $v(A) = z(A)$.

The second type of consequence relation, among the other things, is meant to capture the idea of co-variance, something which characterises the concept of supervenience, but which seems not correctly expressed by classical logical entailment.

We will not directly work on Definition 2, but our analysis falls indeed within the same general approach.

2 Introduction: Assumption II – Supervenience of the Normative vs Normative Supervenience

Let us assume that normative properties are generically those properties that constitute being what one ought to do.[3] If so, a simple preliminary definition relating supervenience and normativity can be the following:

Definition 3 (Supervenience and normativity (Version I)) NS is a binary relation between properties such that normative properties of kind A supervene on non-normative properties of kind B.

From the logical point of view, this definition has the advantage of relating NS to the general relation of supervenience: what makes NS *normative* is simply the fact that the supervenient properties are normative. Definition 3 is pictorially illustrated by Fig. 1. This would formally mean to distinguish two sorts of predicates. However, such a definition can be seen as problematic for those who dispute about the plausibility of normative properties or about the fact that such properties are intuitively, and fundamentally distinguishable, e.g., from the natural ones.

Fig. 1 Supervenience and normativity (Version I: Definition 3)

[3]Notice that this assumption is generic and it does not necessarily mean that individual normative properties directly provide grounds for single prescriptive statements. We simply assume that such properties are normative insofar as they are true in the context of ideal worlds. For instance, one can argue that the sentence "This piece of paper counts as a five euro bill" is normative without directly stating that something here is obligatory: indeed, this sentence presupposes the existence of a certain human institution which (i) refers to a set of ideal worlds where some properties apply to certain individuals, (ii) is globally oriented to guide human behaviour (see Sect. 4).

A rather different way for defining NS does not amount to partitioning the set of predicates into two sorts, but to identifying a *normative way* through which possible worlds (where predicates are made true of individuals) are related—as standardly done in possible-world semantics for deontic logic (cf. Gabbay et al. 2013).

Definition 4 (Supervenience and normativity (Version II)) NS is a logical entailment that makes properties normative and that corresponds to ways for identifying the set of normative possible worlds (normative necessity).

We can thus distinguish two concepts of NS:

- NS in a broad sense, or **supervenience of the normative**, as proposed in Definition 3;
- NS *strictu sensu*, **normative supervenience**, as proposed in Definition 4.

We will technically explain in the subsequent sections how the idea in Definition 4 can be framed to reconstruct the concept of NS. Here it suffices to say that normative properties in any world *w* are nothing but those properties that are true of individuals in worlds that are selected as the most-preferred (or ideal) ones with respect to *w*: hereafter, NS will be denoting the concept of normative supervenience of Definition 4.

The basic philosophical and logical move behind NS is pictorially rendered in Fig. 2.

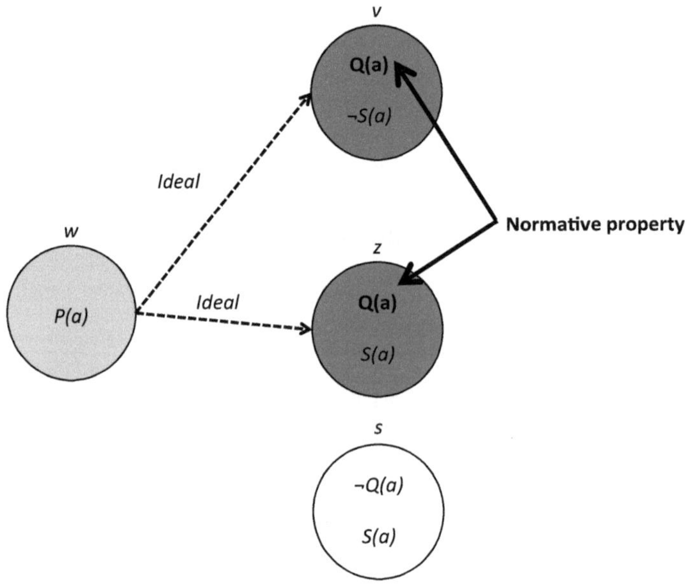

Fig. 2 Supervenience and normativity (Version II: Definition 4)

Figure 2 shows four possible worlds w, v, z, and s. The worlds v and z are normatively ideal with respect to w, while s is not. In v and z the individual a is Q, thus Q can be seen as a normative property with respect to w and a. We will show how this idea is suitable for defining Q as supervenient, e.g., with respect to P.

3 Layout of this Essay

In this essay we will see how alternatives of classical logic can grasp specific aspects of NS.

- Our assumptions are:
  - Formal aspects of supervenience can be captured by suitable forms of non-classical entailment;
  - Supervenience-based entailment is modelled as NS and not as supervenience of the normative.
- We will examine two cases:
  - The idea of institutional supervenience corresponding to the *counts-as relation*;
  - A meta-theory of NS and different *modal logics for jumping or generating the normative dimension of supervenient properties*.

4 The Counts-As Relation

4.1 Introduction

John Searle famously introduced the counts-as relation in the context of his theory of the rule-based nature of social institutions (Searle 1969, 51–52):

> A marriage ceremony, a baseball game, a trial, and a legislative action involve a variety of physical movements, states, and raw feels, but a specification of one of these events only in such terms is not so far a specification of it as a marriage ceremony, baseball game, a trial, or a legislative action. The physical events and raw feels only count as parts of such events given certain other conditions and against a background of certain kinds of institutions. Such facts as are recorded in my above group of statements I propose to call institutional facts. They are indeed facts; but their existence, unlike the existence of brute facts, presupposes the existence of certain human institutions. [...] These "institutions" are systems of constitutive rules. Every institutional fact is underlain by a (system of) rule(s) of the form "X counts as Y in context C." Our hypothesis that speaking a language is performing acts according to constitutive rules involves us in the hypothesis that the fact that a man performed a certain speech act, e.g. made a promise, is an institutional fact.

In other words, institutions emerge from an independent ontology of "brute", natural facts through *constitutive rules* of the mentioned counts-as form "X counts as Y in context C", where X is any object satisfying certain conditions and Y is a label that qualifies *X* as being something of an entirely new sort. In Searle's terms, these rules may be seen as assigning a status to *X*, and with it, a function that *X* does not already have before just in virtue of its being an *X*. Systems of such kind of rules, which are more or less implicit ingredients of stable social practices, "create the very possibility of certain activities" within those systems (Searle 1995, 28).[4]

To sum up:

Definition 5 (Informal 1; Searle 1969, 1995) The *counts-as* (constitutive) *rules* have the following canonical form:

X COUNTS AS *Y* in the context *C*

where, typically, *X* denotes a "brute" fact and *Y* an "institutional" fact.

Definition 6 (Informal 2; Searle 1969, 1995) The *counts-as rules* establish a *counts-as relation* that assigns a status *Y* to *X*, and with it, a function that *X* does not already have before just in virtue of its being an *X*.

Two paradigmatic examples of counts-as relations are

This piece of paper counts as a five euro bill (1)

X counts as a presiding official in a wedding ceremony. (2)

The most we formally learn from Searle (1995, 28, 44, 45) is that

1. counts-as contexts are *intensional* in the usual sense of failing the substitutivity test, and
2. the *X* and *Y* terms in the counts-as relation are *causally unrelated*.

These properties seem to capture crucial features of Searle's counts-as construction. For example, if *X*= 'US president's declaration' and this counts as a certain *Y*, it is not hard to understand that 'Donald Trump's declaration' in itself may not count as *Y* since Trump's declaration is institutionally relevant insofar as Donald Trump is the president of US. Also point 2 is reasonable, especially when we consider the peculiarities of institutional ontology as opposed to the domain of brute (empirical)

[4]As Searle (1995) strongly emphasises, in all such cases the ascription of a status-function through the appropriate rule is not enough to establish such types of facts. To establish these facts we have to believe, or otherwise accept, acknowledge, collectively intend, etc., that *X* has the status-function assigned by the corresponding rules. This means that, in order to do their job these rules have to be agreed upon or believed in by members of the relevant community *qua* members of a collective. The reason for this is that it is a merely contingent fact that some *X* stands in a certain counts-as relation to some *Y*, because the only connection between *X* and *Y* obtains in virtue of collective belief or acceptance, and intention—or, to put it in Searle's words, satisfying the *X* term *is not by itself sufficient* for being money, and the *X* term does not specify causal features that would be sufficient to enable the stuff to function as money. In order to function as money, human agreement has to be involved. Roughly, this is nothing but the idea that the ontology of institutional facts relies on a kind of "epistemic objectivity".

facts. In this perspective, a US president's declaration is not a causal reason for obtaining Y. In fact, Searle does not seem to argue that the occurrence of X determines the existence of Y along with a broad causal interpretation of constitutive rules (Searle 2001, sec. II): these simply specify the "constitutive features of the *actuality* [...] of [...] institutional facts".[5]

This analysis offers some general directions for clarifying the logical nature of counts-as link:

- First, since the counts-as relation is intensional, it can be reconstructed in the context of modal logics; this thesis is in line with most literature on supervenience and, more specifically, with the intuition we have proposed in Sect. 2, according to which NS corresponds to a normative way through which we select ideal worlds;
- Second, since the counts-as relation does not correspond to a causal link, its logical reconstruction cannot enjoy the same formal properties that causal relations usually have; we will see that Searle's view is just an option and that alternative philosophical (and logical) views are possible. Such alternatives are perhaps better for reconstructing the counts-as relation as NS.

4.2 Is the Counts-As Relation a Type of NS?

The counts-as link exhibits some intuitive similarities with supervenience. Consider this legal example:

Electronic signature COUNTS AS handwritten signature
IN CONTEXT Italian contract law

Indeed, for the sake of illustration let us now assume the following standard definitions:

Definition 7 (Indiscernibility and Weak Supervenience (Kim 1993))

Indiscernibility: If B is a set of properties, any two individuals x and y are *B-indiscernible* iff $P(x) \rightarrow P(y)$ for all P's belonging to B.

Weak supervenience: B-properties weakly supervene on A-properties iff, for any two individuals x and y that belong to the same possible world w, if x and y are A-indiscernible in w, then they are also B-indiscernible in w.

[5]It would sound perhaps more reasonable to emphasise the causal role that mental attitudes, such as collective intentionality, play in bringing into existence institutional reality. But even in this case, Searle (2001, sec. II) argues that "collective intentionality is not something which just causes institutional reality, it is constitutive of that reality precisely because it is constitutive of the ontology according to the constitutive rules".

The just mentioned legal example illustrates well at what extent counts-as relations are similar to (weak) supervenience (McLaughlin 1995). Indeed, if we consider any two individuals x and y, we can conceptually admit the following cases (*Esign* and *Hsign* stand for electronic signature and handwritten signature, respectively):

$$\begin{array}{ll} 1.\ Esign(x), Esign(y) & Hsign(x), Hsign(y) \\ 2.\ \neg Esign(x), \neg Esign(y) & Hsign(x), Hsign(y) \\ 3.\ \neg Esign(x), \neg Esign(y) & \neg Hsign(x), \neg Hsign(y) \end{array}$$

Given Definition 7, these cases are *formally* admissible.

What about the following?

$$\begin{array}{ll} 4.\ Esign(x), \neg Esign(y) & Hsign(x), Hsign(y) \\ 5.\ \neg Esign(x), \neg Esign(y) & \neg Hsign(x), Hsign(y) \end{array}$$

These cases should be in principle ruled out, as they do not meet Definition 7. In addition, individuals y (case 4.) and x (case 5.) either

(a) are true instances of handwritten signatures: they are not electronic signatures because they are just brute handwritten signatures; or
(b) are not even brute instances of handwritten signatures (but, e.g., smoke signals): i.e., the fact that they count as handwritten signatures depends on a different counts-as relation (e.g., stating that smoke signals count as handwritten signatures).

The second case does not help here, as it simply refers to another counts-as rule. The first case, instead, suggests that we should reject that, for any property P, P's count as P's, especially if P is not an institutional property. Hence, under the analysis above, case 2., too, should be ruled out: if so, the remaining cases for the counts-as relation satisfy Definition 7.[6]

In the specific legal example, if we use $\Rightarrow$ to denote the counts-as link

$$Hsign(x) \Rightarrow Hsign(x)$$

must be assumed to be invalid. In other words, under the hypothesis that the counts-as link is NS, whenever brute facts are related with institutional facts we have to reject the general view (McLaughlin and Bennett 2014, par. 3.2) that NS is reflexive as the classical logical entailment instead is: if the counts-as must ensure co-variance and thus is genuine NS, it may be argued that counts-as relations do not enjoy the following schema:

$$A \Rightarrow A. \qquad \text{(Reflexivity)}$$

[6]In addition to the intuitive observation that cases 2., 4., and 5. speak of being a handwritten signature as a brute fact, we should also recall that NS, in the sense of Definition 4, does not rely on distinguishing in the formal language different sorts of predicates or propositional letters.

4.3 A Formal Analysis of the Counts-As Relation

The logical nature of counts-as rules has been investigated following several directions (for e general overview, cf. Grossi and Jones 2013). Here, we will consider two options that express the counts-as link as a non-classical (modal) conditional.[7]

In their seminal paper, Jones and Sergot (1996) develop an analysis of the notion of institutionalised power by introducing a new conditional connective '$\Rightarrow_s$'. This connective expresses the counts-as connection holding in the context of an institution s. In short, this approach is roughly in line with Goldman's theory of actions generating actions (Goldman 1970). In this perspective, it may be argued that the generation of institutional facts via counts-as rules is quite close to the idea of a causal relation—contrary to Searle's argument—and assumes that reflexivity does not hold—as required above.

A second formalisation, though openly inspired by Jones and Sergot, proposes some substantial changes in the light of a different philosophical interpretation of the counts-as relation (Gelati et al. 2004). Counts-as rules are meant to capture the constitutive, but classificatory character of institutional ontology. Accordingly, their function is to represent the constitutive ingredients of institutional facts, whose nature is conceptually distinct from that of the empirical facts. On the other hand, counts-as rules have a normative status. They are norms insofar as their conditional nature exhibits some basic properties enjoyed by the usual normative links.

4.3.1 Counts-As Link as NS: A Generative (Dynamic) Relation

Jones and Sergot developed a formal approach to the notion of institutionalised power by introducing a conditional connective $\Rightarrow_s$ to express the counts-as connection holding in the context of an institution s. Accordingly, an expression like $A \Rightarrow_s B$ means that A counts as B, where A is viewed a sufficient condition for obtaining B within s.

Jones and Sergot characterise the logic for $\Rightarrow_s$ as a classical conditional logic (RCEA, RCEC) (Chellas 1980), plus the axioms

$$((A \Rightarrow_s B) \wedge (A \Rightarrow_s C)) \rightarrow (A \Rightarrow_s (B \wedge C)) \quad (3)$$

$$((A \Rightarrow_s B) \wedge (C \Rightarrow_s B)) \rightarrow ((A \vee C) \Rightarrow_s B) \quad (4)$$

$$(A \Rightarrow_s B) \rightarrow ((B \Rightarrow_s C) \rightarrow (A \Rightarrow_s C)) \quad (5)$$

[7] According to Sect. 2, a formal analysis of NS may require to use predicate logics. For the sake of simplicity, we will work in this section with a propositional language, referring the reader to Delgrande (1998)'s investigations on quantification in conditional logics.

In addition, Jones and Sergot's analysis is integrated by introducing the normal **KD** modality D_s, such that D_sA means that A is a "constraint on the institution s". More precisely, this is suggested to capture all (logical, causal, deontic, etc.) constraints on s which include the counts-as connection. Accordingly, a formula like $D_s(A \rightarrow B)$ means "it is a constraint of (operative in) institution s that if A then B" or "it is incompatible with the constraints operative in s that A and not-B". When linked to D_s through the following schema

$$(A \Rightarrow_s B) \rightarrow D_s(A \rightarrow B) \tag{6}$$

counts-as links thus express institutional constraints (on s) to the effect that within s the realisation of A (e.g., performing certain acts as a presiding official in a wedding ceremony) counts as a sufficient condition of creating B (the status of married people).

It is important to note that this approach guarantees a restricted form of detachment of "institutional consequents" from antecedents in the form: if $A \Rightarrow_s B$ holds and it is the case that A, then it is the case in s that D_sB according to the constraints operative in s. This is done by adopting also the following schema:

$$(A \Rightarrow_s B) \rightarrow (A \rightarrow D_sA). \tag{7}$$

4.3.2 Counts-As Link as a Classificatory Relation

Following Gelati et al. (2004), we can argue that the counts-as link—in Searle's sense—is a normative classificatory relation involving institutional facts. As such, it enjoys, among others, Reflexivity: if $\Rightarrow_s$ is a classificatory relation, how can we reject that some A holds as itself in a given institution (i.e., $A \Rightarrow_s A$)? If so, there is at least another way to model counts-as relations:

- let us introduce a generic, normative, and classificatory, conditionality $\Rightarrow$; in other words, any expression $A \Rightarrow B$ means that A is normatively falling within type B; and
- let us use a non-normal "institutional" modality D_s, to strictly denote the domain of institutional facts. More precisely, an expression such as D_sA is to be read as "it is an institutional fact within s that A".

The machinery reframes the counts-as link as follows:

$$(A \Rightarrow_s B) =_{def} (A \Rightarrow D_sB) \wedge (D_sA \Rightarrow D_sB). \tag{8}$$

This statement accounts for the structuring of institutional facts, with regard to an institution s, in a hierarchy of counts-as relations linking (a) brute facts with institutional facts (s-facts) and (b) s-facts with other s-facts.

The formal theory of the counts-as conditional is provided by a logic corresponding at least to Kraus et al. (1990)'s system of nonmonotonic cumulative logic.

The axiomatisation adopted for '$\Rightarrow$' is as follows:

$$A \Rightarrow A \tag{9}$$

$$(A \Rightarrow B) \wedge (A \wedge B \Rightarrow C) \rightarrow (A \Rightarrow C) \tag{10}$$

$$(A \Rightarrow B) \wedge (A \Rightarrow C) \rightarrow ((A \wedge B) \Rightarrow C). \tag{11}$$

As expected, the logic for $\Rightarrow$ is closed under RCEA and RCK (Artosi et al. 2002). In addition, it is possible to add

$$(A \Rightarrow C) \wedge (B \Rightarrow C) \rightarrow ((A \vee B) \Rightarrow C). \tag{12}$$

Finally, the logic for D_s is closed under logical equivalence and contains the following schemata:

$$D_s A \rightarrow \neg D_s \neg A \tag{13}$$

$$(D_s A \wedge D_s B) \rightarrow D_s(A \wedge B). \tag{14}$$

Since this modality is meant to strictly represent the institutional facts holding within s, the necessitation rule is not adopted. In fact, it would sound strange that $\top$ may be viewed as an institutional fact for any institution s.

4.3.3 Semantics for $\Rightarrow$

A rather standard semantics for conditionals is based of selection-function models (Stalnaker 1968, 33–34):

> Consider a possible world in which A is true, and which otherwise differs minimally from the actual world. "If A, then B" is true (false) just in case B is true (false) in that possible world.

From a normative point of view, we can reframe the idea of minimal difference between possible worlds into the one of normative most-preferred worlds:

Definition 8 (Selection function semantics) Selection function semantics is based on the following notions:

- A *selection function frame* is a tuple $\mathscr{F} := \langle W, f \rangle$ where W is a non empty set and f is a function assigning to each sentence and world in W a subset of normatively most-preferred worlds in W.
- A *selection function model* is a tuple $\mathscr{M} := \langle W, f, V \rangle$ where $\langle W, f \rangle$ is a selection function frame and V is an evaluation function.
- The condition to evaluate $A \Rightarrow B$-formulae is as follows. For any $w \in W$:
  $w \models_V A \Rightarrow B$ iff $f(A, w) \subseteq ||B||$ ($||B||$ is the set of all worlds making B true).

The section function thus picks up the best normative states with respect to a certain world and a true propositional condition. This normative interpretation of conditional is far from new: see the discussion in Nute (1997).

The basic system for $\Rightarrow$ of Gelati et al. (2004) is characterised by the following semantic conditions (Artosi et al. 2002):

Definition 9 (Selection function semantics (cont'd)) For all $w \in W$ and any A and B, conditions for schemata are

- if $||A|| = ||B||$ then $f(A, w) = f(B, w)$
- if $f(A, w) \subseteq ||B||$ then $f(A \wedge B, w) \subseteq f(A, w)$
- if $f(A, w) \subseteq ||B||$ then $f(A, w) \subseteq f(A \wedge B, w)$

We can similarly proceed with Jones and Sergot's system and identify suitable semantic conditions characterising it (see Jones and Sergot 1996, sec. 4).

4.3.4 Discussion

Jones and Sergot are clearly inspired by Goldman's theory of action generation. As is well-known, the action generation may be characterised as a kind of conditionality where the occurrence of the antecedent A, which corresponds, typically, to an action description, generates the occurrence of a different action description B, if some background conditions are satisfied. In particular, A and B are modelled as simultaneous and A is not strictly part of doing B. Goldman (1970, 25ff.) considers, among other things, a specific case where the consequent B is generated by A by convention. This type is quite close to the idea of "counts as", since we may speak of conventional generation exactly when, for example, we state that a chess player wins the game by checkmating her opponent.

Jones and Sergot (1996)'s connective $\Rightarrow_s$ is standing for a peculiar kind of conventional generation. In fact, such a connective is stated to be non-reflexive and transitive, two properties that, among others, are typically assigned to characterise any conditionality expressing forms of causality or generation (Shoham 1990). In particular, rejecting or adopting reflexivity of counts-as relations constitutes perhaps one of the most decisive aspects that seem to differentiate the two logical approaches recalled in above. As noted by Jones and colleagues, with regard to the counts-as link, "it is precisely the property of non-reflexiveness that distinguishes a generation relation as such". Reflexivity affects the meaning ascribed to the counts-as link. First of all, as is well-known, if 'A counts as A' holds we have good reasons to argue against transitivity since its presence plus reflexivity imply monotonicity (Kraus et al. 1990). The problem is then to decide whether reflexivity must prevail over transitivity or the other way around. This inevitable choice cannot be avoided insofar as non-monotonicity is a crucial feature of counts-as conditionals:

Example 1 Suppose that in an auction if the agent x raises one hand, this may count as making a bid. It is clear that this does not hold if x raises one hand *and* scratches his own head. If 'x scratches his own head' is true, there are good reasons to conclude that x does not make any bid.

Whether normative relations enjoy reflexivity can be a thorny question (cf. the discussion in Parent 2001). For example, arguments against reflexivity are quite serious when we deal with dyadic obligations (Hansen 2005). On the other hand, one may tend to view a normative conditional by integrating a generic connective $\Rightarrow$ with suitable monadic operators and, especially, with a suitable institutional classificatory operator. According to Gelati et al., a formula like $A \Rightarrow A$ simply states the systematic claim that any formula A is a consequence of itself. Also, notice that this view, according to (8), does not lead to full reflexivity, but only to $D_s A \Rightarrow D_s A$, which means nothing but that an institutional fact is an institutional fact.

In fact, if the counts-as link means that "*A is to be classified as B* within *s*", rejecting reflexivity may be problematic: Defeasible classificatory relations, such as typicality, normally enjoy reflexivity. Actually, counts-as rules are not only regulative; they are primarily constitutive insofar as they express the constitutive elements of institutional reality. As we have seen, this is not only a well-known thesis developed by Searle, but seems to correspond to the idea that such rules may encode as well classificatory relations between categories within any institution.

Of course there are sound arguments to accept transitivity (instead of reflexivity). If we know that raising one hand counts as making a bid, and bidding counts as buying a good, then raising one hand counts as buying a good. This is basically Jones and Sergot's perspective, which is based on the idea that the occurrence of the antecedent of a counts-as relation is a (defeasible) *sufficient* reason for getting the consequent. But, as in the case of causality, some pathological examples may be put forward. In Jones and Sergot's view, counts-as sufficient conditions are defeasible. If so, given a rule such as $r_1 : X \Rightarrow_s Y$, we may say that X is sufficient to imply Y if some implicit background conditions S_1 are satisfied. Each rule of this kind is conceptually linked to a number of implicit conditions. Now imagine we have another rule $r_2 : Y \Rightarrow_s Z$ where the background conditions are S_2. The acceptability of $r_3 : X \Rightarrow_s Z$ depends on the compatibility of $S_1 \cup S_2 \cup X$ with respect to Z. In fact, when S_1 and S_2 are made explicit conjunctively in the corresponding antecedents, we have $X \wedge S_1 \Rightarrow_s Y$ and $Y \wedge S_2 \Rightarrow_s Z$. If so, since '$\Rightarrow_s$' is defeasible, nothing prevents us from having that $S_1 \cup S_2 \cup \{X\} \Rightarrow_s \neg Z$. In a different perspective, when $S_1 \cup S_2$ is inconsistent, we would get the disruptive conclusion to infer trivially any formula. To be sure, these are a logical possibilities that may in theory jeopardise the adoption of full transitivity for counts-as relation. Let's see an example. Consider the following rules:

r_1: x's electronic signature *counts as* x's handwritten signature

r_2: x's handwritten signature *counts as* evidence of *x's handwriting*.

Of course, we cannot conclude that

r_3: x's electronic signature *counts as* evidence of x's handwriting.

The intuitive background presuppositions behind rules r_1 and r_2 are clearly and conjunctively incompatible with regard to Z. So, if counts-as is applied to fact-descriptions, full transitivity cannot in general be accepted.

If the argument above is correct, what we can do is just to drop Jones and Sergot's (5) and adopt at most restricted transitivity (cumulativity), namely (10).

4.3.5 Conclusions

The previous discussion has shown that the counts-as relation can be logically viewed as a conventional type of NS. In particular, to sum up:

- **Option 1:**
  - If the counts-as link does not enjoy reflexivity, then
    - it is a generative (dynamic) relation;
    - it is a form of conventional NS, which semantically refers to the best normative worlds specific to given institutions.
- **Option 2:**
  - If we do not drop reflexivity and transitivity, then
    - we validate the following schema:

$$(A \Rightarrow B) \rightarrow ((A \wedge C) \Rightarrow B) \qquad \text{(Strengthening of the antecedent)}$$

    - Thus, the counts-as relation amounts in fact to classical implication (classificatory, non-generative/non-dynamic, based on subset inclusion), and so it is not NS (see Sect. 1).
- **Option 3:**
  - If we drop transitivity but not reflexivity, then
    - we obtain a defeasible classificatory (non-generative, non-dynamic) institutional relation;
    - the counts-as only partially meet the formal requirements of weak supervenience.

5 Meta-theory for NS: Which Modal Logic?

5.1 Introduction

In the previous section we showed that NS can be analysed in terms of suitable consequence relations and non-classical entailments. In this perspective, under suitable conditions the counts-as link is an interesting type of NS-relation.

Let us now move to a more abstract level of analysis and consider two well-known logical reconstructions for weak and strong supervenience (cf. Kim 1993):

Definition 10 Weak supervenience$_{\mathbf{m}}$ (WS$_{\mathbf{m}}$) A set of properties A weakly supervenes$_m$ on a set of properties B iff

$$\Box\forall x(\bigwedge_{A_j\in A=\{A_1,\dots,A_n\}}(A_j(x)\rightarrow\bigvee_{B_i\in B=\{B_1,\dots,B_m\}}(B_i(x)\wedge\forall y(B_i(y)\rightarrow A_i(y)))))$$

Strong supervenience$_{\mathbf{m}}$: (SS$_{\mathbf{m}}$) A set of properties A strongly supervenes$_m$ on a set of properties B iff

$$\Box\forall x(\bigwedge_{A_j\in A=\{A_1,\dots,A_n\}}(A_j(x)\rightarrow\bigvee_{B_i\in B=\{B_1,\dots,B_m\}}(B_i(x)\wedge\Box\forall y(B_i(y)\rightarrow A_i(y)))))$$

Whatever meta-theoretical model we are inclined to accept, a crucial question arises: What is the logics for $\Box$? If universal quantification over possible worlds is taken to be equivalent to $\Box$, then at least the following system, S5, must be adopted, which traditionally corresponds to a form of *metaphysical necessity* (cf. Forbes 1985):

$$\Box(A\rightarrow B)\rightarrow(\Box A\rightarrow\Box B) \quad (\mathbf{K})$$

$$\Box A\rightarrow A \quad (\mathbf{T})$$

$$\Box A\rightarrow\Box\Box A \quad (\mathbf{4})$$

$$\Diamond A\rightarrow\Box\Diamond A. \quad (\mathbf{5})$$

However, S5 raises a number of problems. Consider Bacon (1986)'s objection:

Remark 1 (Bacon 1986) Under the assumption of diagonal closure (given any set B of properties, if for every world w, ψ is coextensive in w with some property in B, then $\psi\in B$), weak supervenience entails strong supervenience whenever $\Box$ in the definitions of supervenience is based on standard modal logic S4 consisting of $\mathbf{K}\oplus\mathbf{T}\oplus\mathbf{4}$.

This analysis shows that the choice for an appropriate logic for $\Box$ is not irrelevant. Indeed, that weak supervenience entails strong supervenience can be viewed as counterintuitive: given two individuals x and y, strong supervenience clearly rules out the case where x and y are A and B in a world w but, in another world v, x is still A and B while y is A and not B, something that weak supervenience in principle admits.

For this reason, several philosophers maintained that some axiom schemata of S4 (and so of S5 as well) do not make sense in the perspective of reconstructing supervenience (cf. Schmitt and Schroeder 2011). Wedgwood (2007), among others, presented a number of reasons for rejecting **4**, a choice which blocks Bacon's argument.

In general, suppose to work in the context of the quantified modal logic FOL $\oplus$ X—where X is some modal system—and thus assume to have constant domains of individuals across possible worlds—i.e., in normal modal logics, that Barcan schemata are valid (cf., e.g., Corsi 2002):

- Assume $X = \mathsf{T}$ and, for simplicity, $A = \{A_j\}$, $B = \{B_i\}$. For any world w and evaluation V, and for some individuals b and c:

$$\{WS_m\} \models^w_V (A_j(b) \rightarrow (B_i(b) \wedge (B_i(c) \rightarrow A_j(c)))).$$

- Assume $X = \mathsf{K}$ (the minimal modal logic based on Kripke semantics) and, for simplicity, $A = \{A_j\}$, $B = \{B_i\}$. For for some individuals b and c, any evaluation V and some world w:

$$\{SS_m\} \models^w_V (\Box A_j(b) \rightarrow (\Box B_i(b) \wedge (\Box\Box B_i(c) \rightarrow \Box\Box A_j(c))))).$$

- Assume $\mathsf{S5}$:

$$\models SS_m \equiv \forall x \Box (\bigwedge_{A_j \in \{A_1,\ldots,A_n\}} (A_j(x) \rightarrow \bigvee_{B_i \in \{B_1,\ldots,B_m\}} (B_i(x) \wedge \forall y \Box y(B_i(y) \rightarrow A_i(y))))).$$

Do these cases make sense for NS? Although they look harmless, they in fact rely on a logic for $\Box$ that does not fit a sound idea of normativity, something that is required according to the interpretation of NS outlined in Definition 4. Indeed, it is well known, for instance, that schemata such as **T** are not of any use for characterising the idea of ought (see the discussion in McNamara 2014).

In general, it seems that the choice for the best logic for NS requires to identify suitable systems of quantified modal logics for the ought. However, if we do not want to commit to any strong logical system (i.e., those including the schemata mentioned above), one rather basic option is developing a non-normal quantified deontic logic[8] using, e.g., machineries such as the ones recently studied by Calardo and Rotolo (2016), which we briefly and partially recall in the next section.

Another condition that we could relax is the assumption of constant domains of individuals. On the one side, we may have good arguments to keep this assumption as valid, since

- the distinction between *de dicto* and *de re* normative (deontic) statements looks controversial, namely, between formulae with and without free occurrences of variables within the scope of the ought operator **Ought** (von Wright 1951; Castañeda 1981);
- Why does the truth of formulae such as $\exists x$**Ought**$(x = a)$ should vary from world to world (Goble 1973)? In other words, what does it mean that an individual exists in some deontically preferred worlds but does not in other ideal worlds?

[8]Non-normal deontic logics have been considered a solution to avoid many drawbacks of standard deontic logic (i.e., deontic **KD**), which does not tolerate deontic conflicts and gives rise to a number of paradoxes and puzzles (Goble 2005; Jones and Carmo 2002).

The above arguments, however, could be rejected. In particular:

- Why should we assume that exactly the same individuals populate all (normatively) ideal worlds? Indeed, it is known that the assumption of constant domains is often associated with precise metaphysical views, such as—but not only—logical atomism (cf. Cocchiarella 1984); it is far from obvious whether this is required from the normative viewpoint.
- The equivalence between *de dicto* and *de re* statements is not in general guaranteed by the assumption of constant domains:
  - Barcan schemata alone are not sufficient in general to eliminate *de re* modalities, namely, to prove that, given any modal logic S, for each formula ϕ, there exists a *de dicto* formula ϕ' such that $\mathsf{S} \vdash \phi \equiv \phi'$. This can be done only adding some extra-conditions and within strong modal systems such as $\mathsf{S5}$ (see, e.g., Fine 1978; Kaminski 1997);
  - Barcan schemata are not in general characterised in non-normal modal logics by constant domains (Calardo and Rotolo 2016).

5.2 *Quantified Non-normal Modal Logics for the Ought*

Let us recall a piece of Calardo and Rotolo (2016)'s machinery and define an appropriate semantics for quantified non-normal modal logic.

Definition 11 (Multi-relational frames) A multi-relational frame is a tuple $\mathscr{F} := \langle W, \mathscr{R}, D, U \rangle$ where:

- W is a non empty set of worlds;
- $\mathscr{R}$ is a (possibly infinite) set of binary relations over W;
- D is a function associating to each world $w \in W$ a set D_w of individuals (the inner domain of w);
- U is a function associating to each world $w \in W$ a set U_w of individuals (the outer domain of w) such that for any $w \in W$, $U_w \neq \emptyset$ and $D_w \subseteq U_w$ and if wRv for some R, then $U_w \subseteq U_v$.

Models, assignments, and the concepts of *satisfaction, truth, validity* are defined in the standard way.

Definition 12 (Multi-relational models) A multi-relational model is a tuple $\mathscr{M} := \langle W, \mathscr{R}, D, U, I \rangle$ where $\langle W, \mathscr{R}, D, U \rangle$ is a multi-relational frame and I is a function $I : \mathscr{L} \times W \mapsto \bigcup_{w \in W} U_w$ such that:

- $I_w(P^n) \subseteq (U_w)^n$
- $I_w(c) \in U_w$.

Definition 13 (Assignments) For any $w \in W$, a w-assignment σ is a function $\sigma : Var(\mathscr{L}) \mapsto U_w$.

An x-variant τ of a w-assignment σ is a w-assignment which may differ from σ for the value assigned to x.

Definition 14 (σ-interpretation) Given a w-assignment σ, define

(a) $I^{\sigma}_{w}(c) = I_w(c)$, and
(b) $I^{\sigma}_{w}(x) = \sigma(x)$.

Definition 15 (Truth conditions) Let $\mathcal{M} := \langle W, \mathcal{R}, D, U, I\rangle$ be any multi-relational model, σ any assignment, and $w \in W$. Truth evaluation clauses are as follows:

- $\mathcal{M} \models^{\sigma}_{w} P^n(t_1, \ldots, t_n)$ iff $\langle I^{\sigma}_{w}(t_1), \ldots, I^{\sigma}_{w}(t_n)\rangle \in I_w(P^n)$
- $\mathcal{M} \not\models^{\sigma}_{w} \bot$
- $\mathcal{M} \models^{\sigma}_{w} \forall x A$ iff for every x-variant τ of σ such that $\tau(x) \in D_w$, $\mathcal{M} \models^{\tau}_{w} A(x)$
- $\mathcal{M} \models^{\sigma}_{w}$ **Ought**A iff $\exists R_i \in \mathcal{R} : \forall v \in W(wR_i v \Rightarrow \mathcal{M} \models^{\sigma}_{v} A)$.

A model $\mathcal{M}$ *satisfies* a set of formulae Δ iff for some world w and some w-assignment σ, $\mathcal{M} \models^{\sigma}_{w} A$ for all $A \in \Delta$. A formula A is *true in a world* w of a model $\mathcal{M}$, $\mathcal{M} \models_w A$, iff for any w-assignment σ, $\mathcal{M} \models^{\sigma}_{w} A$. A formula A is *true in a model* $\mathcal{M}$, $\mathcal{M} \models A$, iff for all w, $\mathcal{M} \models_w A$. A formula A is *valid* on a frame $\mathcal{F}$, $\mathcal{F} \models A$, iff for any model $\mathcal{M}$ on $\mathcal{F}$, $\mathcal{M} \models A$. Given a class of frames $\mathbb{F}$, a formula A is $\mathbb{F}$-*valid*, $\mathbb{F} \models A$, iff for any frame $\mathcal{F} \in \mathbb{F}$, $\mathcal{F} \models A$. $\mathcal{M}$ is a model for a logic L iff $\mathcal{M} \models A$ for all $A \in \mathsf{L}$.

We assume all individual terms to be rigid designators.

The above semantics characterises the system $\mathsf{Q}^{\circ}.\mathsf{MN}$, which contains the following axioms and inference rules:

- Propositional tautologies;
- $\mathbf{UI}^{\circ} := \forall y(\forall x A(x) \rightarrow A(y/x))$
- $\forall x \forall y A \leftrightarrow \forall y \forall x A$
- $A \rightarrow \forall x A$, x not free in A
- $\forall x(A \rightarrow B) \rightarrow (\forall x A \rightarrow \forall x B)$
- $\mathbf{M} := \mathbf{Ought}(A \wedge B) \rightarrow (\mathbf{Ought}A \wedge \mathbf{Ought}B)$
- $\mathbf{N} := \mathbf{Ought}\top$
- $\mathbf{MP} := A \rightarrow B, A/B$
- $\mathbf{RE} := A \equiv B/\mathbf{Ought}A \equiv \mathbf{Ought}B$
- $\mathbf{UG} := A/\forall x A$

We must notice that the propositional modal schemata and inference rules in $\mathsf{Q}^{\circ}.\mathsf{MN}$ amount to a deontic system proposed by Goble (2001, 2004).

5.3 *Discussion About NS*

Multi-relational semantics was originally proposed by Schotch and Jennings (1981) and Goble (2001, 2004) in the domain of deontic logic. Semantic structures consist of

- **a plurality of worlds**, with possibly infinitely many deontic alternatives,
- **a plurality of accessibility relations**, with possibly infinitely many normative standards (codes, individual or collective preferences, ...) that select the most-preferred (or ideal) worlds.

In deontic logic the Kripke accessibility relation selects for each world those states of affairs that are (morally, legally, etc.) ideal with respect to it: hence, if **Ought**A is true in a world w, this simply means that A is the case in all ideal alternatives to w. The interpretation of multi-relational models, as given in deontic logics, is thus that each accessibility relation corresponds to a particular "standard of value" or a set of norms that selects those ideal worlds; however, it is not guaranteed that such worlds are still ideal according to different standards of value or norms, namely, according to different accessibility relations. In this perspective, different relations correspond to different deontic standards or that conflicting norms are obtained from otherwise consistent different systems of norms. As Goble argues, when both **Ought**A and **Ought**$\neg A$ "are true it is because A is prescribed by one set of norms or regulations while $\neg A$ is prescribed by another, distinct set. [...] Each set of norms or regulations is presumed to be internally consistent, and conflicts only emerge as a result of rivalry between sets of norms" (Goble 2001). In short, multi-relational models can provide a semantic analysis of *normative pluralism*, according to which different normative systems may generate obligations.

The assumption of a plurality of relations, in particular, allows us to provide some useful comments on NS and offers interesting conceptual tools for distinguishing weak and strong NS. Let us recall them using **Ought** and working two sets of predicates consisting of singletons:

$$\mathbf{Ought}\forall x(A(x) \to (B(x) \wedge \forall y(B(y) \to A(y)))) \qquad (WNS_1)$$

$$\mathbf{Ought}\forall x(A(x) \to (B(x) \wedge \mathbf{Ought}\forall y(B(y) \to A(y)))). \qquad (SNS_1)$$

Let us consider the following model[9]:

Example 2

$$\mathscr{M} := \langle W, \mathscr{R}, D, U, I \rangle$$

where

- $W = \{w_1, w_2, w_3, w_4, w_5\}$;
- $\mathscr{R} = \{R_1 = \{\langle w_1, w_2\rangle\}, R_2 = \{\langle w_1, w_2\rangle, \langle w_1, w_3\rangle\}, R_3 = \{\langle w_3, w_4\rangle\}, R_4 = \{\langle w_2, w_5\rangle\}\}$;
- $D_x = U_x = \{a, b\}$, $\forall x \in \{w_1, w_2, w_3, w_4, w_5\}$.

I is defined as follows:

- $I_{w_1}(A) = \{a, b\}$, $I_{w_2}(A) = \{a, b\}$, $I_{w_3}(A) = \{a\}$, $I_{w_4}(A) = \{b\}$,$I_{w_5}(A) = \{a, b\}$;
- $I_{w_1}(B) = \{a, b\}$, $I_{w_2}(B) = \{a, b\}$, $I_{w_3}(B) = \{b\}$, $I_{w_4}(B) = \{a\}$,$I_{w_5}(B) = \{a, b\}$;
- $I_x(a) = a$, $I_x(b) = b$, $\forall x \in \{w_1, w_2, w_3, w_4, w_5\}$.

[9]We assume, for the sake of simplicity, to work with constant domains. This assumption makes things simpler but is not conceptually required and thus is not essential for our purposes. It is a rather straightforward, but pedantic exercise to extend the analysis to varying domains.

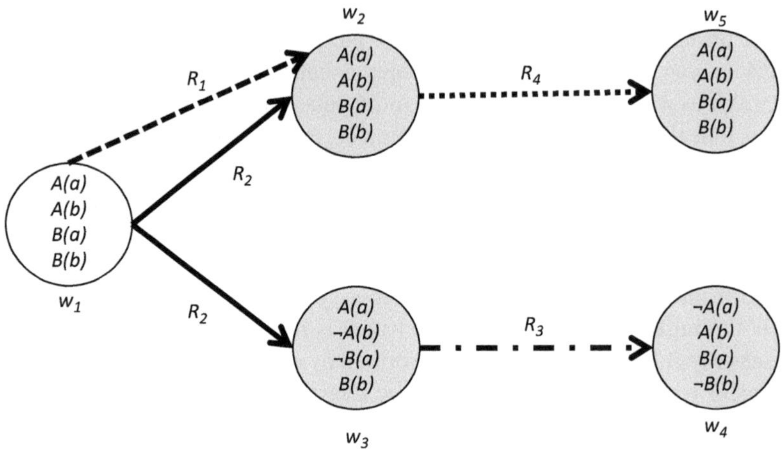

Fig. 3 Model from Example 2

It is straightforward to verify that both WNS_1 and SNS_1 are true at world w_1: see Fig. 3. In particular, let us examine WNS_1: indeed, there exists a normative system/standard, i.e., the accessibility relation R_1, which selects a set of worlds (just consisting of w_2) at which all predicates are made true of all individuals.[10] Notice that the other relation R_2, departing from w_1, does not do the job: this means that, at w_1, we only need to have one normative system/standard for saying that A weakly supervenes on B. Things are partially similar, at w_1, in regard to SNS_1: here, the evaluation works as before in regard to the x, while for y we have to consider another (nested) occurrence of **Ought**, which semantically states that there exists at least one normative system/standard, not necessarily R_1, selecting worlds that make true the formula in the scope of this second **Ought**. In fact, R_4 does the job, thus validating SNS_1.

Example 3 (Normative pluralism and NS) Normative pluralism is a philosophical view according to which, either there is a fundamental plurality of ways of being good that cannot be reduced to something they all have in common, or, less radically, that there exists a plurality of bearers of value (see Mason 2015). Hence, that something is morally due might change depending on whether we examine different moral standards. E.g., if we consider (i) religious morality, and (ii) liberal morality, then we could plausibly have two normative standards.

[10]Of course, we could have other models that make trivially true the conditionals by falsifying the antecedent.

Suppose now

- to change the model in Example 2 by imposing that $I_{w_5}(A) = \{a\}$;
- that

$$\text{(i) } R_1 = \text{liberal morality,}$$
$$\text{(ii) } R_4 = \text{religious morality;}$$

- that

$$\text{(a) } A = \text{valuable}$$
$$\text{(b) } B = \text{desired}$$

In the revised model, WNS_1 is still true at w_1, whereas SNS_1 is falsified: there, being valuable weakly—but not strongly—supervenes on being desired, because this relation does not hold for religious moral standards.

In conclusion, we should observe that the iteration of **Ought** in SNS_1 requires to possibly consider more normative standards; under this assumption, if we assume to work with normative pluralism, strong NS exhibits interesting differences with respect to weak NS. Accordingly, the relative strength of SNS_1, in comparison with WNS_1, is not based on a strong modality, but conceptually depends on the fact that supervenient properties must be checked against more normative systems.

Finally, while the axiom schema **4**, i.e., **Ought**$A \rightarrow$ **OughtOught**A, does not look as appropriate in logics for the ought, it is also partially useless to make SNS_1 and WNS_1 closer, since the semantic property charactering in multi-relational semantics axiom **4** is not standard transitivity; this schema requires that whenever there are two relations R_1 and R_4 connecting respectively any world w_1 with any world w_2 and any such w_2 with any world w_5, then we must ensure that w_5 is always reachable from w_1 with *any* relation (and not necessarily with those which connect w_1 with w_2, and w_2 with w_5) (Calardo and Rotolo 2014). Hence, we reiterate here the same limit we have just noticed above.

6 Summary

In this essay we proposed a logical discussion on NS. Despite the idea that supervenience is taken sometimes to be different from entailment, we argued much depends on what we mean by this last concept. In particular, there is room for an analysis that sees alternatives of classical logic which can grasp specific aspects of NS. We discussed

- the distinction between normative supervenience and supervenience of the normative, the former selecting ideal worlds where properties hold, the latter selecting normative properties holding in all possible worlds;

- how NS can be analysed in terms of suitable consequence relations and non-classical entailments, remarking that the counts-as relation is an interesting, but *sui generis* type of NS, and that weak, but suitable modal logics for the Ought may affect the formal and conceptual behaviour of standard definitions of weak and strong supervenience.

References

Artosi, A., G. Governatori, and A. Rotolo (2002). Labelled tableaux for nonmonotonic reasoning: Cumulative consequence relations. *Journal of Logic and Computation 12*(6), 1027–1060.

Bacon, J. (1986). Supervenience, necessary coextension, and reducibility. *Philosophical Studies 49*(2), 163–176.

Beall, J. and G. Restall (2000). Logical Pluralism. *Australasian Journal of Philosophy 78*, 475–493.

Calardo, E. and A. Rotolo (2014). Variants of multi-relational semantics for propositional non-normal modal logics. *Journal of Applied Non-Classical Logics 24*(4), 293–320.

Calardo, E. and A. Rotolo (2016). Quantification in some non-normal modal logics. *Journal of Philosophical Logic*, 1–36.

Castañeda, H.-N. (1981). The paradoxes of deontic logic: The simplest solution to all of them in one fell swoop. In R. Hilpinen (Ed.), *New Studies in Deontic Logic*, pp. 37–86. Dordrecht: D. Reidel.

Chellas, B. F. (1980). *Modal Logic*. Cambridge University Press.

Cocchiarella, N. B. (1984). Philosophical perspectives on quantification in tense and modal logic. In D. Gabbay and F. Guenthner (Eds.), *Handbook of Philosophical Logic: Volume II: Extensions of Classical Logic*, pp. 309–353. Dordrecht: Reidel.

Corsi, G. (2002). A unified completeness theorem for quantified modal logics. *Journal of Symbolic Logic 67*(4), 1483–1510.

Delgrande, J. P. (1998). On first-order conditional logics. *Artificial Intelligence 105*(1), 105–137.

Fine, K. (1978). Model theory for modal logic - Part II: The elimination of *de re* modality. *Journal of Philosophical Logic 7*, 277–306.

Forbes, G. (1985). *The metaphysics of modality*. Clarendon library of logic and philosophy. Clarendon Press.

Gabbay, D., J. Horty, X. Parent, and L. van der Torre (Eds.) (2013). *Deontic Logic Handbook*. London: College Publications.

Gelati, J., A. Rotolo, G. Sartor, and G. Governatori (2004). Normative autonomy and normative co-ordination: Declarative power, representation, and mandate. *Artificial Intelligence and Law 12*(1–2), 53–81.

Goble, L. (1973). Opacity and the Ought-To-Be. *Noûs 7*(4), 407–412.

Goble, L. (2001). Multiplex semantics for deontic logic. *Nordic Journal of Philosophical Logic 5*(2), 113–134.

Goble, L. (2004). Preference semantics for deontic logic — Part II: Multiplex models. *Logique et Analyse 47*, 113–134.

Goble, L. (2005). A logic for deontic dilemmas. *Journal of Applied Logic 3*(3–4), 461–483.

Goldman, A. (1970). *A theory of human action*. Prentice-Hall.

Grossi, D. and A. Jones (2013). Constitutive rules and counts-as conditionals. In X. P. D. Gabbay, J. Horty and L. van der Torre (Eds.), *Deontic Logic Handbook*. London: College Publications.

Hansen, J. (2005). Conflicting imperatives and dyadic deontic logic. *Journal of Applied Logic 3* (3–4), 484–511.

Humberstone, L. (1993). Functional dependencies, supervenience, and consequence relations. *Journal of Logic and Computation 2*, 309–36.

Humberstone, L. (2002). The modal logic of agreement and noncontingency. *Notre Dame Journal of Formal Logic 2*, 95–127.
Jones, A. and J. Carmo (2002). Deontic logic and contrary-to-duties. In D. Gabbay and F. Guenthner (Eds.), *Handbook of Philosophical Logic* (2nd ed.). Dordrecht ; Boston: Kluwer Academic Publishers.
Jones, A. J. I. and M. J. Sergot (1996). A formal characterisation of institutionalised power. *Logic Journal of the IGPL 4*(3), 427–443.
Kaminski, M. (1997). The elimination of *de re* formulas. *Journal of Philosophical Logic 26*, 411–422.
Kim, J. (1993). *Supervenience and Mind: Selected Philosophical Essays*. Cambridge Studies in Philosophy. Cambridge University Press.
Kraus, S., D. Lehmann, and M. Magidor (1990, July). Nonmonotonic reasoning, preferential models and cumulative logics. *Artificial Intelligence 44*(1–2), 167–207.
Mason, E. (2015). Value pluralism. In E. N. Zalta (Ed.), *The Stanford Encyclopedia of Philosophy* (Summer 2015 ed.). Metaphysics Research Lab, Stanford University.
McLaughlin, B. (1995). Varieties of supervenience. In E. Savellos and U. Yalcin (Eds.), *Supervenience: New Essays*. Cambridge University Press.
McLaughlin, B. and K. Bennett (2014). Supervenience. In E. N. Zalta (Ed.), *The Stanford Encyclopedia of Philosophy* (Spring 2014 ed.).
McNamara, P. (2014). Deontic logic. In E. N. Zalta (Ed.), *The Stanford Encyclopedia of Philosophy* (Winter 2014 ed.). Metaphysics Research Lab, Stanford University.
Nute, D. (Ed.) (1997). *Defeasible Deontic Logic*. Dordrecht: Kluwer.
Parent, X. (2001). Cumulativity, identity and time in deontic logic. *Fundamenta Informaticae 48*(2–3), 237–252.
Schmitt, J. and M. Schroeder (2011). Supervenience arguments under relaxed assumptions. *Philosophical Studies 155*(1), 133–160.
Schotch, P. K. and R. E. Jennings (1981). Non-Kripkean deontic logic. In R. Hilpinen (Ed.), *New Studies in Deontic Logic*, pp. 149–162. Reidel.
Searle, J. (1969). *Speech Acts: An Essay in the Philosophy of Language*. Cambridge: Cambridge University Press.
Searle, J. (1995). *The Construction of Social Reality*. Harmondsworth: Penguin.
Searle, J. (2001). Neither phenomenological description nor rational reconstruction: Reply to Dreyfus. *Revue Internationale de Philosophie 55*, 277–284.
Shoham, Y. (1990). Nonmonotonic Reasoning and Causation. *Cognitive Science 14*, 213–252.
Stalnaker, R. (1968). A theory of conditionals. In *Studies in Logical Theory*, Volume 2, pp. 98–112. Blackwell.
von Wright, G. H. (1951). *An Essay in Modal Logic*. Amsterdam: North-Holland.
Wedgwood, R. (2007). *The Nature of Normativity*. Oxford: Oxford University Press.

Propositional and Doxastic Justification: Their Relationship and a Questionable Supervenience Claim

Giorgio Volpe

Abstract Propositional justification pertains to propositions: it is the sort of justification that a proposition enjoys for an agent when the agent is epistemically justified to believe it. By contrast, doxastic justification is justification of beliefs, i.e., of doxastic states actually instantiated by an agent. The 'orthodox' view of the relationship between propositional and doxastic justification is that the latter should be explained in terms of the former, so that an agent's belief is (doxastically) justified just in case (i) it is a belief in a proposition that is (propositionally) justified for the agent and (ii) it is held on the basis of that which (propositionally) justifies its content. This view has been challenged by John Turri in his paper 'On the Relationship between Propositional and Doxastic Justification' (Philosophy and Phenomenological Research, 80, 2010, pp. 312–326). There he offers two putative counterexamples to the orthodoxy and goes on to argue that the order of explanation should be reversed: it is propositional justification that should be explained in terms of doxastic justification, and not vice versa. Though I share Turri's feeling that there is something amiss with the way a number of contemporary epistemologists talk of propositional and doxastic justification, I do not believe he has managed to put his finger on the real trouble. So the first point I make is that his counterexamples fall short of refuting the orthodox view, which I argue should be maintained. Then I try to diagnose the real source of the trouble. It lies, I suggest, in the way a number of recent epistemologists talk of propositional justification, a way which commits them to the questionable view that the basis upon which facts concerning propositional justification supervene does not include facts concerning the doxastic states of agents, but only facts concerning the evidence to which agents have access. So I observe that there are different degrees of idealisation involved in judgments of 'propositional justification', propose to distinguish what an agent is propositionally justified to believe given his overall doxastic state from what an agent is propositionally justified to believe irrespective of his overall doxastic state, and argue that, whenever it is the former relation that is at stake, an agent can be propositionally justified to believe a proposition p at time t only if it is reasonably easy for him to form a doxastically justified belief in p at t. It is most likely an

G. Volpe (✉)
University of Bologna, Bologna, Italy
e-mail: giorgio.volpe@unibo.it

B. Brożek et al. (eds.), *Supervenience and Normativity*, Law and Philosophy Library 120, DOI 10.1007/978-3-319-61046-7_2

awareness of this fact – or of some fact in the vicinity – that encourages the belief that propositional justification should be explained in terms of doxastic justification. But I suggest that this fact, far from being evidence that the notion of doxastic justification is in any sense more fundamental than that of propositional justification, can be accounted for by paying attention to the relationship that links the relevant sort of (epistemic) justification to (epistemic) responsibility. So I conclude that there is an important sense in which facts concerning epistemic justification supervene not merely on facts concerning the evidential states of agents, but on facts concerning their overall doxastic states.

1 Introduction

Common epistemological wisdom has it that epistemic facts supervene on non-epistemic ones – which is usually thought to be just a particular instance of the general truth that evaluative facts supervene on non-evaluative ones (Turri 2010a). More specifically, it is widely held that facts concerning the epistemic justification of beliefs supervene on facts concerning beliefs' non-epistemic properties. It is not my purpose here to add to the literature on this topic: the issue with which I will be concerned has to do, rather, with the relationship between facts concerning one particular kind of epistemic justification, that is, *propositional* justification, and facts concerning people's doxastic states. For a number of contemporary epistemologists seem to believe that the basis upon which facts concerning propositional justification supervene only includes facts concerning the reasons or evidence to which agents have access – a suggestion that deserves closer scrutiny, if only because it is in tension with the way epistemic justification has been conceived in much traditional epistemology. The supervenience issue on which I propose to shed some light in this paper is then different from the issue that is at stake in familiar debates on epistemic supervenience. Moreover, I will address it in a slightly indirect way, by focussing on the question of the order of explanation between propositional and doxastic justification. By discussing a recent challenge to the answer that is usually given to this question I hope I will eventually put in an interesting perspective the specific issue concerning the supervenience basis of propositional justification that I am interested in in this paper.

The challenge I have in mind is posed by John Turri in his paper 'On the Relationship between Propositional and Doxastic Justification' (Turri 2010b). As I explain in Sect. 2, in that paper Turri offers two counterexamples to the 'orthodox' view that doxastic justification should be explained in terms of propositional justification and goes on to suggest that the order of explanation must be reversed: it is propositional justification that should be explained in terms of doxastic justification, and not vice versa. Though I share Turri's feeling that there is something amiss with the way a number of contemporary epistemologists talk of propositional and doxastic justification, I do not believe he has put his finger on the real trouble. So in Sect. 3 I argue that his counterexamples fall short of refuting the orthodox view, but I also suggest that the conception of propositional justification with which the orthodox view (which I believe should be maintained) is often conjoined needs clarification. In Sect. 4 I observe that there are different degrees of idealization involved in judgments of propositional justification and emphasize that the type of justification that is at issue when we reach the higher degrees may be in a clear sense unavailable to the agent for which a proposition is said to possess it. In Sect. 5 I propose to distinguish what an agent is propositionally justified to believe *given his overall doxastic profile* from what an agent is propositionally justified to believe *irrespective of the evidentially idle features of his doxastic profile*, and argue that, whenever the former relation is at stake, an agent can be propositionally justified to believe a proposition p at time t only if it is reasonably easy for him to form a doxastically justified belief in p at t. It is most likely an awareness of this fact – or of some fact in the vicinity – that encourages the belief that propositional justification should be explained in terms of doxastic justification. But in Sect. 6 I argue that this fact, far from being evidence that the notion of doxastic justification is more fundamental than that of propositional justification, can be accounted for by adverting to the relationship that links the relevant sort of (epistemic) justification to (epistemic) responsibility. So I conclude that there is an important sense in which epistemic justification supervenes not merely on the agents' reasons or evidence, but on their overall doxastic profile.

2 Turri's Criticism of the Orthodox View

The distinction epistemologists have in mind when they oppose propositional to doxastic justification is reasonably clear.[1] *Propositional* justification pertains to *propositions*: it is the sort of justification enjoyed by a proposition when an agent is epistemically justified to believe it.[2] A proposition may enjoy this kind of justification even if the relevant agent does not believe it, or does not believe it on the basis of that which (propositionally) justifies it. By contrast, *doxastic* justification is justification of *beliefs*, which means that an agent can have a (doxastically) justified belief in a certain proposition only if he believes it. The usual story is that doxastic justification is the sort of justification enjoyed by a belief just in case (i) it is a belief in a proposition that is (propositionally) justified for the agent and (ii) it is held on

[1]The terminology is due to Firth (1978, 217 f.). Some writers, including Feldman and Conee (1985, 24), Feldman (2002, 46) and Pryor (2004, 365), talk of *well-founded* rather than of *doxastically justified* beliefs. Here, however, I shall follow the most common usage and stick to the latter phrase.

[2]Depending on circumstances, an agent may instead be justified to *disbelieve*, or to *withhold belief from*, a proposition. For simplicity, in what follows I will not discuss the justificational status of such attitudes, nor will I attend to the complications raised by considering degrees of belief, or different kinds of propositional attitudes, such as trust or acceptance. These omissions will not affect the thrust of the argument.

the basis of that which (propositionally) justifies its content. It is this story, not the underlying distinction, that Turri sets out to debunk in his paper.

To be sure, the target of his criticism is just one side of the biconditional, namely

> (**Basis**) IF (i) *p* is propositionally justified for S in virtue of S's having reason(s) R and (ii) S believes *p* on the basis of R, THEN S's belief that *p* is doxastically justified.[3] (Turri 2010b, 314)

But of course, showing that Basis is false is sufficient to refute the overall picture.

As it will soon become clear, Turri assumes that reasons have propositional content. But nothing of what I have to say in this paper depends on this assumption, or on the assumption that reasons are the sort of thing that can be given, or cited, in defence of a claim. Moreover, although a reason that an agent can have and use as a basis for a belief is naturally regarded as something accessible from, or internal to, the agent's perspective on the world, only part of what I maintain in Sect. 6 is flatly inconsistent with externalist views of epistemic justification. Everything I say in this paper could in fact have been phrased more neutrally in terms of 'justification-makers' or 'justifiers'; but for ease of exposition, I follow Turri's lead and talk of reasons throughout.

Let's then consider his attack on the orthodox view. He introduces his point by noting that a doxastically justified belief is in some important respects like a well built deck. A carpenter, he observes, may be equipped with the finest tools and lumber, but if he puts them together in the wrong way, the result is bound to be disappointing: 'Merely having the right equipment for the job, and using it to perform the job, does not guarantee a job well done' (Turri 2010b, 315). Similarly for belief: merely having one or more reasons R that make *p* propositionally justified (for oneself) and using them as a basis for believing *p* does not guarantee a doxastically justified belief in *p*.

As I have already hinted at, Turri's criticism turns on two counterexamples, which are designed to put in sharp relief the importance of the way in which an agent makes use of his reasons. The first counterexample features two jurors, Miss Proper and Miss Improper, sitting in judgment of Mr. Mansour (ibid., 315 f.). Both jurors know the following things:

(P1) Mansour had a motive to kill the victim.
(P2) Mansour had previously threatened to kill the victim.
(P3) Multiple eyewitnesses place Mansour at the crime scene.
(P4) Mansour's fingerprints were all over the murder weapon.

---

[3]Turri keeps switching between formulations in which '*p*' appears to function as an objectual variable (as in 'S believes *p*') and formulations in which it occurs as a sentential variable, or perhaps a sentence letter (as in 'S's belief that *p*'). This oscillation doesn't cause any real harm, but in this paper I consistently adopt the former usage.

Premises (P1–P4) make it overwhelmingly likely that <Mansour is guilty> is true.[4] So <Mansour is guilty> is (propositionally) justified for both jurors, and as a matter of fact each of them comes to believe that Mansour is guilty as the result of an episode of conscious reasoning that features (P1–P4) essentially. However, the respective trains of thought follow significantly different routes. Miss Proper's reasoning is as follows:

> (Proper Reasoning) (P1–P4) make it overwhelmingly likely that Mansour is guilty. (P1–P4) are true. Therefore, Mansour is guilty.

On the other hand, Miss Improper reasons like this:

> (Improper Reasoning) The tea leaves say that (P1–P4) make it overwhelmingly likely that Mansour is guilty. (P1–P4) are true. Therefore, Mansour is guilty.

Although each juror bases her belief that Mansour is guilty on the reasons that make its content (propositionally) justified for her, it seems clear that only Miss Proper's belief is doxastically justified. Contra Basis, then, having one or more reasons R that make *p* propositionally justified (for oneself) and using them as a basis for one's believing *p* is not sufficient for having a (doxastically) justified belief in *p*.

This counterexample, notes Turri, is also fatal to a natural strengthening of Basis:

> (**Basis**$^{+}$) IF (i) *p* is propositionally justified for S in virtue of S's having reason(s) R and (ii) S believes *p* on the basis of R *as evidence for p*, THEN S's belief that *p* is doxastically justified. (Turri 2010b, 314)

For both Miss Proper and Miss Improper treat (P1–P4) *as evidence* for the proposition that Mansour is guilty. Apparently, however, another way of strengthening Basis is more effective:

> (**Austere Basis**) IF (i) *p* is propositionally justified for S in virtue of S's having reason(s) R and (ii) S believes *p* on the basis of R *and only R*, THEN S's belief that *p* is doxastically justified. (Turri 2010b, 314)

Austere Basis is unscathed by Turri's first counterexample, which is why he goes on to tell his second story, featuring Mr. Ponens and Mr. F.A. Lacy (Turri 2010b, 317). Both characters know two things:

(P5) The Spurs will win if they play the Pistons.
(P6) The Spurs will play the Pistons.

From these two premises – and only from them – Mr. Ponens and Mr. F.A. Lacy draw the conclusion that the Spurs will win. But here again, the two characters form their beliefs by significantly different routes. While Mr. Ponens gets to the conclusion that the Spurs will win by an application of *modus ponens*, Mr. F.A. Lacy reaches it by an application of *modus profusus*, that is to say, by applying the rule that, for any *p*, *q* and *r*, allows to infer <*r*> from <*p* and *q*>. The intuition the counterexample is designed to fuel is of course that Lacy's belief, unlike Ponens',

[4] As usual, substitution-instances of '<*p*>' are used to abbreviate corresponding substitution-instances of 'the proposition that *p*'.

is doxastically unjustified, as it is reached by applying a rule of inference that is blatantly invalid. Contra Austere Basis, then, having one or more reasons R that make *p* (propositionally) justified (for oneself) and using them *and only them* as a basis for one's believing *p* is *not* sufficient for having a doxastically justified belief in *p*.

Turri emphasizes that his examples have nothing to do with the 'Gypsy-lawyer' cases that occur in many discussions of the epistemic basing relation and explains that his argument does not commit him to any definite view of the nature of such relation (ibid., 318 f.). The conclusion he wants to draw from his cases is just that Basis and its strengthenings miss

> something *deep and important* about the relationship between propositional and doxastic justification. The way in which the subject performs, the manner in which she makes use of her reasons, fundamentally determines whether her belief is doxastically justified. Poor utilization of even the best reasons for believing *p* will prevent you from justifiedly believing or knowing that *p*. (Turri 2010b, 317 f.)

Turri, however, does not stop here. For he takes his counterexamples to Basis and its strengthened versions to motivate a wholesale rejection of the orthodox view of the relationship between propositional and doxastic justification – a rejection that leads him to endorse the claim that it is propositional justification that should be explained in terms of doxastic justification, and not vice versa. His proposal does not amount to a specification of individually necessary and jointly sufficient conditions for propositional justification, but comes in the form of a less ambitious conditional:

> (**PJ**) Necessarily, for all S, *p*, and *t*, if *p* is propositionally justified for S at *t*, then *p* is propositionally justified for S at *t* BECAUSE S currently possesses at least one means of coming to believe *p* such that, were S to believe *p* in one of those ways, S's belief would thereby be doxastically justified. (Turri 2010b, 320)

Turri's claim is in fact that the causal clause in the consequent of **PJ** specifies a condition which is both *necessary* and *explanatory* for propositional justification. Subsequent discussion (Turri 2010b, 320–323) makes it clear why he does not venture to say that the condition is also sufficient, offers a number of reasons that should command **PJ** to our attention, and introduces a deeper (if vaguer) principle that takes care of some possible counterexamples to **PJ**. It is not my purpose here to assess what Turri has to say on such matters: whatever the merits of **PJ** and of the deeper principle that lies behind it, I think something has gone wrong with his argument at an earlier stage, for the cases that are taken to motivate his own proposal fall short of providing a refutation of the orthodox view of the relationship between propositional and doxastic justification.

3 Why Turri's Cases Fail to Refute the Orthodox View

Turri's purported counterexamples turn on cases of inferential justification. So one might be tempted to discount them by arguing that, whenever inferential justification is at stake, the reasons in virtue of which a proposition is justified for an agent will obviously include the circumstance that the truth of certain premises entails, or renders overwhelmingly likely, the truth of the proposition in question. Thus, for example, one may be tempted to maintain that, if the proposition that the Spurs will win is justified for Mr. Ponens, it cannot enjoy such a status merely in virtue of his knowing (or justifiedly believing) P5 (that the Spurs will win if they play the Pistons) and P6 (that the Spurs will play the Pistons). If the proposition is justified for Mr. Ponens, it must be so also in virtue of his knowing (or justifiedly believing) that it is the conclusion of a valid argument – an instance of *modus ponens* – that has P5 and P6 as its premises.[5] If this claim is correct, Turri's cases fail to refute Basis and its strengthenings because the beliefs of their heroes do not satisfy the antecedents of the relevant conditionals: Mr. F.A. Lacy does not believe that the Spurs will win on the basis of all the reasons in virtue of which that proposition is justified for him – and Miss Improper does not believe that Mansour is guilty on the basis of all the reasons in virtue of which that proposition is justified for him.

Tempting as it is, this argumentative strategy invites the reply that the objection mixes up things of different kinds. One way of bringing out this point is to invoke the paradox of Achilles and the tortoise (Carroll 1895) with its moral that the inference rules employed in an argument should not be counted among the argument's premises. But perhaps it is not inevitable to model the reasons in virtue of which a proposition is (inferentially) justified for an agent as premises of a (semi-)formal argument. So it may be instructive to look at the matter from a different angle.[6] The relevant distinction will not be that between the premises of an argument and the rules of inference employed to reach its conclusion, but that between reasons

[5]As I said in Sect. 2, it is natural to regard a reason that an agent can have and use as a basis for belief as something accessible from, or internal to, the agent's perspective on the world – which naturally leads to Turri's assumption that having reason(s) amounts to *knowing* (or *justifiedly believing)* certain facts or propositions. Here, however, nothing important depends on accepting an internalist construal of justifiers, and the argument of this paragraph could be easily reformulated in terms more acceptable to externalistically-minded philosophers.

[6]Eugenio Orlandelli has tried to convince me, both in conversation and in correspondence, that Turri's cases appear to pose a challenge to the orthodox view only because they are set on the background of a misleading account of the nature of that in virtue of which a proposition may be inferentially justified for an agent. Orlandelli's alternative account may be sketched by applying it to the basketball case. His view is, in a nutshell, that the proposition that the Spurs will win, far from being (propositionally) justified for Mr. Ponens and Mr. F.A. Lacy in virtue of their knowing (or justifiedly believing) P5 and P6, is justified for them in virtue of their being (propositionally) justified to believe *that it follows via* modus ponens *from P5 and P6*. Orlandelli's diagnosis is then that Lacy's belief that the Spurs will win fails to be doxastically justified precisely because it is not based on *that* justification. For reasons that will become apparent in due course, I doubt that this account of inferential justification is correct. In any case, it seems able to make sense of our intuitions concerning Turri's basketball case only on the assumption that Mr. F.A. Lacy neither *knows* nor has a doxastically justified *belief* to the effect that the proposition that the Spurs will win follows via *modus ponens* from P5 and P6 – if he did, why would he employ *modus profusus* to draw the conclusion? This seems somewhat arbitrary, especially if one considers that in the more usual framework adopted by Turri it is possible to make the rather plausible claim that Mr. F.A. Lacy knows (or justifiedly believes) the reasons in virtue of which the proposition that the Spurs will win is justified for him.

and requirements of (subjective) rationality. For the *reasons* in virtue of which a proposition is justified for an agent seem to be one sort of thing, the logical and probabilistic *requirements* that rationality imposes on an agent's (subjective) attitudes quite another. The distinction is due to Broome (1999),[7] but here I will quote Niko Kolodny:

> Normativity involves two kinds of relation. On the one hand, there is the relation of being a reason for. This is a relation between a fact and an attitude. On the other hand, there are relations specified by requirements of rationality. These are relations among a person's attitudes, viewed in abstraction from the reasons for them. (Kolodny 2005, 509)

There is of course an ongoing debate on the relationship between reasons and rational requirements: 'reductionists' maintain that the relation of *being a reason for* can be explained in terms of rationality, 'nonreductionists' deny it.[8] For present purposes, it is not necessary to take a stand on this issue. Nor is it necessary to subscribe to the claim that reasons are *facts*. Many philosophers would regard them rather as *contents* available from an agent's point of view on the world (and of course the representatives of a prominent epistemological tradition have long been used to argue that 'only a belief can justify another belief'). Be that as it may, one may concur with Turri that (propositional) justification is something that a proposition possesses, or lacks, for an agent at a time in virtue of the agent's having one or more *reasons* to believe it.[9] If that much is admitted, it is inevitable to sense something amiss with assimilating the requirements that rationality imposes on our doxastic attitudes in virtue of the logical and probabilistic relations that obtain among their contents (or among the levels of confidence with which these are held) to the reasons in virtue of which certain propositions are justified for a specific agent – for example, to return to Turri's basketball case, with counting the *requirement* that one believe that the Spurs will win if one believes P5 and P6 among the *reasons* in virtue of which the proposition that the Spurs will win is justified for Mr. Ponens and Mr. F.A. Lacy. As soon as one recognizes the relevance of Broome's distinction, it appears clear that, in an important sense, the existence of a valid argument from P5 and P6 to the proposition that the Spurs will win cannot be listed among the *reasons* in virtue of which this proposition is justified for our agents – which is apparently grist for Turri's mill, because it supports the view that, after all, Mr. F.A. Lacy *does* believe that the Spurs will win on the basis of all the reasons in virtue of which this proposition is justified for him.

---

[7]A related but not identical distinction between the 'vertical' relations that obtain between mental states and the world and the 'horizontal' relations that obtain among mental states is made by Zangwill (2005, 4).

[8]For references to the debate, and a defence of nonreductionism, see Kolodny (2005, 510 f.).

[9]As I said in Sect. 2, for the purposes of this paper it is not necessary to assume that the things that lend justification to propositions have propositional content, can be given or cited in defence of a claim, or are accessible from, or internal to, a specific agent's perspective on the world. What I think one should grant to Turri is then, in more neutral terms, that (propositional) justification is the epistemic status that a proposition may enjoy for an agent at a time in virtue of there being one or more justification-makers (justifiers) for the agent to believe it.

Yet, a little reflection shows that taking seriously the distinction between reasons and requirements of rationality does not mandate the conclusion that Turri's cases are fatal to Basis and its strengthenings. Even if such cases show, as he claims, that poor utilization of even the best reasons for believing a proposition will prevent an agent's believing that proposition from being epistemically justified or an instance of knowledge, this admission only warrants the rejection of those formulations of the orthodox view that do not give due weight to the way reasons are used to support belief. Something strikes us as deeply inappropriate in the way Miss Improper and Mr. F.A. Lacy handle the (good) reasons they have for believing the propositions they end up believing, and that makes us reject the claim that they are doxastically justified in believing those propositions. In itself, however, the fact that inappropriate utilization of the reasons that (propositionally) justify an agent to believe a proposition precludes the formation of a (doxastically) justified belief whose content is that proposition has no tendency to show that there is anything wrong with the usual view of the order of explanation between the two kinds of justification. The intuition elicited by Turri's cases is just that one cannot form a doxastically justified belief by making inappropriate use of the reasons in virtue of which the belief's content is justified, and this intuition is fully consistent with the view that doxastic justification should be explained in terms of propositional justification – that is, in terms of propositional justification *plus rationally appropriate belief-formation*.

There is, however, a difficulty to be addressed. The way Miss Improper and Mr. F.A. Lacy handle their reasons certainly strikes us as rationally inappropriate, but in what exactly does the inappropriateness consist? It is not clear that they violate the requirements that rationality imposes on the way they use their respective reasons. On the face of it, neither of them can be accused of adopting a set of doxastic attitudes that is either logically or probabilistically inconsistent: each of them infers and comes to believe the conclusion that is rationally mandated by the premises they respectively know (or justifiedly believe). So what is it exactly that makes Miss Improper's and Mr. F.A. Lacy's beliefs rationally inappropriate – inappropriate, that is, in the way that prevents a belief that is held on the basis of (all) the reasons that justify its content from being a doxastically justified belief?

If it is not sufficient for a belief to be *rationally appropriate* that it not be logically or probabilistically inconsistent with the agent's overall set of doxastic attitudes (or perhaps with the subset of that set that contains the doxastic attitudes with which it is most closely related), what else is required? Here are two possible answers. The first is that a rationally appropriate belief must, in addition, be held as a result of the exercise of a genuine probabilistic or logical competence: Miss Improper's and Mr. F.A. Lacy's beliefs are rationally inappropriate because their hitting on the truth cannot be *attributed* to any such competence.[10] This answer has an externalist

[10]This idea was suggested to me by some related considerations made by Lalumera (2013). For the relevant notion of epistemic competence, see Sosa (2007, 22 ff.).

ring to it. An internalist answer might be that a rationally appropriate belief must, in addition, result from a train of reasoning that is (or could be) justifiedly believed to be capable of transmitting the justification enjoyed by its premises to its conclusion: Miss Improper's and Mr. F.A. Lacy's beliefs are rationally inappropriate because they are held as a result of trains of reasoning which are so defective that the epistemic status of their premises cannot justifiedly be believed to *transmit* to their conclusions.[11] There is no need, here, to adjudicate between these – or other – answers. For our purposes it is sufficient to have shown that there are at least two plausible accounts of the sort of inappropriateness that may prevent a belief that is held on the basis of all the reasons that justify its content from being a doxastically justified belief – two accounts that fit well in the framework provided by the distinction between reasons and requirements of rationality, but whose plausibility does not depend, ultimately, on endorsing that framework.

If these considerations are on the right track, the intuition elicited from Turri's cases, far from mandating a reversal in the order of explanation between doxastic and propositional justification, comes out as fully consistent – to tamper a bit with his formulations – both with the claim expressed by

> (**Rational Basis**) IF (i) *p* is propositionally justified for S in virtue of S's having reason(s) R and (ii) S believes *p* in a rationally appropriate way on the basis of R, THEN S's belief in *p* is doxastically justified

and with the stronger tenet articulated by

> (**Rational Austere Basis**) IF (i) *p* is propositionally justified for S in virtue of S's having reason(s) R and (ii) S believes *p* in a rationally appropriate way on the basis of R and only R, THEN S's belief in *p* is doxastically justified.

Rational appropriateness is more demanding than mere conformity to the requirements of rationality. But I have already made clear that I do not wish to commit myself to any specific account of rationally appropriate belief. So I happily acknowledge that Rational Basis and Rational Austere Basis provide at best the *structure* of the desired conditional: much will depend on the way the notion of rationally appropriate belief is fleshed out. In any case, the version of the orthodox view that results from conjoining Rational Austere Basis with its converse is clearly too strong – it is very rarely the case that we believe a proposition in a rationally appropriate way *only* for those reasons that justify it. On the face of it, Rational Basis looks more promising. But again, it is not my purpose here to work out a formulation that gets every detail exactly right. My point is just that the general idea that (specifications of) Rational Basis and Rational Austere Basis attempt to capture

[11] For an overview of the literature on the transmission of justification and the ways in which it can fail, see Moretti and Piazza (2013). Miss Improper and Mr. F.A. Lacy adopt ways of belief-formation that, employed on a regular basis, would almost inevitably lead them to believe logically inconsistent propositions. So one might also suggest that the former's belief about Mansour and the latter's belief about the Spurs are irrational because they are formed by methods of belief-formation which are essentially flawed.

is not refuted by Turri's cases: such cases provide no compelling reason to give up the orthodox view of the order of explanation between propositional and doxastic justification.

4 Five Ways of Construing Propositional Justification

There is, I think, something potentially misleading in the way a number of contemporary epistemologists talk of propositional and doxastic justification, something which I suspect has been misdiagnosed by Turri as a reversal of the order of explanation between these two properties (or, rather, relations). In my view, the nub of the matter has less to do with the relationship between propositional and doxastic justification than with some features of the conception of propositional justification with which the orthodox view is frequently conjoined.

These features arise, I believe, from a tendency to consider propositional justification in abstraction from certain aspects of the epistemic situation of the specific agents for which propositions are said to be, or not to be, justified. The judgments of propositional justification that are formulated as a result of indulging in this tendency are, in themselves, perfectly legitimate; but the attendant idealization can lead to some serious confusion when it is not explicitly acknowledged or too hastily generalized. So I shall start this discussion by rehearsing the obvious point that saying that *p* is justified for S at *t* is just a convenient way of saying that S is justified *to believe p* at *t* – where of course the existence of the justification in question does not depend on S's actually believing *p* at *t*.[12] Epistemic justification can be treated as a relation between a proposition, an agent and a time – the relation that holds between S, *p* and *t* just in case S is justified to believe *p* at *t* – only because there is some *attitude* that an agent can have (or fail to have) toward a proposition at a time. Various logical and probabilistic relations can obtain among propositions atemporally and irrespective of the doxastic states of any agent whatsoever, and sometimes the language of epistemic justification is used loosely to talk of such relations, but in the strict and proper sense that is in play when we employ sentences of the form 'The proposition that *p* is justified for S at *t*', it is *believing* a proposition that is epistemically justified for an agent at a time. Propositions are inherently the contents of propositional attitudes, and it is hard to see how they could entertain any

[12]To many speakers, saying that S is justified to believe *p* at *t* sounds significantly different from saying that S is justified *in believing p* at *t*. Bach (1985, 251) maintains that statements to the effect that someone is justified *in believing* a proposition at a time express claims of *personal*, as opposed to doxastic, justification, while Kvanvig and Menzel (1990, 240–247) argue that claims of personal justification are in fact logically equivalent to claims of doxastic justification. Be that as it may, it seems clear that the truth of statements to the effect that someone is justified *to believe*, unlike (possibly) that of statements to the effect that someone is justified *in believing*, a proposition at a time does not depend on the agent's actually believing the proposition at the relevant time.

genuine relation with agents and times other than through the attitudes of which they are supposed to be the contents. Epistemic justification, then, is inherently justification *to believe* a proposition.[13]

Let us turn to the role of idealization in judgments of propositional justification. This is also a subject to which Turri pays his attention, for he builds his argument for the deeper principle that he maintains lies behind **PJ** on the intuitions elicited by two cases – Ron's case and Cedric's case – which he takes to show that our judgments of propositional justification involve idealizing to a typical intellectual performance either of a competent member of the agent's kind or of the specific agent that is in question.[14] Here, however, I am more interested in distinguishing two different ways in which the various degrees of idealization involved in judgments of propositional justification may cause the justification that a proposition enjoys for an agent at a time to be unavailable to the agent in question. So I propose to address the issue from a different angle: I shall start by introducing a case which is in many respects similar to, but also significantly different from, Turri's first case, and then I will turn to a related claim concerning the rational availability of propositional justification which has found its way in recent epistemological literature.

The protagonist of the case I want to introduce is Peppe, an Italian political activist who is reflecting on how to overcome the current economic crisis. He knows both that Italy's leaving the euro would be a disaster,[15] and that if Italy's leaving the euro would be a disaster, then Italy should not leave the euro. Peppe is, let us suppose, sufficiently familiar with *modus ponens*. However, he is currently under the effects of a drug that impairs his logical skills. As a consequence, Peppe will not exploit *modus ponens* to form the belief that Italy should not leave the euro (nor, for that matter, any other belief), but will defer to the outcome of an online survey asking the question, 'Should Italy leave the euro?' Now, we

---

[13]As I said, for simplicity I ignore the complications raised by the possibility of considering degrees of belief or different kinds of doxastic and propositional attitudes, as they are immaterial to the problem under consideration.

[14]Here is a brief description of the two cases. *Ron's case*. Ron knows both that invading Iran would be catastrophically stupid, and that if invading Iran would be catastrophically stupid, than the U.S. ought not to invade Iran. But although perfectly familiar with *modus ponens*, he will not exploit such pattern of reasoning to form the belief that the U.S. ought not to invade Iran because massive exposition to right-wing propaganda has made him incapable of believing that the U.S. ought not to invade *any* country, much less Iran. The intuition elicited by this case is meant to be that the proposition that the U.S. ought not to invade Iran is (propositionally) justified for Ron even if he is currently incapable of forming a (doxastically) justified belief in it. *Cedric's case*. Cedric is the most brilliant logician in the world: for any given proposition and any given set of axioms, he is able to discover with relative ease whether the former is a theorem of the latter by applying some clever algorithm he devised. The intuition elicited by this case is meant to be that the true proposition that (say) T is a theorem of A is (propositionally) justified for Cedric even if most competent human reasoners are obviously incapable of forming a (doxastically) justified belief in it. See Turri (2010b, 322–324).

[15]If you do not believe that it would, just assume it for the sake of the example.

are inclined to think that, whatever the outcome of the survey, the proposition that Italy should not leave the euro is justified for Peppe even if he is currently incapable of forming a (doxastically) justified belief with that content. In forming this judgment, we abstract from his momentary logical disability. For, as Turri observes at the end of his discussion of the first of his own two cases, in idealized judgments of propositional justification we typically 'have in mind a competent intellectual performance by a normal human adult, who doubtlessly would be able to competently and effortlessly reason his way to the relevant conclusion' (ibid., 324).

Turri's diagnosis is framed in terms of doxastic justification, but the point can be formulated equally well in terms of propositional justification. We have seen that, when we say that *p* is justified for S at *t*, what we mean is normally that

(i) S is justified to believe *p* at *t*.

Substitution-instances of (i) typically express judgments of *concrete* propositional justification, i.e., judgments of propositional justification that do not abstract away from specific aspects of the agent's epistemic situation – anyway, this is how I shall interpret them henceforth. Now, it should not be taken for granted that what is at stake when a proposition is said to be (or not to be) justified for an agent at a time is always concrete propositional justification. In some cases, especially when the agent in question displays some form of cognitive disability, when we say that *p* is justified for S at *t* what we are likely to mean is rather that

(ii) *Any normal human reasoner* whose total evidence and overall doxastic profile are relevantly similar to S's total evidence and overall doxastic profile is justified to believe *p* at *t*,

where of course the justification that any normal human reasoner that meets the relevant conditions is supposed to possess with respect to believing *p* at *t* is just the concrete sort of justification that is at issue in judgments expressed by substitution-instances of (i). Thus, the reason why we are inclined to say that the proposition that Italy should not leave the euro is justified for Peppe even if he is currently incapable of forming a (doxastically) justified belief with that content is precisely that *any normal human reasoner whose total evidence and overall doxastic profile are relevantly similar to Peppe's total evidence and overall doxastic profile* is justified to believe that proposition.

There is nothing wrong in the judgments about *moderately idealized* propositional justification expressed by the substitution-instances of (ii) – nor is there anything intrinsically objectionable in putting them concisely by saying that a certain proposition is (propositionally) justified for a specific agent at a given time. However, one should not be misled by this turn of phrase into believing that, in formulating such judgments, we are talking of a justification that the relevant agent can easily become aware of and use as the basis of a doxastically justified belief. As Peppe's case makes clear, *p*'s being justified for S at *t* in this moderately idealized sense is perfectly compatible with S's being incapable of recognising *p*'s justifiedness and of forming in a rationally appropriate way a (doxastically) justified belief in p. The type of justification that is at issue when we introduce this moderate degree of idealization may well be *unavailable for rationally appropriate belief-formation* to the relevant agent.

Now, someone might be inclined to regard the distinction between judgments of concrete propositional justification and judgments of moderately idealized propositional justification as spurious. Perhaps the reason why we are disposed to say that the proposition that Italy should not leave the euro is justified for Peppe is just that *all* judgments of propositional justification involve the moderate degree of idealization that is associated with ignoring the most blatant weaknesses or failings in the agents' cognitive abilities and powers. Perhaps it is precisely in terms of propositional justification of this moderately idealized sort that doxastic justification is to be explained. If this were the case, the conclusion of the last paragraph would apply across the board – there would be no unified species of propositional justification that one might be legitimately inclined to regard as inherently available, in virtue of its concreteness, for rationally appropriate belief-formation. As the ensuing discussion will make clear, I find the idea that there is just one variety of propositional justification unappealing. Here, however, I will not pause to criticize it in general terms. In the remaining part of this section I will single out some further varieties of propositional justification, each associated with an increasing degree of idealization; what follows will make it clear, I hope, that ignoring the differences that set apart such varieties of justification by focussing on just one of them is unlikely to provide philosophical illumination.

As I said, other reasons may be cited in support of the conclusion that the justification that a proposition enjoys for an agent at a time may on occasion be unavailable to the agent in question. Some philosophers have suggested that this may happen not because of any weaknesses or failings of the agent's cognitive abilities and powers, but as a result of some specific doxastic attitudes the agent happens to have. The idea has been put forward by Jim Pryor and Martin Davies,[16] who have argued in slightly different ways that the justification that a proposition has for an agent at a time can be *rationally unavailable* to the agent in question because of some unjustified beliefs or doubts he happens to have. Thus, Pryor writes that an agent 'can *have some justification* to believe p, but be unable to *rationally* believe p on the basis of that justification, because of some (unjustified) beliefs and doubts he also has' (2004, 365).[17] And Davies maintains that if 'warranted doubt

[16]A similar idea is found in work by Crispin Wright, who takes a proposition to be 'rationally *available*' to an agent when it is 'consistent with what they believe' (Wright 2004, 181). See also Coliva (2015, 22).

[17]Pryor's idea is, essentially, that an agent is prevented from forming a *rational* belief in p on certain grounds whenever he holds a belief in q, such that justification for q would undermine the justification those grounds give him for p (Pryor 2004, 364 f., 2012, 285 f.). Pryor applies this idea to Moore's proof of an external world, whose failure is in his view merely dialectical, a consequence of the fact that whoever rejects its premises or even doubts whether they are true cannot rationally believe its – propositionally justified – conclusion. See Pryor (2004, 368–370, 2012, Section 5).

would undermine a warrant, W, to believe a proposition, P, then even an unwarranted doubt would make it rationally impossible for me to avail myself of W' (2009, 367), preventing me from forming a *rationally based* belief in that proposition. Pryor's notion of rational belief and Davies' notion of rationally based belief have to do, ultimately, with the satisfaction of the logical and probabilistic requirements that rationality imposes on our doxastic attitudes, so they are logically weaker than the notion of rationally appropriate belief introduced at the end of Sect. 3. As a consequence, a justification that is *rationally unavailable* to an agent in Pryor's and Davies' sense will always be a justification that is *unavailable for rationally appropriate belief-formation* to that agent in my sense.

Now, a conspicuous feature of the judgments of propositional justification on which Pryor and Davies (but also Crispin Wright and Annalisa Coliva)[18] focus their attention is that they abstract away not only from any weaknesses and failings in the agent's cognitive abilities and powers, but also from any 'doxastic mistakes' the agent may be making. Here, then, we seem to be faced with a further sense – or perhaps, as we shall presently see, with three further senses – in which a proposition may be said to be justified for an agent at a time. Let us say that an agent is an *unimpeded* reasoner if and only if he (i) is endowed with cognitive abilities and powers that are at least as strong as those of any normal human reasoner, (ii) does not believe any unjustified proposition and (iii) does not disbelieve any (adequately) justified proposition. (For the purpose of characterising unimpeded reasoners, talk of 'justified' and 'unjustified' propositions can be construed indifferently in terms of concrete or moderately idealized justification.) An unimpeded reasoner needn't be either logically or probabilistically omniscient; so there will typically be consequences of justified propositions that an unimpeded reasoner does not believe and contraries of justified propositions that an unimpeded reasoner fails to disbelieve.[19] What is meant by saying that p is justified for S at t may then be that

(iii) *Any unimpeded human reasoner* whose total evidence is relevantly similar to S's total evidence is justified to believe p at t,

where again the justification that any unimpeded human reasoner that meets the relevant condition is supposed to possess with respect to believing p at t is just the concrete sort of justification that is at issue in judgments expressed by substitution-instances of (i).

---

[18]See the works cited in footnote 16 above.

[19]Although there is a sense in which one is *rationally committed* to believe every implication of the propositions one believes (Volpe 2012, 323 f.), it is not the case that one is *justified* to believe every proposition that follows from the propositions that one justifiedly believes. This said, among the consequences of justified propositions that an unimpeded but not logically omniscient reasoner will inevitably fail to believe there will likely be some, even many, *justified* propositions – propositions he might easily have recognized to follow from (or, perhaps, to be made overwhelmingly likely by) propositions he is justified to believe. So an unimpeded reasoner will not be, in general, a reasoner who believes every proposition he is justified to believe (and who disbelieves every contrary of the propositions he is justified to believe).

A proposition may be said to be justified for an agent at a time in the sense captured by (iii) even if its justification is in a clear sense unavailable to the agent in question because of some doxastic mistakes he makes. However, the conception of propositional justification captured by (iii) abstracts away from the agent's mistaken beliefs and disbeliefs, not from the agent's mistaken *doubts*. Moreover, while an unimpeded reasoner needn't be either logically or probabilistically omniscient, different reasoners will have different levels of logical and probabilistic competence, and it is plausible to suppose that reasoners with higher levels of logical and probabilistic competence will have access to larger sets of reasons. So we need to consider (at least) two further degrees of idealization. What is meant by saying that *p* is justified for S at *t* may be that

(iv) *Some human reasoner* whose total evidence is relevantly similar to S's total evidence is justified to believe *p* at *t*,

or even that

(v) A human reasoner whose total evidence were relevantly similar to S's total evidence *might be* justified to believe *p* at *t*.

(I spare the reader the usual explanation about the notion of justification that should be employed in understanding these formulations.)

If propositional justification is construed along the lines of (iv), for a proposition to be justified for an agent at a time it will suffice that there exist just one or two extraordinarily gifted human reasoners whose total evidence is relevantly similar to the agent's total evidence but whose cognitive abilities and powers far exceed those of the vast majority of their fellows, who are justified (in the most basic sense) to believe it. And if it is understood along the lines of (v), for a proposition to be justified for an agent at a time it will suffice that *it be possible* that a human reasoner whose total evidence is relevantly similar to the agent's total evidence is justified (in the most basic sense) to believe it. It is arguably something very close to (v) that a number of recent epistemologists have in mind when they say that propositional justification is justification of propositions 'in the abstract space of warrants' (Davies 2009, 338; cf. Coliva 2010) or 'in the abstract space of reasons' (Coliva 2012, 326, 2015, 16).

Again, there is nothing intrinsically wrong in the increasingly idealized judgments of propositional justification articulated by the substitution-instances of (iii), (iv) and (v). But expressing such judgments by saying that a certain proposition is justified for an agent at a time may be rather misleading – at least if what is being done is not openly declared or made clear by the context. For again, one should not forget that *p*'s being justified for S at *t* in the senses associated with such degrees of idealization is perfectly compatible with S's being incapable of recognising *p*'s justifiedness and of forming in a rationally appropriate way a (doxastically) justified belief in *p* – even if S's cognitive abilities and powers display no particular weaknesses or failings. The type of justification that we are talking about when we reach such degrees of idealization may be in a clear sense *unavailable for rational belief-formation* to the relevant agent.

5 Doxastically Independent Propositional Justification?

The claim that a proposition can be justified for an agent at a time even if its justification is unavailable to the agent in question because of certain (unjustified) beliefs or doubts he happens to have does not logically entail but naturally leads to the thought that which propositions an agent is justified to believe (as opposed to committed to believe by the requirements of rationality) is largely independent of his doxastic states.

I say 'largely independent' to allow for cases in which a doxastic state provides a reason to believe a proposition merely in virtue of the fact that the agent that is in that state knows or justifiedly believes that he is. Think, for instance, of situations in which an agent gains insight into his own psychological makeup by reflecting on the fact that he has certain beliefs (or disbeliefs, or doubts). It seems clear that in situations of this kind the agent is justified to believe the relevant proposition(s) precisely in virtue of his knowing or justifiedly believing that he is in certain doxastic states. However, the question raised in this section is not whether propositional justification is independent of the kind of reasons that doxastic states uncontroversially provide in such situations (which it obviously is not); rather, it is whether propositional justification is independent of the doxastic states that do not provide the agent who is in them with this kind of reasons.

The thought that which propositions an agent is justified to believe is (largely) independent of the agent's doxastic states is of course far from uncontroversial. For one thing, it is clearly inconsistent with many coherentist views of epistemic justification. For another, it sits uncomfortably with reductionist attempts to explain the relation of *being a reason for* in terms of the requirements of rationality. But it is a thought that is likely to attract those epistemologists who, like Pryor, Davies, Wright and Coliva, take pains to emphasize the independence of propositional justification (or of some subspecies of it) from what might be called the 'vagaries of belief'. Let us first consider an unrestricted version of the thought. According to this version, propositional justification is (largely) independent of the relevant agent's doxastic states *generally*:

> (**Unrestricted Doxastic Independence**) Which propositions S is justified to believe at t is largely independent of the doxastic states S is in at t (or, for that matter, at any other time).

This principle might look attractive if the only way in which doxastic states provide agents with reasons for belief were the one that has been described and set aside a few lines earlier. However, if we are to explain along the usual lines how inferential justification is possible, we had better not rule out from the beginning the possibility that *justified* beliefs may furnish agents with reasons by contributing to the inferential justification of propositions that logically follow from, or are made overwhelmingly likely by, suitably related sets of premises. So I propose to focus on a weaker version of the thought. Let us say that a doxastic state is *evidentially idle* (for an agent at a time) just in case it *doesn't* contribute to the inferential justification of any proposition (for that agent at that time).[20] The weaker version of the thought can then be stated as follows:

> (**Doxastic Independence**) Which propositions S is justified to believe at *t* is largely independent of the evidentially idle doxastic states S is in at *t* (or, for that matter, at any other time).

By restricting the relevant sort of independence to evidentially idle doxastic states, this formulation does not rule out the possibility that justified beliefs may influence which propositions an agent is justified to believe by contributing to the inferential justification of some of them. However, it does rule out the possibility that an agent's *unjustified* beliefs and doubts may influence which propositions an agent is justified to believe – other, that is, than in the rather unexciting way that has been described a few paragraphs earlier.

Again, there is nothing intrinsically wrong with Doxastic Independence – as long as it is clear that it is meant to apply uniquely to the highly idealized varieties of propositional justification that are in play when judgments of propositional justification are cashed out in the terms articulated by the substitution-instances of (iii), (iv) or (v). The idea is simply that a human reasoner whose evidential situation were relevantly similar to S's evidential situation at *t* might have access to a wider range of reasons than are actually available to S at *t* – so that there is a sense in which it will be possible for a proposition to be justified for S at *t* even if its justification is unavailable for rational belief-formation to S because of some (unjustified) doxastic states he is in. However, it would be ill-advised to conclude that Doxastic Independence applies to *all* varieties of propositional justification, in particular to the mundane variety that is in play when sentences of the form '*p* is justified for S at *t*' are given their most natural reading. Ignoring the differences that set apart the varieties of propositional justification to which Doxastic Independence arguably applies from those to which it doesn't apply by assuming that when we say such things as that *p* is (or is not) justified for S at *t* we are always engaged in sophisticated exercises of idealization can be utterly misleading.

The main source of my dissatisfaction with the conception of propositional justification in terms of which the orthodox view of the relation between propositional and doxastic justification has frequently been fleshed out in recent years is then that it gives pride of place to varieties of propositional justification that are rather removed from the relations that are at issue in many situations in which we say that a proposition is (or is not) justified for an agent at a time. Putting the emphasis on such robustly idealized varieties of propositional justification may lead to hasty generalisations – in particular, it may prompt the conclusion that *all* varieties of propositional justification supervene only on the evidential situations of epistemic

[20]This is a technical notion: a doxastic state that provides a reason to believe a proposition merely in virtue of the fact that the agent that is in that state knows or justifiedly believes that he is will count as evidentially idle in this sense. Needless to say, whether a doxastic state is evidentially idle for an agent at a time will depend in part on the agent's level of logical and probabilistic competence.

agents and not also on their overall doxastic profiles, including their evidentially idle doxastic states.[21] This conclusion, however, seems to me to be unacceptable. For if *p*'s justification is unavailable for rational belief-formation to S at *t*, S will be unable to form on its basis a *doxastically justified* belief in *p*. And I want to press the intuition that, on a natural and central reading of (the substitution-instances of) '*p* is justified for S at *t*',

> (**EJ**) S can be (propositionally) justified to believe *p* at *t* in virtue of S's having reason(s) R only if it is reasonably easy for S to form a (doxastically) justified belief in *p* at *t*

(if you like, only if there is a world which is easily available – in the relevant sense – to S in which S forms a doxastically justified belief in *p* at *t*). If the overall doxastic profile of S at *t* makes it *too difficult* for S to form a doxastically justified belief in *p* at *t*, then in a natural and important sense S cannot be said to be propositionally justified to believe *p* at *t*.

The intuition articulated by **EJ** coheres well with the view that epistemic justification is just a matter of logical or probabilistic relations between beliefs; for on this view there is apparently little point in talking of what an agent is propositionally justified to believe irrespective of his overall doxastic profile. However, it should be abundantly clear by now that this is not a view I am inclined to accept (nor, for that matter, am I inclined to accept the particular brand of justification-relativism that naturally goes hand in hand with it).[22] My point is simply that if the doxastic states we happen to be in (even unjustified ones) affect the things that we can come to believe in a rationally appropriate way and so the things that can become the content of our doxastically justified beliefs, it is plausible to think that they also affect the things that, in a natural and important sense, we are *propositionally* justified to believe. So Doxastic Independence does not apply across the board.

To a certain extent, the issue is verbal. There are ways of talking of propositional justification that allow for the possibility that the justification a proposition enjoys for an agent at a time might be unavailable to the agent in question due to certain peculiarities of his overall doxastic profile. And there are ways of talking of propositional justification that do not allow for such a possibility. (The line may

---

[21] The term 'evidential situation' is used to refer to the whole set of reasons possessed by an agent at a time, including the agent's evidentially non-idle beliefs.

[22] What I have in mind is not the trivial claim that a proposition that is justified for an agent at a time may fail to be justified for another agent at the same time, or for the same agent at a different time (or that a proposition that is not justified for an agent at a time may be justified for another agent at the same time, or for the same agent at a different time). Nor is it just the claim that the doxastic states of an agent affect what the agent is justified to believe in the sense that a proposition that is justified for an agent at a time might fail to be so justified (or that a proposition that is not justified for an agent at a time might be so justified) if the agent's overall doxastic profile at that time were relevantly different. It is, rather, the claim that the doxastic states of an agent affect what the agent is justified to believe in the sense that, had his overall doxastic profile been sufficiently different from the overall doxastic profile that he is in at some given time, an agent might have been justified to believe propositions that are *inconsistent* with the propositions he is actually justified to believe. Nothing of what I say in this paper commits me to subscribe to this form of justification-relativism.

not be so sharp, but for present purposes we can ignore this complication.) So there are in fact two different notions of propositional justification that turn up and are sometimes confused with each other in recent epistemology: the notion of what an epistemic agent is (propositionally) justified to believe *irrespective of the evidentially idle features of his doxastic profile*, and the notion of what an epistemic agent is (propositionally) justified to believe *given his overall doxastic profile*.[23] **EJ** articulates a central feature of this latter notion – or so I maintain.

6 The Point of the Notion of Propositional Justification

Should we leave it at that? It might be thought that the notion of what an epistemic agent is propositionally justified to believe given his overall doxastic profile is more fundamental than the notion of what an epistemic agent is propositionally justified to believe irrespective of the evidentially idle features of his doxastic profile because it involves a lower degree of idealization (it does not abstract away from the agent's evidentially idle doxastic states). Moreover, taking the former notion as more fundamental might lead one to agree with Turri that propositional justification should be explained in terms of doxastic justification and not vice versa – if what explains *p*'s justifiedness for S at *t* is S's currently possessing at least one means of forming a doxastically justified belief in *p*, then small wonder that S's evidentially idle doxastic states at *t* may affect what S is propositionally justified to believe at *t*.

However, I think that **PJ** is mistaken, and not merely in the qualified sense that it is an approximation and a guide to some deeper and more general principle (Turri 2010b, 323–325). If *p* is (propositionally) justified for S at *t*, it is not, I claim, *because* S currently possesses at least one means of forming a (doxastically) justified belief in *p*. **EJ** stands on its own feet, and the fact that, on a rather natural construal of the notion of epistemic justification, S can be justified to believe *p* at *t only if* it is reasonably easy for S to form a justified belief in *p* at *t* should not be taken as evidence that the notion of doxastic justification is in any sense more fundamental than that of propositional justification.

It is possible, I think, to sketch an alternative account of why **EJ** holds – an account that explains why it does not hold unrestrictedly, but only relative to the sort of justification that supervenes on the agents' reasons *together* with their overall doxastic profile. My bid is that **EJ** holds with respect to this sort of justification because it is this sort of justification that occupies centre stage when the issue is whether it would be *epistemically responsible* for an agent to believe a

[23] A third notion might be considered: that of what an epistemic agent is (propositionally) justified to believe *irrespective of his overall doxastic profile*. But this notion would be of any interest only if Unrestricted Doxastic Independence were true.

that it cannot prove valuable in addressing other significant epistemological issues, such as, for instance, the architecture of epistemic justification, the conditions for the transmission of justification and many familiar sceptical paradoxes. But when it comes to the two issues that have been traditionally at the centre of epistemological inquiry, it seems clear that the crucial notion will be that of what an epistemic agent is propositionally justified to believe *given his overall doxastic profile* – a notion whose employment goes hand in hand with the assumption that the basis upon which facts concerning propositional justification supervene is not restricted to facts concerning the evidential situation of agents.

Acknowledgments Earlier versions of this paper were presented at a philosophy of language conference held in Gargnano (Brescia) in June 2013 and at Cogito's Epistemology seminar (Bologna) in January 2014. Thanks to all present for discussion. I am especially grateful to Andrea Borghini, Delia Belleri, Annalisa Coliva, Elisabetta Lalumera, Sebastiano Moruzzi, Ernesto Napoli, Eugenio Orlandelli, Elisa Paganini, Michele Palmira, Marco Santambrogio, Giuseppe Spolaore and Luca Zanetti for many helpful comments and suggestions.

References

Bach, Kent (1985). 'A Rationale for Reliabilism'. *The Monist*, 68, 246–263.

BonJour, Laurence (1985). *The Structure of Empirical Knowledge*. Cambridge, MA: Harvard University Press.

Broome, John (1999). 'Normative Requirements'. *Ratio*, 12, 398–419.

Carroll, Lewis (1895). 'What the Tortoise Said to Achilles'. *Mind*, 4, 278–280.

Coliva, Annalisa (2010). 'Moore's Proof and Martin Davies' Epistemic Projects'. *Australasian Journal of Philosophy*, 88, 101–116.

Coliva, Annalisa (2012). 'Liberals and Conservatives. Is There a Third (Wittgensteinian) Way?'. In Id. (ed.), *Mind, Meaning and Knowledge: Themes from the Philosophy of Crispin Wright*. Oxford: Oxford University Press, 323–351.

Coliva, Annalisa (2015). *Extended Rationality*. Basingstoke: Palgrave Macmillan.

Davies, Martin (2009). 'Two Purposes of Arguing and Two Epistemic Projects'. In Ravenscroft, Ian (ed.), *Mind, Ethics, and Conditionals: Themes from the Philosophy of Frank Jackson*. New York: Oxford University Press, 337–383.

Feldman, Richard (2002). *Epistemology*. Upper Saddle River, NJ: Prentice Hall.

Feldman, Richard & Conee, Earl (1985). 'Evidentialism'. *Philosophical Studies*, 48, 15–34.

Firth, Roderick (1978). 'Are Epistemic Concepts Reducible to Ethical Concepts?'. In Goldman, Alvin I. and Kim Jaegwon (eds.), *Values and Morals: Essays in Honor of William Frankena, Charles Stevenson, and Richard Brandt*. Dordrecht: Reidel, 215–229.

Foley, Richard (2005). 'Justified Belief as Responsible Belief'. In Steup, Matthias and Sosa, Ernest (eds.), *Contemporary Debates in Epistemology*. Malden, MA: Blackwell, 313–326.

Ginet, Carl (1975). *Knowledge, Perception and Memory*. Dordrecht: Reidel.

Greco, John (2005). 'Justification Is not Internal'. In Steup, Matthias and Sosa, Ernest (eds.), *Contemporary Debates in Epistemology*. Malden, MA: Blackwell, 257–270.

Goldman, Alvin I. (1999). 'Internalism Exposed'. *The Journal of Philosophy*, 96, 271–293.

Kolodny, Niko (2005). 'Why Be Rational?'. *Mind*, 114, 509–563.

Kvanvig, Jonathan & Menzel, Christopher (1990). 'The Basic Notion of Justification'. *Philosophical Studies*, 59: 235–261.

Lalumera, Elisabetta (2013). 'Doxastic Justification and the Competence Condition'. Ms.

Moretti, Luca & Piazza, Tommaso (2013). 'Transmission of Justification and Warrant'. In Zalta, Edward N. (ed.), *The Stanford Encyclopedia of Philosophy* (Winter 2013 Edition), URL = <http://plato.stanford.edu/archives/win2013/entries/transmission-justification-warrant/>.

Plantinga, Alvin (1993). *Warrant: The Current Debate*. New York: Oxford University Press.

Pryor, James (2004). 'What's Wrong with Moore's Argument?'. *Philosophical Issues*, 14, 349–378.

Pryor, James (2012). 'When Warrant Transmits'. In Coliva, Annalisa (ed.), *Mind, Meaning, and Knowledge: Themes from the Philosophy of Crispin Wright*. Oxford: Oxford University Press, 269–303.

Sosa, Ernest (2007). *A Virtue Epistemology*. Vol. 1: *Apt Belief and Reflective Knowledge*. Oxford: Clarendon Press.

Turri, John (2010a). 'Epistemic Supervenience'. In Dancy, Jonathan, Sosa, Ernest and Steup Matthias (eds.), *A Companion to Epistemology*. 2nd ed. Oxford: Blackwell, 340–343.

Turri, John (2010b). 'On the Relationship between Propositional and Doxastic Justification'. *Philosophy and Phenomenological Research*, 80, 312–326.

Volpe, Giorgio (2012). 'Cornerstones: You'd better Believe Them', *Synthese*, 189, 317–336.

Wright, Crispin (2004). 'Warrant for Nothing (and Foundations for Free)?', *Aristotelian Society Supplementary* Volume, 78, 167–212.

Zangwill, Nick (2005). 'The Normativity of the Mental', *Philosophical Explorations*, 8, 1–19.

Moral Properties: Some Epistemological, Ontological, and Normative Dimensions

Robert Audi

Abstract Moral properties lead a double life. We invoke them as high authorities when we feel mistreated or want to redirect others; but we also doubt their authority—or even their existence—when we seek to understand them philosophically. Some philosophers would say that even this open-ended contrast between respect and skeptical doubt presupposes too much: ontological neutrality requires speaking not of moral properties but instead of moral *predicates*. Nonetheless, even if we confine the contrast to those, a comparable duality is evident. For nearly everyone, moral terms are apparently quite well understood when it comes to bringing up children—an activity in which our true colors surely show—but deeply puzzling when it comes to the attempt at analysis. In this, to be sure, moral language is not so different from many other kinds: we learn how to use moral terms, much as we do psychological and other "descriptive" terms, and in that crucial way we know what they mean, yet even most philosophers are unable to give definitions that capture their meaning. This plainly applies to psychological language embodying action-explaining terms, and it clearly applies to at least a great many physical terms, perhaps all those not ostensively "definable." This kind of parity between moral and descriptive language is one among many reasons to explore the moral domain on the tentative assumption of realism. This paper does not argue directly for moral realism, but if the framework it presents for understanding moral discourse and practice is plausible, that will perhaps constitute an indirect argument for the view that moral judgments belong to the realm of the true and the real, not simply to that of attitudinal expression and behavioral regulation.

1 Moral Properties and Their Normativity

We are obligated to live up to our solemn agreements. It is wrong to violate them, as it is to lie in making them. We can be blameworthy for an accident we should have prevented and praiseworthy for risking our lives to pull a fallen child from

R. Audi (✉)
University of Notre Dame, Notre Dame, IN, USA
e-mail: audi.1@nd.edu

B. Brożek et al. (eds.), *Supervenience and Normativity*, Law and Philosophy Library 120, DOI 10.1007/978-3-319-61046-7_3

the path of an approaching train. We sometimes ask what would be the right thing to do in response to plagiarism, or we might say that a certain profitable action would be the wrong thing to do. In such uses, the terms of assessment—'obligated', 'wrong', right', 'blameworthy', and 'praiseworthy'—are moral. I take them to express properties, though of course their (non-conditional) attributive uses ordinarily also express pro and con attitudes. I also consider it clear that we apply moral terms not capriciously but on various kinds of grounds. We are indeed expected to be able to cite one or more of such grounds if asked to explain or justify our moral judgment.

I have so far concentrated on deontic vocabulary, roughly that of right and wrong. But ethics—conceived as moral philosophy—concerns the axiological domain, that of the good and the bad, as well as the right and the wrong. Here too, there are paradigms of broadly ethical ascriptions: rescuing the child from the onrushing train is a good deed; failing to live up to one's agreements is a bad thing; and so forth. Moreover, in the axiological case as in the deontic, there are grounds we are expected to have for our valuational ascriptions, and we may be called on to cite these to explain or justify them. All this makes it natural to think of moral ascriptions—including valuational ones, as attributing properties and as truth-valued.

In the history of moral philosophy, major figures have tended to conceive their ethical theories as either good-based, as with Bentham and Mill, or right-based, as on most interpretations of Kant. Here I make no assumption of reducibility either way. This is not to deny the possibility of *equivalences* across the two domains; for instance, what is intrinsically good might be equivalent to what we *ought* to love or care about, or the right might be equivalent to what accords with a rule whose universal internalization maximizes goodness or accords with virtue, conceived as goodness of character. Although my interest is in both rightness and goodness—indeed, in normative properties generally, including such aesthetic properties as beauty—I will concentrate on the deontic realm. Deontic notions (at least obligatoriness and wrongness) are, in certain familiar contexts, clearly moral, and scarcely anyone doubts that their application in some particular situation implies some reason for action. In that implication, the deontic and the axiological are each normative. Let me say something about normativity in general before proceeding to outline an account of the ontology and epistemology of moral properties.

The kinds of things that can be properly called normative are highly various. Reasons are an immensely important case of the normative, and on some views normative phenomena are, broadly, those involving reasons, in a certain way, whether for action or for some attitude. Cognitive attitudes are an important case here. Justifiedness, for instance, is an important normative property beliefs may have. Paradigms of normative ascription in the practical as opposed to cognitive realm are propositions to the effect that something ought to be done or that something has intrinsic, as opposed to instrumental, value. These are the kinds of normative ascriptions that are of main concern in this paper.

There is wider agreement about normativity on the negative side than on what constitutes it. One thing that many philosophers are inclined to say of normative properties (and the corresponding terms and concepts) is that they are not *descriptive* but rather, say, prescriptive, evaluative, or expressive (or some combination of these). Descriptive properties of the most familiar sorts are observable. In more complex cases, the term is used for properties that, whether observable or not, are (a) causal, (b) of a kind appropriate to constituting subjects of (empirical) scientific investigation, and (c) capable of figuring directly in prediction and explanation of events, roughly in the sense that something's possessing one is capable of explaining or predicting some fact. This threefold claim is controversial, however, and I will rest no major contention on it.[1] It should be stressed, however, that the descriptive need not be identified with the "factual" (fact-stating, if you like). Moral realists take moral claims to be capable of truth, hence of being factual, though they do not treat them as descriptive in the sense in question.

What is probably not controversial is that things possess normative properties in virtue of possessing other properties—those constituting the base of the former properties—that seem descriptive in the sense sketched. Even anti-realists in ethics may grant that normative *ascriptions* must meet a parallel condition: being applied on the basis of such properties. This condition leaves open whether normative properties (or terms) are themselves ultimately descriptive. But the consequentiality ("in virtue of") relation is not only common ground between non-naturalists and (cognitivistic) naturalists; it is also a basis for anchoring moral judgments in what almost everyone would grant are intersubjectively accessible facts. Whether the relation is a priori, as rationalists commonly take it to be in normative cases, or empirical, as empiricists would likely consider it to be in all cases, is a matter of continuing disagreement.

It is essential for understanding normativity that we distinguish two different kinds: *normativity in content*—which could also be called normativity in (conceptual) constitution—from *normativity in upshot*.[2] Consider the concept of pain. Taken generically, the notion is psychological: pain is (as a matter of conceptual truth) a psychological phenomenon with behavioral as well as phenomenal (at least

[1]Moore, in *Principia* (1903) is plausibly thought to have held this. It might be denied by, e.g. Boyd (1988), Sturgeon (1985), and Brink (1989), "Cornell Realists" who, even if they might grant that normative *concepts* are not natural, hold that normative properties are.

[2]The distinction between these two kinds of normativity is one I have long made and have most recently discussed in "Knowledge, Justification, and Normativity" (2013). I should add here that normativity in content is apparently not equivalent to normativity in *ontic* constitution, as it may be to normativity in conceptual constitution. Obligatoriness may be argued to be ontically constituted by such properties as being promised, being an avoidance of lying, and others. These are relevant to the content of the concept (as will be apparent below), but I am not assuming that they are internal to its content.

normally introspectible) aspects. Yet instances of pain—of the property of being pained—also cry out for a palliative response: a creature's being in pain makes such a response fitting and often fully justifies it. It is also an a priori truth that pain has this property—supporting a palliative response. On this second count—providing, a priori, a reason for action, such as a response that, like cooling a burned hand, is fitting and, often, fully justified—pain is normative in upshot.[3]

The reason-giving power of pain has great normative significance—enough to make it quite appropriate to speak of normativity in upshot as a kind of normativity. But, in content, the concept of pain is not deontic or axiological or normative in any other contentual respect, and its normativity is not a basic for it. The concept is fundamentally psychological and descriptive; but because the fact that some being is in pain provides—and a priori entails (indeed, arguably self-evidently entails)—that there is a reason (however slight) to do something that would eliminate it, it bears an important relation to the normative "proper"—what is normative in content. Pain has a normative upshot, but I do not believe it has a normative nature. What is normative in upshot is reason-grounding, but it is not conceptually normative.[4]

One response to this distinction is to say that pain (for instance) is normative in upshot *because* it is normative in content. It is true that if a normative attribution—say that something is intrinsically bad—is true, then, connected with it, there *is* a reason for action. But being intrinsically bad is—as a matter of conceptual truth—not a brute property; and if one did not have a sense of why the things that are intrinsically bad are so, one would not understand why something's being intrinsically bad entails there being a reason for action in relation to it. By contrast, pain directly provides a reason for action; and someone's being in pain *explains* why palliative action is called for. The statement 'Jan is in pain, but that implies no reason for anyone to do anything to relieve it' is at best conceptually puzzling. Related to this, an attribution of obligation or intrinsic value is an exercise of a normative concept and, more specifically, cannot be adequately understood apart

---

[3]The apriority of the reason-giving relation is controversial, I have defended it in some detail, e.g. in Audi (2004) and will extend the case below in Sect. 2. As characterized here, the normative in upshot can also be normative in content, but I use the term only for what is not normative in content.

[4]In my terminology, what is normative in upshot is not also normative in content, though I leave open whether what is normative in content can also share with the normative in upshot the important property of being reason-grounding. There are of course other conceptions of normativity. Wedgwood holds that intentional phenomena are normative; e.g. "(i) It is essential to *beliefs* that they are causally regulated by standards of rational or justified belief, and (ii) the ultimate purpose or point of conforming to those standards is not just to have rational or justified beliefs for their own sake but to ensure that one believes the proposition in question if and only if that proposition is true" (2007), p. 154. This apparently yields an extremely broad notion of normativity—one we might call *essential teleological appraisability.* Stones lack it, but pain apparently does not: it might be "regulated" by standards of rational behavior (since it tends to signal danger or potential harm and lead to avoiding it) and might have the (evolutionary?) purpose of self-preservation. There are also serious questions about whether belief is *causally* regulated in the relevant way and about how purpose figures in such regulation. For Wedgwood's defense of the view, see *Normativity* (2007) esp. pp. 155–73.

from having a concept of a reason and a related concept of the appropriateness of criticism for denying there being one; whereas attribution of a property normative in upshot does not meet this condition. One could attribute pain fully comprehendingly without having—and certainly without exercising—the concept of a reason or any equivalent. It is only when one *also* has such a concept that, say, attributing pain and denying that there is any reason for action should seem to one to be deviant. For here one is using both concepts; and one's denying the relation between them can be attributed not to the content normativity of the former but to a failure to see an a priori connection between the former and the latter. This connection is indeed important for understanding the normative content of the latter. Imagine that someone sincerely denied that pain provides any reason for action. This would be strong evidence of a lack of full understanding of the concept of a reason for action.

Given the wide range of things that can be intrinsically good or bad—commonly taken to include people, seasides, artworks, elegant proofs—one might wonder whether anything at all, say a rock, can be normative in upshot. I have not implied that just anything whatever can be normative in upshot. Only what a priori entails the presence of a property normative in content (and is not itself such a property) is normative in upshot. As to my presupposing here that there is a wide range of things of intrinsic value, of course the history of philosophy has many attempts to show, as hedonists attempt to, that there is a limited range of things of intrinsic value, or at least of the basic kind(s). It will already be apparent that I have presupposed that even normativity in upshot entails that there is an a priori connection between possession of the property in question, such as pain, and its normative upshot, here a reason to palliate. Being a rock does not a priori entail any reason for action, though *in* an appropriate context—say one in which we are pledged to save rocks from being pulverized to make a desired power—a normative consequence may be derived. This, however, requires a connective premise that entails the normative significance of rocks, as where they are needed to fulfill promissory obligations, and it shows only that what is normative in upshot, such as promising, can endow anything with what might be called *derivative normative importance*.

2 The Non-moral Grounds of the Moral: Supervenience and Consequentiality

There is wide agreement on the broad idea that normative properties are supervenient on non-moral properties. Consider just the moral case. A plausible supervenience thesis might be this:

> *The supervenience of moral properties*: Necessarily, for any given object or person, x, and any moral property, M, if x has M, then there is a unique set of non-moral properties, N, such that (necessarily) any given object or person, y, has M if and only if it has at least one property in N.

A number of comments are needed here.[5] First, we might illustrate with a simple case such as being obligated to keep a promise to a friend, where the obligation, as is normal, is prima facie rather than absolutely indefeasible, and is to do something—call it *A* to represent an act-type. One has this property—or in any case an obligation of fidelity to *A*—if and only if one has a commitment to the friend to *A*, normally by *making* that commitment.[6] There is more than one way to make a commitment: we can say, for instance, 'I promise to *A*' or simply 'yes' when asked by the friend whether one is promising. We must, then, either take the property N to be disjunctive or simply take the property of promising to be instantiated if and only if at least one of the properties in the set is instantiated. Secondly, it is plausible to consider N to be a natural property. On that assumption, we may further hold that, necessarily, no two things (including persons) can share all their natural properties and differ in their moral properties.

If there are plausible exceptions to the view that the base properties are natural, they likely come from theology: divine command theorists would argue that obligatoriness ultimately supervenes on divine commandedness. Thus, in our example the obligation to *A* is supervenient on the act-type, one's A-ing, being required (directly or indirectly) by God's command. Divine commandedness need not be conceived as a normative property; but although it may be conceived as a descriptive property, it is not plausibly held to be a natural property. This is not the place to consider divine command ethics,[7] and in what follows I assume that the base properties for normative properties are not only descriptive and non-normative but also natural.

This brings us to a third point. The supervenience thesis does not indicate that anything explains something's possessing a moral property. Surely something does. Acts are not brutely obligatory or wrong, nor good things brutely good. As our examples and numerous others kinds of cases illustrate, these properties belong to their bearers on the basis of other properties. Indeed, the very terminology of

---

[5]My formulation is much like Jaegwon Kim's in *Physicalism or Something Near Enough* (Princeton, 2005). In "Supervenience as a Philosophical Concept," (1990) he maintained that supervenience as I've characterized it is a kind of covariance and used 'strong supervenience' for (necessary) covariance conjoined with dependence—something close to what I call 'consequentiality' below. At present, however, 'supervenience' is commonly—though not consistently—used for what Kim called *strong* supervenience. This is inappropriate on the assumption (which I believe Kim and many others accept) that covariance—which, for many, is equivalent to supervenience, is too weak to do major metaphysical work (as I hold consequentiality does). For recent detailed discussion of supervenience, see the entry of that title by Karen Bennett and Brian McLaughlin in *The Stanford Encyclopedia of Philosophy,* http://plato.stanford.edu.entries/supervenience/ (July 2005), 1–42.

[6]Normally because commitments can be acquired without being *made*, as where one becomes someone's friend and simply by being in that relationship has a prima facie obligation of to give support of certain kinds.

[7]In ch. 6 of *Rationality and Religious Commitment* (2011) I propose a theory of the difference between divine commandedness and divine commandability as grounding properties for obligatoriness and there consider other views of theological grounding, especially that of Adams (2000).

"base" properties and of a supervenience base suggests this. The thesis we should be considering, then, and one prominent, at least by implication, in ethical theory since at least G. E. Moore, is something like this:

> *The consequentiality of moral properties*: Necessarily, for any given object or person, x, and any moral property M, if x has M, then (1) there is a unique set of non-moral properties, N, such that x has M *in virtue of* having one (or more) properties in N, and, necessarily, (2) for any given object or person, y, that has one or more properties in N, y has M, and has it in virtue of having, that property (or those properties).[8]

The consequentiality relation may also be called *grounding* and, apart from its causal associations, *resultancy.*[9] Again, several comments are needed.

It should be plain that the consequentiality relation is metaphysically explanatory (as opposed to causally or purely logically so). For instance, that I have promised to *A* explains why I should *A* and does so both non-causally and in such a way that it is necessary that the making of the promise explains why I have an obligation. Granted, my obligation may be defeated, but that I have some obligation—in a sense implying a moral reason to *A*—seems quite clear.[10] A second point is that the consequentiality thesis not only implies but explains the supervenience view.[11] Take a simple analogy to indicate why the former relation is explanatorily more powerful. For integers, being even supervenes on being a member of the series 2, 4, 6, 8 . . . But the set-theoretic property of membership in this series does not explain why (say) 144 is even. This can (in some sense) be explained by indicating that it is divisible by 2 without remainder. Moreover, the general fact of supervenience of even integers on membership in the series can itself be explained by taking the property of being even to be grounded on that of being divisible by 2 without remainder. I am not sure that this grounding view about evenness is correct (since being even may be, in a certain definitional way, constituted by being divisible by 2 without remainder); but it has enough plausibility to illustrate how a consequentiality view can explain the corresponding supervenience thesis (which would also hold for a constitution view of evenness).

---

[8]Here, as with the supervenience formulation, I am ignoring, for ease of exposition something that figures later in the paper: that the base properties may not constitute an a priori closed list, hence may not be referred to as belonging to a (non-fuzzy) set.

[9]The term 'resultancy' has been used by Jonathan Dancy and others and is not inappropriate if we keep in mind that its usual association with causal determination is inappropriate; grounding is a non-causal relation.

[10]This implication has been contested, e.g. by Dancy. For defenses of the view taken here, see my "Ethical Generality" (2008) Cf. Stangl (2010) for a contrasting view.

[11]Kim seems to think that intuitionists, at least, cannot explain the supervenience of the normative: "An ethical intuitionist like G. E. Moore would see normative supervenience as a fundamental synthetic a priori fact not susceptible of further explanation; it is something we directly apprehend through our moral sense" (2005, p. 13). This claim surely does not hold for intuitionists in general. For one thing, direct apprehensibility is an epistemic property and surely does not by itself entail unexplainability.

A third point is that, important though consequentiality is, it does not solve certain important questions in the epistemology of ethics. It does, however, accomplish several things of both epistemological and ethical importance. First, it imposes a welcome consistency requirement on moral ascriptions: it rules out claims that although two cases are descriptively alike, say two shootings of noncombatants by soldiers on the same patrol, they are morally different. (This much follows from the supervenience thesis alone.) Second, it requires openness to the question *why*, as directed to any given moral judgment, where the question is answerable by citing a grounding property for the moral property ascribed by the judgment. Third, it promises to help in dealing with moral disagreements: it opens up the possibility of using agreement on the grounding properties—whose presence can, at least in principle, be ascertained using common-sense and scientific procedures—to resolve moral disagreements.

These points are correct but limited in scope. First, no two cases are *exactly* alike descriptively. The two soldiers differ in certain ways, for instance. Second, knowing that a ground is available in principle to explain a moral judgment does not imply knowing what it *is* or that there should be agreement on its force. Thirdly, even though the availability of objective procedures to ascertain grounds of a moral judgment should both help and constrain rational persons who understand the consequentiality relation, it does not follow that there must be rational agreement on what the relevant grounds are or that we can always determine whether they are present. Some problems raised by these limitations will be addressed in the next section.

3 The Epistemology of Moral Properties

We have so far seen in outline how moral properties are *ontically dependent* on (non-moral) descriptive properties. This dependence is implicit in the grounding relation. We have also seen why it is plausible to consider the former *epistemically dependent* on the latter as well. Roughly, this is to say that our knowledge that something has a moral property depends on our knowledge of its having, or at least on our possessing adequate ground for ascribing to it, an appropriate descriptive property, and our justification for ascribing a moral property to something, depends on our justification for ascribing to it an appropriate descriptive property.[12]

It should be no surprise that there are philosophical differences over whether the knowledge and justification in question—knowledge of, and justification for

[12]There is a possible exception: our having "natural knowledge"—roughly, knowledge without a justifying ground—of something's having a moral property, such as might be implanted in us by an omnipotent being. For discussion of such knowledge, which, since the knower lacks a ground for it, does not require justification, see ch. 10 of *Epistemology*, 3rd ed. 2010).

believing, certain moral generalizations—are empirical. Moreover, there can be agreement on necessity without agreement on apriority. My own view in this matter is a moderate rationalist intuitionism, on which such knowledge has both properties. Let me sketch a case for the apriority of the grounding principles for moral properties, with a focus mainly of obligatoriness, since this is representative of such properties. (I leave axiology out here; but a similar strategy is applicable there.) My case will not depend on providing an analysis of obligatoriness, but I do not consider that needed for it.[13] My strategy here is to support the apriority of the propositions in question by showing that they play certain pivotal roles in the language and thought of relevantly sophisticated people, especially their descriptive, classificatory, explanatory, and inferential discourse. The arguments support the conclusion that relations expressed by the propositions are both necessary, conceptual, and ascertainable by adequate reflection.

3.1 The Argument from Moral Education

It is instructive to consider how people commonly educate their children about right and wrong (I do not exclude even people in "undeveloped countries" or tribal people, though the latter may educate for life in the in-group and less representative). Consider as a plausible set of grounds the kinds that go with W. D. Ross's famous list of prima facie obligations (prima facie "duties"): justice and non-injury, veracity and promissory fidelity, beneficence and self-improvement, and reparation and gratitude.[14] For ease of exposition, I will consider mainly fidelity, veracity, and beneficence—understood as reducing pain or suffering or enhancing pleasure. These are understandable descriptively and are sufficiently representative for our purposes. Begin with veracity. Even parents who are not morally upright are likely to demand of their children that they not lie *to them.* And if these parents lied to their children except in limited ways (or prevented their exposure to discourse in which terms are use with some consistency and in appropriate ways), it is not clear how they could teach the children a natural language.

A related point is this: where we can properly speak of moral education at all, we expect some range of prohibitions of lying to be instilled; and, related to this, where people may be said to use the concepts of (moral) right and wrong at all, we expect them to tend apply an equivalent of 'wrong' to their children (as well as others) when they find the latter lying to them. The case with promising is quite similar. When it comes to beneficence, we expect parents to teach their children that

[13] I have argued that the self-evident is a priori and need not be analytic in (2010) ch. 5 and "Skepticism about the A Priori" (2008).

[14] See ch 2 of Ross's (1930) and ch 5 of my (2004), which explains how to understand the grounds of these obligations descriptively.

they *must,* on pain of the kind of principled criticism that bespeaks moral judgment, act in the relevant positive way toward at least some people, say the family, the tribe, or some wider community. The *scope* of the requirement and the modes of its enforcement, are highly variable; but moral education is partly centered on instilling the standards in question as applying in certain types of situations.

Moral education commonly teaches more than the kind of sufficiency relation so far illustrated between the presence of a ground and that of a moral obligation. Once this relation is grasped, children are in a position to see that the relation is not unqualifiedly sufficient for *overall,* as opposed to prima facie, obligation. Suppose a child fails to pick up toys strewn around the living room. The mother might critically note, "You promised to put those away." If the child replies, "I had to help Daddy," a normal response would be, "Oh, then I'll excuse you, but next time you tell me why you couldn't do what I asked." The excuse shows the defeasibility of the initial overall obligation; a promissory ground is not invariably sufficient for overall obligation. That no particular ground (an element normative in upshot) is *necessary* for overall obligation is also commonly taught. Suppose a child of ten is asked to help a cousin with yardwork and declines, saying "I never promised to help." A parent may say, "I know that, but you should help her anyway—she's your cousin and you have no need to do anything else." This would be readily understood as indicating both that promising is not necessary for an obligation to someone else and that another obligation, such as that of beneficence, suffices for it. The same example also indicates how the plurality of obligations may be gradually introduced to children.

3.2 The Argument from Moral Sensibility

If we stub our toe, we dislike it; but if an abuser tramps on the toe, we are indignant, even morally outraged. Similarly, if we forage in search of strawberries and don't find them, we are disappointed; but if we are lied to about their location, don't find them on searching for them, and conclude we were lied to, we resent that act. A broken promise may leave us disapproving or even indignant. Indignation, resentment, and the relevant kind of disapproval are moral sentiments, and the use of moral terms is associated with the sense that these sentiments are appropriate in certain cases.[15]

I am not implying that *only* conceptually sophisticated persons can have such sentiments; but it is the responses of those persons that seem to me to give some support to the a priori character of the moral principles in question. For instance, suppose someone with a mastery of ordinary English, without special

[15]For an indication of the importance of resentment in understanding reasons and in explaining (and I would say also grounding) obligation, see Stratton-Lake (2011).

explanation, did not tend to have such sentiments in such situations or—especially—took them as inappropriate to those situations. This would tend to manifest a lack of understanding or (as in the case of a comprehending amoralist) a failure to have internalized moral standards. Such people would not be players in the moral game, even if they might know how the game is played. The correlations I note here are empirical; but their role in the constitution of moral concepts seems to me a priori.

3.3 The Aretaic Argument

Consider what constitutes a morally virtuous person. Is it not largely a matter of an appropriate pattern of responses to the kinds of descriptive grounds we are exploring? The very names Ross used for basic duties suggest this—for instance, 'fidelity' and 'beneficence'. Much as we can identify right and wrong actions in terms of, say, lying on the negative side, and, on the positive side, helping those who suffer, we can identify morally virtuous people—as well as people with moral vices—in terms of *patterns* of such behavior, provided we may assume the normal range of underlying motivational explanations (a range also characterizable in descriptive terms). Someone who often lies has the *vice* of being a liar; someone who regularly (and without an "agenda") does good turns for people (and nothing significant of a contrary kind) has the virtue of beneficence; and so on.

This is not to assume without argument that deontic concepts or axiological concepts such as the intrinsically good and bad are more basic than aretaic concepts. My point requires only the close relations among them that indicate how the relevant descriptive grounding properties figure constitutively in the nature of moral properties. Certain moral virtues are partly constituted by action tendencies in the domain of Rossian grounds, whatever else may constitute these virtues. Other moral virtues, such as the higher-order virtue of moral uprightness, may be seen as largely derivative from these.

3.4 The Argument from Partial Analysis

Whether or not we agree with G. E. Moore about the indefinability of *good*, we should recognize that the history of ethics since Moore has confirmed that our basic normative terms do not admit of any simple philosophical analysis, if they admit of any analysis at all. I assume this here. It does not follow that we cannot give partial analyses. Indeed, do we not know some of the elements that must go into an analysis of the concept of the morally obligatory? An obvious way to begin is to say that, in reference to acts, what is obligatory is what it is wrong not to do. This may be correct, but wrongness needs explication as much as obligatoriness. We could say that what is wrong is what we are blameworthy for doing (at least if we have no excuse), but the same point applies. We have enlarge the circle but not broken out of it. To break out of it, we most naturally turn to paradigms. Keeping our promises is obligatory; not harming those around us is obligatory; doing some good deeds toward at least those close to us is; telling the truth is. Each of these points indicates part of what would go into an illuminating definition if we can find one that is also correct.

To indicate the point differently, what other ways are there to bring out the content of the concept of the obligatory or, correspondingly though not equivalently, the nature of the property of obligatoriness? One possibility is to ask what must go into the "complete" thought of obligatoriness, the kind of thought that would contain all its constituent concepts. I doubt we can frame such a thought if the demand is to capture *all* of the basic constituents. But can one think of what, at the most basic level, conceptually constitutes obligation to do something without thinking of it as promised or as doing something beneficent, or as avoiding harms to others, or as abstaining from lying, and so forth for Rossian grounds of obligation? It seems not. The same point about the constitution of obligatoriness seems implicit in any attempt to list paradigms. A good way to see the point is to ask how one would explain to an inquiring child what an obligation is. Here we cannot presuppose an understanding of other normative terms, but we would have no difficulty citing examples and telling mini-stories. It is these examples that reflect the work the notion of obligation does, and there is no doubt that such examples commonly teach the child how to understand that notion and other moral notions.

3.5 The Argument from Norms of Discourse

This is a good place to indicate a related argument that proceeds from facts about our critical practices. Positively, in many kinds of cases we expect people to draw inferences from propositions ascribing grounds of obligation to judgments of obligation. If you tell me that a small child has fallen onto the train tracks, I will immediately judge that someone (or I) must quickly get the child to safety. If, when I firmly shake your hand, you cry out and tell me that this hurt your bruised finger, I will apologize and say I didn't know about the bruise. I must excuse the injury. I draw inferences as expected given the a priiori relevance of the Rossian grounds to the normative properties consequential on them.

Negatively, how would we react to denials of such judgments given the kinds of descriptive grounds in question? It is hard to imagine anyone's saying that the potential harm to the child is no reason to help, or that no one nearby and able has any obligation to help. In someone who knows English, we would need a special explanation to avoid concluding that this person doesn't understand reasons or obligation. And does anyone who apparently understands moral discourse at all ever say such things as 'I know you promised to *A*, but that is no reason at all to do it' or 'Driving through the crowd to get quickly to your destination would kill a few people, but that doesn't make it wrong'?

3.6 *The Testability Argument*

Still another route to seeing the importance of the descriptive grounds we are considering is to inquire into the testability of moral judgments. Whether or not one takes them to be ultimately ascriptions of natural properties, one is likely to agree that instantiating some such properties is either necessary or sufficient (or both) for their truth (or, for noncognitivists, their appropriate assertibility). Suppose someone explaining why a woman is divorcing her husband says that time and again he wronged her and never made amends. We consider this explanation testable; and if it is to be sustained, it surely must cite such things as injuries, lies, and broken promises. The mention of not making amends, moreover, indicates recognition of the obligation Ross called "the duty of reparation." Descriptively understood, it is in good part doing something to enhance happiness or reduce suffering, in response to having done a harm or having violated some other prima facie obligation.

We can also see the implications of testability from the point of view of descriptive sufficient conditions. Suppose a moral psychologist hypothesizes that wrongdoing adversely affects psychological health. Is there any plausible way to ascertain instances of the independent variable here, wrongdoing, apart from relying on the descriptive grounds we have been exploring? If there is, it will surely be dependent on establishing a high correlation with such grounds. One implication of this is that the philosophical work of identifying constitutive grounds of moral properties can facilitate the scientific work of testing empirical generalizations important for understanding ethical behavior. Moral philosophy and moral psychology make good partners.

These arguments support, though none of them strictly proves, the view that the principles of obligation we have been considering are a priori and indeed a priori in the basic way the self-evident is: such that an adequate understanding of them suffices for justification for believing them. Moreover, the data forming the basis of the arguments are best understood on that view. This view can also explain the necessity of the moral principles in question. The arguments bring out that the principles figure in governing discourse and inference is the way one would expect on this apriorist view of them. They represent *criteria,* in a conceptual sense of the term, for obligatoriness. We apparently know a priori that an act is (morally) obligatory if it satisfies any one of them; this is *criterial sufficiency*. We also apparently know a priori that an act is obligatory only if it satisfies the disjunction of them—or of them and certain similar conditions. This criterial necessary condition is put more broadly because I do not take it that the set of grounds I consider criterial is a priori closed.

A compromise position is that the principles of obligation are simply conceptually and ontically constitutive: they need not be considered a priori to play this role, but we can still maintain that part of what it is to be obligatory is to satisfy one of the descriptive conditions in question. We can even say that obligation is apparently constituted by the criterial set as a whole. One could take the constitution relation to be, as ontological, necessary but leave open apriority. I do not accept this view, but it is not without some explanatory power. In any case, we should ask whether, ontologically, the property of being (prima facie) obligatory might be identical with the disjunction of the constitutive grounds. This is a question I will pursue after considering further facts about moral obligation.

4 The Problem of Normative Defeasibility

As common as undefeated obligations apparently are in daily life, it is not clear that any can be non-trivially claimed to be indefeasible. Ross seemed to take this view and, apparently in part for that reason, resorted to 'prima facie duty' as his main term for the normative status conferred on an act by one or more of the grounds. Aware that one could be obligated to do something other than what is a prima facie duty, he said that prima facie duty is not equivalent to duty "proper." The point is perhaps this: unless a prima facie duty is in fact undefeated, the act in question, though supported by a moral consideration, may not be right on balance, as where a promise must be broken for the sake of finding a lost child and one is therefore obligated to break it. Is there a better terminology than Ross's? Perhaps not for purposes of philosophical theory. Merely substituting 'obligation' for 'duty' is of some help but does not affect the logic of the terminology. There is, however, a notion that, for moral philosophy, may be clarifying.

Suppose we give high priority to capturing the connection of the grounds of obligation—or of "prima facie duty"—with what morally one *ought* to do, with practical judgment, with what it is right to do, and so forth for other deontic notions. I suggest that here the notion of a moral reason seems apt. We could also speak of an ought-making consideration, but that may be no better. In exploring the argument from norms of discourse, we noted that even if one may deny that (e.g.) one ought to do something one promised to do, especially where one has a clearly overriding contrary obligation, it does not follow, and seems untrue, that one may deny having any reason whatever to do the thing. To be sure, it may be that breaking the promise is constituted by telling a lie, in which case there are two reasons not to do it. The overrider might also be complex; an obligation of reparation to the lost child's mother might join that of beneficence calling for breaking the promise to find the child. The overridingness of the latter grounds may be quite clear, but it is equally clear that numbers are not crucial. Moral reasons for a given act combine non-additively. Overall reason, we might say, is organic.

The organicity view is a kind of holism: many factors may go into determining overall obligation, where (as is usual) the determination is a strong sufficiency relation though not self-evident entailment, if an entailment at all. One might also call the view a kind of particularism about overall moral judgment: such judgment is justifiable only in the light of the particular situation of action or prospective action, which may crucially involve a plurality of grounds organically combinable. The view is not a strong particularism on which the *valence*—the positive or negative thrust—of the constitutive grounds of obligation changes from one situation to the other. On the view in question, the constitutive criteria for what we might call the basic moral properties (perhaps above all that of being supported by a moral reason) are invariant and objective, and this gives a kind of stability and clarity to the institution of morality. But the criteria for the non-basic property of overall obligatoriness are variable and, in some cases, open to rational disagreement. This accounts for a justifiable if limited pluralism in moral matters.

It is natural to wonder whether holism about overall obligation implies that not all moral propositions are consequential on descriptive properties after all. That does not follow from the holism sketched here. That it does not is suggested by fact that even for overall obligation, supervenience holds: if two cases of moral choice are exactly alike except for the identity of the agents, who are perfect duplicates, what is overall obligatory for one must be so for the other. If such strong supervenience could hold for overall obligation only if the corresponding consequentiality thesis also holds for obligation, we could conclude that holistic obligation is a consequential property. That entailment is not self-evident. But recall that moral properties are not brute. This applies to overall obligation as much as to prima facie obligation. The overall obligation to break a promise in order to search for a lost child is based (in part) on the potentially great loss if the child dies, and no one would accept the judgment of obligation here without some such explanation. The point is not that there is any question of consequentiality; it is that there may be no description we can hope to formulate, at least with precision, such that *any* act satisfying it is an overall obligation. There might be such a description, as where the promissory obligation is simply to meet for a daily short walk after class and no other obligation opposes the obligation to search for the child. But there need not be so few relevant variables or such a simple comparative weighting of them.

The organic holism just outlined complicates moral theory in a way that some, say certain hedonistic consequentialists, might argue it need not be complicated. But the view accounts better than its alternatives for both moral practice and the major elements in ethical theory that command wide agreement. Arguably, the view also opens the way for skepticism about moral judgment. But skepticism is possible even for simple cases of moral judgment.[16] Here I can only say that I take humility about overall moral judgment to be often a good thing. It reduces dogmatism and facilitates rational discussion. It does not undermine a fallibilist objectivism.

5 Are Moral Properties Natural (or Naturalizable)?

One further question should be addressed I conclude. It concerns whether the intuitionistic position advanced here can be naturalized. Early twentieth-century intuitionists—famously Moore—were avowedly anti-naturalistic. But the ontology of moral properties proposed here is not. Should it be?

---

[16] Sinnott-Armstrong's *Moral Skepticisms* (2006) makes clear why this is so, but in a way that otherwise seems compatible with the view taken here.

It might seem that, if the list of constitutive grounds of obligation is not a priori closed, and indeed cannot be plausibly closed unless the ground-designating terms are taken with artificially extended vagueness, naturalization is not possible. But there is no entailment here. It is not clear that what we might call an open-ended, multiple-criterion property cannot be natural. Consider the properties of being a theory, a poem, a religion, or, in the scientific realm, even acidic or magnetic. Each of these is to be understood in terms of a number of properties (some relational, of course, as with the magnetic), but a case can be made that none is fundamentally normative in content. Nonetheless, with an open-ended list of criteria for obligatoriness, we must find it at best difficult to determine what candidate naturalizations are plausible. What might the natural property be?

Here we must resist the tendency to think that unless we can name candidate properties, there are none. Suppose, however, that we bypass the felt need for some kind of name. Still, we cannot plausibly attempt to naturalize the property of obligation without taking account of the constitutive grounding properties. How might a naturalization project do this?

A plausible starting point, I think, is to appeal to disjunction. For anyone who agrees that hedonic considerations, promises, avoidances of lies, and other descriptively identifiable states of affairs can provide reasons for action, it may be natural to claim that the property of obligatoriness is reducible to a *disjunctive* property. Being obligatory, for example, might be the property (of an act) of *either* having been promised or being a reducing of suffering or an avoidance of lying or . . . , and so forth for all the types of basic normative grounds. (The last disjunct might be something open-ended like 'or having a property conducive to human cooperation'.) Even apart from the question whether a property description this open-ended kind could designate a natural property, we should ask whether there are disjunctive *properties,* as distinct from something obviously possible: disjunctive ascriptions of properties. Even if there are disjunctive properties, not just any disjunction of property-ascribing terms can be assumed to express them. I doubt that there are disjunctive properties,[17] and, if there are, they are certainly not basic and, in part for that reason, reduction to the kind just indicated might not take us all the way to a naturalization with significant ontological value.

It may be evident that I have presupposed that equivalence of property-expressive predicates (their necessary coextensiveness) does not entail identity of the properties, in the sense that they expresses the same properties. If 'obligatoriness' designates a property, as I hold, then if it is equivalent to 'being promised or . . . ' that disjunction expresses the same property. But recall our numerical example. The predicate 'being an even integer' is necessarily equivalent to 'having membership in the infinite class of numbers in the series 2, 4, 6 . . . ', but the properties in question surely differ. Perhaps one point here could be put as follows: one is an arithmetic property belonging to individual numbers; the other is a set-theoretic property, which seems of a different kind. In any case, assuming they do express properties,

[17] For a detailed case against countenancing disjunctive properties, see P. Audi (2013).

no naturalistic analysis along the lines in question is compelling. Similar points hold for 'being a circle' and 'being the kind of plane figure whose circumference is pi times its diameter'. A disjunction might, then, express an equivalent of a property, but even if that should imply expressing some property, it does not imply expressing the same property.

Here one might think of determinables and their determinates, since these might provide a model on which, even if reduction to the constitutive disjunction fails, there is sameness of ontological category. Being colored is consequential on the color(s) in virtue of which a thing has color at all. Now there may be no disjunction of colors such that satisfying it is equivalent to being colored or, if there is, that disjunction my not express the property of being colored. But being colored is surely as much a natural property as being, say, red. I doubt that being obligatory is a determinable,[18] but a case might be made that it has enough in common with determinables to be categorially similar: to share the same ontological category as its grounds. I have said that the grounds of obligatoriness are non-moral and can grant that they are natural. Why not, then, grant that obligatoriness is also a natural property?[19]

Here I can only reiterate that my overall view is neutral with respect to the possibility that obligation is some natural property. Its being so would not change the metaphysical or epistemological picture I have presented. We still have consequentiality, apriority, and, I think, objectivity. Indeed, the latter is supported, since there are descriptive sufficient conditions and there is a disjunction of conditions at least one of which is at least normally necessary. I leave naturalization open, then, but do not see it as well supported. I have granted, however, the possibility of a natural constitution thesis. This may be enough for those who think that realism (at least about properties of concrete entities) must be naturalistic; but even thoroughgoing naturalists can be accommodated within the realist ontology and intuitionist moral epistemology defended in this paper.

Moral discourse is constitutively governed by facts. The fundamental governing facts are descriptive, pervasive in human life, and important for social coordination and indeed survival itself. I refer to such facts as that people make promissory commitments, statements whose truth others depend on, and distributions of scarce resources. More dramatically, children are suffering and dying, and tribal warfare is killing thousands of noncombatants. The factual governance I have described here is based on the consequentiality of moral properties on non-moral, descriptive properties. That relation implies supervenience but goes beyond it. It is not only a necessary relation but an explanatory determination relation. On my view, moreover, it is a priori, but it can be in a strong sense constitutive even if it is not a priori.

[18]Color and the specific colors are significantly *intra-categorial*—all being properties of surfaces. Compare sound. Sounds may be pianistic, thunderous, howling (as with wind), crackling, vocal, and much else. Is sound a determinable? And is obligatoriness, even as applied to actions alone, any less varied in kinds than sounds?

[19]Cf. Butchvarov (1989) on *good* as a determinable. He does not consider disjunctive properties or categorial similarity.

This consequentiality relation can also be objective without being a priori. But its apriority best explains its necessity and its role in the functioning of the moral concepts in question. This is not to claim that the concept of the obligatory is a priori closed or that moral disagreement can be easily dispelled by those with good information about relevant grounds. But the framework I have sketched allows us to approach moral disagreement with a sense that there is a truth of the matter, a realm of genuine properties to argue about, and an objective method for approaching agreement on at least many of the divisive questions of human life.[20]

References

Adams, Robert Merrihew (2000). Finite and Infinite Goods. Oxford: Oxford University Press.

Audi, Robert (2004). The Good in the Right: A Theory of Intuition and Intrinsic Value. Princeton: Princeton University Press.

Audi, Robert (2008). Skepticism About the A Priori: Self-Evidence, Defeasibility, and *Cogito* Propositions, John Greco, The Oxford Handbook of Skepticism. Oxford: Oxford University Press, 2008, 149–175.

Audi, Robert (2010). Epistemology: A Contemporary Introduction to the Theory of Knowledge. London: Routledge.

Audi, Robert. (2011) Rationality and Religious Commitment. Oxford: Oxford University Press.

Audi, Paul (2013). How to Rule Out Disjunctive Properties. Nous 47, 4. (2013), 748–766.

Audi, Robert (2013). Knowledge, Justification, and Normativity. Res Philosophica 90, 2, 125–145.

Bennett, Karen, and Brian McLaughlin (2005). "Supervenience." *The Stanford Encyclopedia of Philosophy*, http://plato.stanford.edu.entries/supervenience/.

Boyd, Richard (1988). How To Be a Moral Realist.Geoffrey Sayre McCord, Essays on Moral Realsim. Ithaca: Cornell University Press, 181–228.

Brink, David O. (1989). Moral Realism and the Foundations of Ethics. Cambridge: Cambridge University Press.

Butchvarov, Panayot. (1989). Skepticism in Ethics. Bloomington and Indianapolis: Indiana University Press

Kim, Jaegwon (1990), "Supervenience as a Philosophical Concept." *Metaphilosophy* 1–2, 21, 1-

Kim, Jaegwon (2005). Physicalism or Something Near Enough. Princeton: Princeton University Press.

Moore, G. E. (1903). Principia Ethica. Cambridge: Cambridge University Press. Sturgeon. (1985),

Ross, W. D. (1930). The Right and the Good. Oxford: Oxford University Press.

Sinnott-Armstrong (2006), Moral Skepticisms. Oxford: Oxford University Press.

Stangl, Rebecca (2010). Asymmetrical Virtue Particularism, Ethics 1, 121, 37–57.

Stratton-Lake, Philip (2011). Recalcitrant Pluralism, Ratio XXIV 4, 364–383.

Sturgeon, Nicholas (1985). Moral Explanations, David Copp David Zimmerman, Morality, Reason, and Truth. Totowa, NJ: Roman and Allanheld, 49–78.

Wedgwood, Ralph (2007). Normativity. Oxford: Oxford University Press.

[20]Earlier versions of this paper were presented at a meeting of Oxford University's Moral Philosophy Society and at the University of Minnesota, Minneapolis, and I have benefited from discussing the issues on those occasions. Roger Crisp and Brad Hooker were among the helpful discussants in Oxford, and Paul Audi has helped me in dealing with some of the ontological issues.

Reasons and Supervenience

Daniel Laurier

Tout le monder n'est pas Cézanne Nous nous contenterons de peu

(Louis Aragon)

In philosophy, it is hard to improve intelligibility while retaining the excitement

(Donald Davidson)

Abstract In this paper, I will (i) introduce a distinction between a weaker and a stronger sense in which something (be it a proposition, a state of affairs, a concept or a property) may be said to be normative, (ii) distinguish between conceptual and metaphysical versions of what is known as "individual" supervenience (iii) explain why we should concentrate on the conceptual supervenience claims, (iv) discuss the plausibility of various conceptual supervenience claims concerning some specific kinds of normative concepts, namely, concepts that can be constructed out of the concept of a (normative) reason and (v) argue that reasons-concepts of a certain kind conceptually supervene on mental ones and that this is compatible with a form a realism with respect to reasons-propositions.

1 Introduction

Discussions of supervenience with respect to normativity tend to be conducted in very general terms, to focus on specifically moral properties/concepts and to proceed without any clearly stated way of distinguishing the normative/moral properties/concepts from those they are claimed to supervene (or not to supervene) on. Thus, it is asked whether the normative *in general* supervenes on anything other

D. Laurier (✉)
University of Montreal, Montreal, Canada
e-mail: daniel.laurier@umontreal.ca

B. Brożek et al. (eds.), *Supervenience and Normativity*, Law and Philosophy Library 120, DOI 10.1007/978-3-319-61046-7_4

than itself, and if so, whether this is true *a priori*, and whether the supervenience base is best thought of as being the "natural", the "factual" or the "non-normative". However, there is no generally agreed upon conception of exactly how to single out normative or moral properties/concepts or of what sets them apart from other kinds of properties/concepts. Indeed, it is not even clear that there is any single, substantive and non-trivial criterion of the normative (or the moral) to be had. In this paper, I will try to avoid some of these pitfalls by discussing the significance and plausibility of various supervenience claims pertaining to one specific kind of uncontroversially normative propositions, namely, propositions about (normative) reasons, or more precisely, propositions involving what I am going to call "reasons-concepts".

This paper has three parts, followed by a brief conclusion. In Sect. 2, I introduce a distinction between "reasons" propositions which have normative force and others that have normative content without having normative force, and a correlative distinction between "reasons-concepts" which are normative force conferring and others that are not. In Sect. 3, I introduce a distinction between different forms of "metaphysical" supervenience relations and corresponding forms of "conceptual" supervenience relations and comment on their relations. In Sect. 4, I suggest that in order to avoid begging the question against certain kinds of metaethical views, we should concentrate on the "conceptual" supervenience relations. I then distinguish between several kinds of "reasons-concepts" which are normative force conferring and several corresponding kinds that are not, and ask for some of the most basic of them whether there is any interesting kind of concepts on which they could conceptually and non-trivially supervene. I come out with a negative answer in all cases but one. For the reader's convenience, I give, at the end of the paper, a list of the main claims that I will have been making along the way.

2 Normative Force vs Normative Content

It is nearly uncontroversial that such propositions (or propositional schemas) as

1. There is a (or some) reason for S to do X

count (in some of their uses) as normative. There are, of course, many other kinds of propositions which would rightfully be counted as normative, and there is no guarantee that they could all somehow be reduced to or explained in terms of propositions involving the concept of a "reason", though several people[1] have suggested or at least seriously considered the view that the concept of a reason is the basic normative concept in terms of which all others can be defined or explained. However that may be, in this paper I will be concerned only with those normative propositions that are somehow reducible to propositions about reasons.

All propositions involving the concept of a reason thus count as normative, insofar as they thereby have normative *content*. But what is it that is distinctive

[1]See, e.g., Scanlon (1998, 2014), Skorupski (2010), Dancy (2009), Schroeder (2007), and Parfit (2011).

of these propositions and sets them apart from others? Or in other words, what is so special about the concept of a reason? Well, it has the power to confer what I call "normative force" to *some* of the propositions involving it. A proposition (or set of propositions) has normative force when it entails (its members jointly entail) that some individual has some normative status with respect to something, such as being permitted or obliged to do something, or being such that there is reason for one to do something. Thus, proposition (1) clearly (and trivially) has normative force, while some logically complex propositions, such as

2. If there is a reason for S to do X then Q

and

3. If Q then there is a reason for S to do X,

just as clearly lack normative force (no matter what Q is), even though they have normative content. But then what, in turn, is so special about normatively forceful propositions? The only remotely plausible answer that I know of is the internalist one, according to which there is an intimate connection between *first-personal* normatively forceful propositions and motivation, which manifests itself in the fact that it is irrational for one to judge that there is reason for oneself to do X without having some motivation to do X.[2] In other words, it is irrational to self-ascribe the normative status of being such that there is reason for one to do X without being somewhat motivated to do X.

Just as some, but not all, normative propositions have normative force, some, but not all, normative concepts are normative force conferring. For example, the concept of being such that if there is some reason for one to do X then Q is clearly not normative force conferring, even though it contains the normative force conferring concept of being such that there is some reason for one to do X. So we need to register the fact that when we talk about normative propositions we may be taken to be talking about all normatively contentful propositions, or only about normatively forceful propositions, and that when we talk about normative concepts we may be taken to be talking about all normatively contentful concepts or only about normative force conferring concepts.

[2]In Laurier (2011), I admitted that not all first-personal normatively forceful propositions have this feature. For example, it is not irrational for me to judge that I am permitted to do something without being in the least motivated to do it, even though the proposition that I am permitted to do it clearly has normative force. I then went on to suggest that all first-personal normatively forceful propositions may at least turn out to involve normative force conferring concepts which are somehow explainable in terms of normative force conferring concepts which are such that first-personal normatively forceful propositions involving them do have this internalist feature. For the purposes of this paper, however, it doesn't matter whether this is so, because the only normatively forceful propositions I will consider are those which directly involve the concept of a "reason".

Now let's consider such propositions as

4. That P is a reason for S to do X.

On one way of reading it, it is equivalent to "The fact that P is a reason for S to do X", and may thus be taken to imply that it is true that P; or, it may be read as not implying that it is true that P, and thus as saying merely that the proposition that P entertains the "reason-relation" with S's doing X, or, as I prefer to say, that the proposition that P is "reason-related" to S's doing X. On both readings, however, it entails (by ordinary logic) that there is something which is a reason for S to do X, and thus that there is some reason for S to do X. So it turns out that (1) itself is potentially ambiguous, as between

(1a) There is a true proposition which is reason-related to S's doing X.

and the weaker

(1b) There is a proposition which is reason-related to S's doing X.

Yet, intuitively, only (1a) genuinely has normative force, i.e., entails that S actually has some normative status with respect to doing X. What seems to explain this, is the fact that, while it is irrational for one to judge, in the first-person, that there is some true proposition which is reason-related to one's doing X without being motivated to do X, it is not irrational for one to judge, in the first-person, that there is some (possibly false) proposition which is reason-related to one's doing X without being in the least motivated to do X. Indeed, for any X, it is nearly trivial that some proposition or other is reason-related to one's doing it (which is probably why (1) is spontaneously heard as equivalent to (1a)).

To put it somewhat paradoxically, only true propositions (or "facts") can be reasons but not only true propositions can be reason-related to someone's doing something. Thus, when we say that some proposition is a reason for S to do X we are, strictly speaking, saying more than that this proposition is reason-related to S's doing X, we are also committing ourselves to the truth of this proposition; and when we say that some proposition is reason-related to S's doing X, what we are saying is that this proposition, if true, is or would be a reason for S to do X. This leads me to suggest that such propositions as (4) are best understood as being normatively forceful, and equivalent to

5. P and the proposition that P is reason-related to S's doing X,

where to say that the proposition that P is "reason-related" to S's doing X is just a convenient way of saying that if the proposition that P is (or were) true, then it is (would be) a reason for S to do X. This makes it plain that I take the concepts "is a reason to" and "is reason-related to" to be inter-definable thus:

(DF1) that P is reason-related to S's doing X $=_{df}$ if P then that P is a reason for S to do X
(DF2) that P is a reason for S to do X $=_{df}$ P and that P is reason-related to S's doing X.

The significance of this lies in the fact that the concept "is reason-related to", contrary to the concept "is a reason to", is not normative force conferring. Thus, such propositions as

6. That P is reason-related to S's doing X

clearly are normative, i.e., have normative content, without having normative force. With this in mind, we can now turn to such propositions as

7. That P is no reason for S to do X

which, since (4) is now understood as equivalent to (5), should strictly speaking be understood as saying that the proposition that P is either false or not reason-related to S's doing X. However, depending on the context, (7) may be used to convey either that P is false, or that

8. That P is not reason-related to S's doing X,

which, again (and just as (7) itself), has normative content without having normative force. Accordingly, such propositions as

9. There is no reason for S to do X

are to be understood as saying that every proposition is either false or not reason-related to S's doing X (or, equivalently, that no proposition is both true and reason-related to S's doing X). Hence, no particular instance of (9) has any normative force. Yet it may be tempting to suggest that (9) may nonetheless have normative force, insofar as it may seem plausible to endorse some such principle as that if there is no reason for S to do X then there is some reason for S *not* to do X, or even that if there is no reason for S to do X then *that* is a reason for S *not* to do X. However, these are very strong principles I am not prepared to commit myself to. For, suppose there is no reason for S to do X, it would then follow, not only that there is *some* reason for S not to do X, but that there is *more* reason for S not to do X than to do it, and, indeed, that if S has to choose between doing X and not doing X then there is most reason for S not to do X. Assuming that if there is most reason for S to do something then S ought to do it, it would follow that it is always wrong to do something one has no reason to do. But, even if there certainly are many things one ought not to do unless there is some reason to do them, it seems no less certain that some things are so insignificant that it is permitted to do them even when there is no reason to. But then doesn't it follow that at least *some* instances of (9) have normative force? Not so, because even when it is true that if there is no reason for S to do X then there is some reason for S not to do X, what has normative force is not the proposition that there is no reason for S to do X but the conjunction "there is no reason for S to do X and if there is no reason for S to do X then there is some reason for S not to do X"; and when it is true that that there is no reason for S to do X is a reason for S not to do X, *this* (and not the proposition that there is no reason for S to do X) is what has normative force. So I maintain that *no* instance of (9) has any normative force.

3 Conceptual vs Metaphysical Supervenience

As such recent surveys as McLaughlin and Bennett (2011), Leuenberger (2008), and Shagrir (2013) amply demonstrate, there is a plethora of supervenience relations that are currently investigated in the literature. Nearly all of the time, the focus is exclusively on supervenience relations construed as metaphysical (dyadic) relations and as holding between kinds of *properties* (or facts). While this may well be entirely appropriate in many areas, where it is acknowledged on (nearly) all sides that there *are* properties of the relevant kinds, about which it may be asked whether they entertain some supervenience relation, it becomes questionable (and question-begging) when the very existence of properties of the relevant kinds is in dispute. Yet it is not as if talk of supervenience then suddenly turned out to be out of place or meaningless. As Sturgeon (2009) has recently reminded us, many metaethicists (most prominently, expressivists) are prepared to admit that the normative supervenes (in one sense or another) on the non-normative while denying that there are normative properties or facts (in any metaphysically robust sense).[3] This explains, in part, why, in this paper, I wish to focus on supervenience relations taken as relations between kinds of concepts (or propositions). But the main reason comes from the fact that I take normativity (or at least the sort of normativity which is my concern here, namely the normativity of *reasons*) to pertain primarily to the realm of concepts and propositions and only secondarily and derivatively (if at all) to the realm of properties and facts.

In the previous section, I suggested that one distinctive feature of the concept of a (normative) reason is that it is irrational for one to endorse such first-personal normatively forceful propositions as "There is a reason for me to do X" (or, for that matter, "That P is a reason for me to do X") while having no motivation to do X. However, this feature doesn't transmit to the relation (if any) designated by this concept. For presumably, if the concept of a reason designates a certain relation then there may also be some other (possibly complex) concept C which designates the very same relation; yet there is no guarantee that it would be irrational for one to judge "there is some P such that C applies to P, myself and doing X" without being motivated to do X. This would be irrational only if one realized that the concept C and the concept of a reason designate the same relation. Now, as far as I can tell, there may nonetheless be some other ("intrinsic") feature of this relation which sets it apart from other, intuitively non-normative, relations and makes it normative. But if there is one, I have no inkling what it might be, and if there is no such feature then it will be merely in virtue of being designated by some normative concept (which presumably is an "extrinsic" feature) that it could be counted as "normative". It would, in this sense, only derivatively count as normative.

---

[3] Of course, if the set of normative properties is empty, then normative properties trivially supervene on any non-empty set of properties. But this is clearly not how the metaethicists alluded to understand the claim that the normative supervenes on the non-normative.

This need not always be of much significance, for there are natural assumptions on which it can be taken for granted that[4] if concepts of kind A* supervene (in whatever sense) on concepts of kind B*, then the properties designated by concepts of kind A* supervene (in some corresponding sense) on the properties designated by concepts of kind B*. However, as I will now try to explain, on the most interesting way of construing the distinction between "conceptual" and "metaphysical" supervenience, it is not the case that if concepts of kind A* "conceptually" supervene on concepts of kind B* then the properties designated by concepts of kind A* "metaphysically" supervene on the properties designated by concepts of kind B*.

It is common practice to distinguish between weak, strong and global supervenience. However, in order to keep things as simple as possible, and because it is somewhat disputed how global supervenience is best understood, I will concentrate on the two standard forms of individual supervenience, namely weak and strong supervenience. These are standardly understood as relations between kinds of properties, and defined either in terms of (metaphysically) possible worlds:

> (PWW) Properties of kind A weakly supervene on properties of kind B iff for any possible world w and any individuals x and y in w, if x and y are B-indiscernible in w then they are A-indiscernible in w

> (PWS) Properties of kind A strongly supervene on properties of kind B iff for any possible worlds w_1 and w_2 and any individuals x in w_1 and y in w_2, if x in w_1 is B-indiscernible from y in w_2 then x in w_1 is A-indiscernible from y in w_2

or in terms of the modal operator of (metaphysical) necessity:

> (MOW) Properties of kind A weakly supervene on properties of kind B iff necessarily, if anything x has some property F of kind A then there is at least one property G of kind B such that x has G and everything that has G also has F

> (MOS) Properties of kind A strongly supervene on properties of kind B iff necessarily, if anything x has some property F of kind A then there is at least one property G of kind B such that x has G and necessarily, everything that has G also has F.

As McLaughlin and Bennett (2011: 25–26) point out, the modal operator definitions are stronger than the corresponding possible worlds definitions (when, as is customary, the necessity operator is understood as a universal quantifier over possible worlds) in that they entail that nothing can have any A-property unless it also has some B-property, while the possible worlds definitions don't (i.e., they allow that something has some A-property but no B-property at all). However, since my concern here is limited to whether normative properties supervene on non-normative ones and since it can safely be assumed that everything that has some normative property also has some non-normative property, we may concentrate on the modal operator versions.

[4]As I hope will be obvious, in this section, I will be using "starred" letters, like "F*" and "A*", to refer to concepts or kinds of concepts, and "un-starred" letters, like "F" and "A", to refer to properties or kinds of properties.

Now, corresponding to (MOW) and (MOS), there are at least three other pairs of individual supervenience relations that we may want to consider. One appeals to metaphysical necessity and concerns relations between concepts:

(WC_1) Concepts of kind A* weakly supervene on concepts of kind B* iff necessarily, if anything x falls under some concept F* of kind A* then there is at least one concept G* of kind B* such that x falls under G* and everything that falls under G* also falls under F*

(SC_1) Concepts of kind A* strongly supervene on concepts of kind B* iff necessarily, if anything x falls under some concept F* of kind A* then there is at least one concept G* of kind B* such that x falls under G* and necessarily, everything that falls under G* also falls under F*

Another one appeals to conceptual truth (or conceptual necessity) and concerns relations between properties:

(WC_2) Properties of kind A weakly supervene on properties of kind B iff it is a conceptual (*a priori*) truth that if anything x has some property F of kind A then there is at least one property G of kind B such that x has G and everything that has G also has F

(SC_2) Properties of kind A strongly supervene on properties of kind B iff it is a conceptual (*a priori*) truth that if anything x has some property F of kind A then there is at least one property G of kind B such that x has G and it is a conceptual (*a priori*) truth that everything that has G also has F

And a third appeals to conceptual truth and concerns relations between concepts:

(WC_3) Concepts of kind A* weakly supervene on concepts of kind B* iff it is a conceptual (*a priori*) truth that if anything x falls under some concept F* of kind A* then there is at least one concept G* of kind B* such that x falls under G* and everything that falls under G* also falls under F*

(SC_3) Concepts of kind A* strongly supervene on concepts of kind B* iff it is a conceptual (*a priori*) truth that if anything x falls under some concept F* of kind A* then there is at least one concept G* of kind B* such that x falls under G* and it is a conceptual (*a priori*) truth that everything that falls under G* also falls under F*.[5]

Let's first consider how (MOW) and (MOS) are related to (WC_1) and (SC_1), respectively. Of course, no kind of concepts is a kind of properties; but for each kind of concepts, we may talk of the properties (if any) which are designated by some concept of this kind, and for each kind of properties, we may talk of the concepts (if any) which designate some property of this kind.

Suppose that properties of kind A MOW-supervene on properties of kind B. Then, necessarily, if x has property F of kind A then (there is some property G of kind B such that x has G and everything that has G also has F). On the assumption that all properties of kind B are designated by some concept, it follows

[5]Here is another, perhaps more revealing, way of seeing how these four pairs of definitions relate to one another. Notice that the right-hand side of (MOW) could also be formulated thus: "necessarily, for any F of kind A, if x is F then there is some G of kind B such that x is G and everything which is G is also F". But now suppose that second-order quantification is interpreted substitutionally, instead of objectually, and "necessarily" is replaced by "it is a conceptual truth that". What we get is another formulation of the right-hand side of (WC_1). In other words, we could drop explicit mention of "concepts" and "properties" and vary the interpretation of the second-order quantifiers.

that necessarily, if x falls under some concept F* designating a property of kind A, then (there is some concept G* designating a property of kind B such that x falls under G* and everything that falls under G* also falls under F*). In other words, it follows that the concepts which designate some property of kind A WC_1-supervene on the concepts which designate some property of kind B. Likewise, it will easily be seen that, on the same assumption, if properties of kind A MOS-supervene on properties of kind B then the concepts which designate some property of kind A SC_1-supervene on the concepts which designate some property of kind B.

Now, suppose that concepts of kind A* WC_1-supervene on concepts of kind B*. Then, necessarily, if x falls under some concept F* of kind A* then (there is some concept G* of kind B* such that x falls under G* and everything that falls under G* also falls under F*). On the assumption that all concepts of kind B* designate some property, it follows that necessarily, if x has some property F which is designated by some concept of kind A*, then (there is some property G which is designated by some concept of kind B* such that x has G and everything that has G also has F). In other words, it follows that the properties which are designated by some concept of kind A* MOW-supervene on the properties which are designated by some concept of kind B*. Likewise, it will easily be seen that, on the same assumption, if concepts of kind A* SC_1-supervene on concepts of kind B* then the properties which are designated by some concept of kind A* MOS-supervene on the properties which are designated by some concept of kind B*.

Thus, on the assumption that all concepts of kind B* designate some property of kind B and that all properties of kind B are designated by some concept of kind B*, we can always move from a MOW or MOS supervenience claim to some corresponding WC_1 or SC_1 supervenience claim, and vice versa. I conclude that the supervenience relations introduced by (WC_1) and (SC_1) are not significantly different from those introduced by (MOW) and (MOS), and, in particular, that they are not aptly described as "conceptual" supervenience relations, even though they take concepts as their relata. It seems then that genuinely "conceptual" supervenience must involve some modality other than metaphysical necessity. So let's turn to the two other pairs of definitions.

The first thing to observe is that (WC_2) and (SC_2) are related to (WC_3) and (SC_3) in the same way that (MOW) and (MOS) are related to (WC_1) and (SC_1): they differ only in that the first pair of definitions refers to properties while the second refers to concepts. Accordingly, on the assumption that all properties of kind B are designated by some concept, (i) if properties of kind A WC_2-supervene on properties of kind B then the concepts which designate some property of kind A WC_3-supervene on the concepts which designate some property of kind B, and (ii) if properties of kind A SC_2-supervene on properties of kind B then the concepts which designate some property of kind A SC_3-supervene on the concepts which designate some property of kind B. And, on the assumption that all concepts of kind B* designate some property, (i) if concepts of kind A* WC_3-supervene on concepts of kind B* then the properties which are designated by some concept of kind A* WC_2-supervene on the properties which are designated by some concept of kind B*, and (ii) if concepts of kind A* SC_3-supervene on concepts of kind B* then the properties which are designated by some concept of kind A* SC_2-supervene on the properties which are designated by some concept of kind B*.

So, what we really need to concentrate on is the relation between (WC_3)-(SC_3) and (WC_1)-(SC_1) and the relation between (WC_2)-(SC_2) and (MOW)-(MOS). This calls for some comments on the relation between conceptual truth and metaphysical necessity.

As I understand it, to say that something is conceptually true is to say that its negation is inconceivable (and to say that it is conceptually false is to say that it is inconceivable), though not in the merely psychological sense that no one can think it, but in the sense that thinking it involves some kind of inconsistency. For example, it is inconceivable, in the relevant sense, that some circle be a square, though we must of course be able to entertain the thought (and thus, in another sense, be able to conceive) that some circle is a square, if only in order to deny it. Alternatively, we could say that to be conceptually true is to be true in all "conceivable worlds". This may help to make it clear that "conceptual truth" is a kind of modality (and could just as well be called "conceptual necessity"). Another point worth stressing (obvious though it may be) is that claims of conceivability (inconceivability) are best understood as (at least implicitly) relative to some "conceptual scheme",[6] or better, relative to a person or class of persons and a time.

Thanks to the work of Kripke, it is now widely acknowledged that metaphysical necessity doesn't entail conceptual truth, and thus that what is conceivable (by some people, at some time) need not be metaphysically possible. This is well illustrated by such stock examples as the propositions that "water is H_2 O" and "water isn't H_2 O", neither of which is conceptually true (or false), despite the fact that (as current wisdom has it) the first is metaphysically necessary and the other metaphysically impossible. Thus, some space of "conceivable worlds" (in particular, our current space of conceivable worlds) is not contained in the space of "metaphysically possible worlds". This, I think, is enough to show (i) that WC_1-supervenience and SC_1-supervenience do not entail WC_3-supervenience and SC_3-supervenience, respectively, and (ii) that MOW-supervenience and MOS-supervenience do not entail WC_2-supervenience and SC_2-supervenience, respectively. In a word, metaphysical supervenience doesn't entail conceptual supervenience.

That much will probably not encounter much resistance. But what I now want to claim is that, conversely, (i) WC_3-supervenience and SC_3-supervenience do not entail WC_1-supervenience and SC_1-supervenience, respectively, and (ii) WC_2-supervenience and SC_2-supervenience do not entail MOW-supervenience and MOS-supervenience, respectively. This is a somewhat more delicate matter because in order to defend this, I must contend that just as metaphysical necessity doesn't entail conceptual truth, the latter doesn't entail the former, and thus that what is metaphysically possible need not be conceivable, and it would seem difficult to argue for such a claim "from within" any conceptual scheme.

[6] I should perhaps emphasize that, as I see it, the fact that I help myself to the notion of a "conceptual scheme" doesn't, by itself, commit me to the claim that there might be "incommensurable" conceptual schemes.

So, let me be clear that in denying that conceptual truth entails metaphysical necessity, I don't mean to be denying that if something is metaphysically possible, then there is some conceptual scheme or other relative to which it is conceivable (i.e., there are some people, at some time, for whom it is conceivable), nor that there may be some (ideal) conceptual scheme such that if something is conceptually true relative to that scheme then it is metaphysically necessary, nor even that there may be some (even more ideal) conceptual scheme such that something is conceptually true relative to that scheme if and only if it is metaphysically necessary. What I mean to be denying, is merely that the space of metaphysically possible worlds is contained in every space of "conceivable worlds", i.e. that every metaphysical possibility is somehow reflected in every conceptual scheme. When it is put that way, it admittedly sounds like a pretty trivial thing to say.

What may, however, make the claim that something can be conceptually true without being metaphysically necessary sound odd, is the fact that when we say that something is conceptually true *period*, we usually mean to be saying that, as things now stand with us, it is inconceivable that it be false, or in other words, that it is conceptually true relative to our own current conceptual scheme (i.e., that it is true in all currently conceivable worlds). In any case, this is how (WC_2)-(SC_3) are to be understood. But it would seem that no one could be in a position to *judge* that it is inconceivable, yet metaphysically possible, that not-P (i.e. that one is unable to conceive consistently that not-P, even though it is not metaphysically impossible). However, as G. E. Moore has taught us, the fact that no one can be in a position to judge that one doesn't believe that P but P, does nothing to show that it cannot be the case that one fails to believe that P, while P.

4 Do Normative Reasons Supervene on the Non-normative?

In discussions of supervenience and normativity, it is often asked, not only whether and why the normative supervenes on the non-normative, but also whether it is a priori or a posteriori that it does (or doesn't). Assuming that something is true *a priori* if and only if it is conceptually true, to raise the latter question about any of the metaphysical supervenience relations mentioned in the previous section is to ask whether it is a conceptual truth that a certain proposition is metaphysically necessary, and to raise it about any of the conceptual supervenience relations mentioned there is to ask whether it is a conceptual truth that a certain proposition is conceptually true.

It is not the case that if something is conceptually true relative to some scheme then it is conceptually true relative to that scheme that it is conceptually true relative to that scheme, since a conceptual scheme need not contain the concept of "conceptual truth". However, since I am only concerned with what is conceptually true for us (now), I think we may take it for granted that if the normative *conceptually* supervenes on the non-normative, then it is a conceptual truth that it does. In that case, then, in order to determine whether it is *a priori* that the normative conceptually supervenes on the non-normative, we need only ask whether it is true.

But since something can be metaphysically necessary without being *a priori*, showing that it is *a priori* that the normative *metaphysically* supervenes on the non-normative requires more than showing merely that it is true. Moreover, if I am right in denying that conceptual truth entails metaphysical necessity, this claim should be handled with some care. Strictly speaking, the claim that a conceptual truth need not be metaphysically necessary is compatible with the claim that if it is conceptually true that (it is metaphysically necessary that P) then it is metaphysically necessary that (it is metaphysically necessary that P), and thus with the claim that if it is conceptually true that (it is metaphysically necessary that P) then it is metaphysically necessary that P. However, if we wish to deny this, and maintain that even such propositions as the proposition that it is metaphysically necessary that P may be conceptually true without themselves being metaphysically necessary, then we have to deny that the "S4" principle that what is necessary is necessarily necessary holds for metaphysical necessity. For if this principle held, then from the fact that it is not necessary that (it is necessary that P) it would follow that it is not necessary that P, with the result that if it were conceptually true but not necessary that (it is necessary that P) then it would be conceptually true that (it is necessary that P), yet *not* necessary that P, which would mean that a conceptual truth could be false. But however that may be, I confess that I have no idea how it could ever be shown, of anything, that it is conceptually true that it is metaphysically necessary.

I am thus led to set aside the question of whether it is *a priori* that the normative supervenes on the non-normative, to concentrate on whether it is true.

As I said in Sect. 2, I don't know how to single out any kind of normative properties except as being the properties which are designated by normative concepts of certain kinds. And in Sect. 3, it was, in effect, made clear that if normative concepts of kind A* conceptually supervene (either weakly or strongly) on concepts of a given kind B*, then, *on the assumption that all concepts of this kind B* designate some property*, the properties which are designated by some normative concept of kind A* also conceptually supervene (either weakly or strongly) on the properties which are designated by some concept of kind B*. However, on the same assumption, the properties which are designated by some normative concept of kind A* may well conceptually supervene on the properties which are designated by concepts of kind B* without its being the case that normative concepts of kind A* conceptually supervene on concepts of kind B*, because it may not be the case that all normative concepts of kind A* designate some property. But to assume that all normative concepts of the relevant kind designate some property would beg the question against a number of metaethical positions, while it doesn't seem in any way question begging to assume that all concepts of the "subvenient" kind B* do designate some property. As far as conceptual supervenience is concerned, then, it is best to start by asking whether normative concepts of certain kinds WC_3-or-SC_3-supervene on concepts of some kind or other (as opposed to whether normative properties of certain kinds WC_2-or-SC_2-supervene on properties of some kind or other).

As I stressed in Sect. 2, the normative propositions I want to consider are those which are somehow reducible to propositions about reasons, i.e. propositions involving the concept of a reason. But, if I am right that the concept of a reason and the concept of "being reason-related" are inter-definable, all propositions involving the concept of a reason could as well be seen as involving the concept of "being reason-related" and vice versa. Accordingly, any concept involving one of these two concepts is to be included in the kind of normative concepts I am concerned with, which I will refer to as "reasons-concepts" or "R-concepts".

Now, both the concept of a reason and the concept of being reason-related are relation concepts which apply to at least[7] ordered triples consisting of (i) a proposition, (ii) an individual and (iii) an intentional action or attitude. And this is a source of trouble, in view of the fact that all the supervenience relations we have been considering are forms of individual supervenience, which are defined for monadic concepts only.

A variety of monadic reasons-concepts can be constructed out of the triadic concepts of a reason and of being reason-related, by either abstracting from or quantifying on one or the other of their three argument places. A sample involving the concept "being reason-related" would include the following: "being reason-related to S's doing X", "being such that that P is reason-related to S's doing *it*", "being such that that P is reason-related to *one*'s doing X", "being reason-related to *someone*'s doing X", "being such that *some proposition* is reason-related to S's doing *it*", etc.... And, of course, analogous monadic reasons-concepts can also be constructed with the concept of a "reason". It may, in principle, be asked, about monadic reasons-concepts of any of these kinds, whether they supervene on concepts of any other kind.

It may be worth remarking that, since concepts such as "being reason-related to S's doing X" could only supervene on concepts that apply to propositions, while concepts such as "being such that that P is reason-related to S's doing it" could only supervene on concepts that apply to intentional actions or attitudes, and concepts such as "being such that that P is reason-related to one's doing X" could only supervene on concepts that apply to individuals (or agents), there can be no one "natural" supervenience base (i.e., no one "natural" kind of concepts) on which all (monadic) R-concepts supervene (or in other words, any such *general* supervenience base will have to be a mixed bag including concepts of several different kinds). This, in itself, need not be worrying, since I guess nobody expects non-normative concepts to apply to a single sort of things; but it may be a source of trouble for those who would be tempted to go further and claim that all (monadic) R-concepts supervene on physical or naturalistic concepts.

For let's briefly consider R-concepts of the kind "being reason-related to S's doing X" which, as I have just said, will have to supervene on concepts that apply to propositions, if they supervene on concepts of any other kind. It is very hard to

[7] According to Skorupski (2010: 37) the concept of a reason has two more argument places, one for times and another for degrees of strength, but I am going to leave this implicit.

think of any kind of non-normative concepts applying to propositions (other than such "identity" concepts as "being the proposition that P") on which normative R-concepts of this kind could be said to supervene, and it is even harder to think of "physical" or "naturalistic" concepts applying to propositions[8] that could fill the bill. This, in my opinion, makes it overwhelmingly *implausible* that *all* normative concepts supervene on "physical" or "naturalistic" concepts.

People who raise the question whether normative concepts supervene on non-normative ones are generally concerned either with whether two *persons* who are indiscernible with respect to (some kind of) non-normative concepts can nonetheless satisfy different normative concepts, or with whether two *actions* (or attitudes) which are indiscernible with respect to (some kind of) non-normative concepts can nonetheless satisfy different normative concepts, presumably because they focus on such (monadic) normative concepts as "being good", "being such that *one* ought to do X" or "being such that S ought to do *it*". This suggests that, when it comes to R-concepts, they would be especially interested in supervenience claims concerning such R-concepts as "being such that (the proposition) that P is reason-related to *one*'s doing X" and "being such that (the fact) that P is a reason for *one* to do X", or "being such that (the proposition) that P is reason-related to S's doing it" and "being such that (the fact) that P is a reason for S to do *it*". So let's turn to these, beginning with R-concepts of the first of these four kinds.

I start by asking whether there is any interesting kind of non-normative concepts on which R-concepts of the kind "being such that (the proposition) that P is reason-related to one's doing X" might plausibly and non-trivially WC_3-supervene. It seems intuitively plausible, at first, to suggest that they WC_3-supervene on "motivational" concepts, that is, on concepts which can be constructed out of such concepts as "desiring that Q", with the help of the ordinary logical operators (including, perhaps, the necessity operator). This, of course, would be consistent with the view that in some, or even all, cases, the proposition that P is reason-related to S's doing X only if everyone is such that the proposition that P is reason-related to his/her doing X, no matter what his/her motivational attitudes are. But it is tempting to think that if the proposition that P is reason-related to S's doing X without being reason-related to S1's doing X, it must be on account of the fact that S and S1 differ in some of their motivational attitudes. However, there are at least two obvious problems with this suggestion.

Problem One (Capacity and Opportunity)

It seems that, that a child is drowning in the swimming pool can very well be reason-related to S's stepping into the water without being reason-related to S1's stepping into the water, even when S and S1 are (conceptually) indiscernible in all motivational respects. This may happen, for example, if S1 is in a wheelchairor a

[8] If, indeed, it makes sense to suppose that a "physical" or "naturalistic" concept could apply to such things as propositions.

hundred miles away, or otherwise unable to step into the water, and if "being such that the proposition that P is reason-related to one's doing X" requires that one has the "capacity and opportunity" to do X (or in other words, that doing X is among one's options).

Problem Two (Identity)

Suppose S suddenly finds herself in the middle of a lake, so that she needs to start swimming in order to survive, and desires to survive. That S is in the middle of a lake would then, plausibly enough, be a reason for her to start swimming. But it may very well not be a reason for S1 to start swimming, even if she is motivationally indiscernible from S (so that both S and S1 desire that S survives and that S1 survives) and her capacities and opportunities are the same as S's (perhaps S1 finds him/herself in the middle of a different but very similar lake and is as good or bad a swimmer as S). What matters here, of course, is the identity of the individuals in question. That S is in the middle of a lake is reason-related to S's starting to swim, but not to S1's starting to swim, and similarly, that S1 is in the middle of a lake is reason-related to S1's starting to swim but not to S's starting to swim.

As far as I can see, it would be useless to try to take care of this simply by acknowledging that such concepts as that of "being reason-related to S's doing X" (or, for that matter, as that of "being a reason for S to do X") may apply to (monadic) concepts (or "propositional functions") as well as to propositions. The problem is that any proposition about S can be seen as (vacuously) applying some concept to S1, so that there can be no difference between that proposition's being true and that concept's being true-of S1. On the other hand, denying that these R-concepts ever apply to propositions is not an option, for it certainly is sometimes the case that S's being such-and-such is reason-related to S1's doing a certain thing, and not only to S's doing some (other) thing.[9]

It is of course anything but clear exactly when S and S1 can be said to have the very same "capacities and opportunities". But since one's opportunities (at least with respect to actions) would seem to depend pretty much on one's spatiotemporal location, it is arguable that this could be interpreted in such a strict way that different individuals can have the very same capacities and opportunities only if they inhabit different worlds; or more precisely, in such a way that there is no conceivable world in which different individuals have the very same capacities and opportunities. On this assumption, it would be conceptually but trivially true that if S is such that the proposition that P is reason-related to S's doing X then there is some "capacity and opportunity" concept C such that S is C and everyone who is C is such that that P is reason-related to his/her doing X (because everyone who is C would then be identical to S); or in other words, it would be trivially true that R-concepts of the kind "being such that (the proposition) that P is reason-related to one's doing X" WC_3-supervene on "capacity and opportunity" concepts.

[9]As Smith (1994: 169) puts it, "there are both *de dicto* and *de se* normative reasons".

We can do somewhat better for the special cases where doing X consists, not in performing some action, but in having (or forming) some intentional attitude, such as believing or desiring that Q. Consider R-concepts of the kind "being such that (the proposition) that P is reason-related to one's believing that Q". Some people (e.g., Thomson 2008) hold that if anyone is such that the proposition that P is reason-related to his/her believing that Q, then everyone is, while others think that whether someone is such that the proposition that P is reason-related to his/her believing that Q depends on his/her motivations and interests. Either way, it would seem plausible to suggest that R-concepts of the kind "being such that (the proposition) that P is reason-related to one's believing that Q" WC_3-supervene on "motivational and capacity" concepts (as well as on "capacity and opportunity" concepts); or in other words, that it is conceptually true that if S is such that the proposition that P is reason-related to his/her believing that Q, then there is some "motivational and capacity" concept C such that S is C and everyone who is C is also such that the proposition that P is reason-related to his/her believing that Q. As far as I can see, the same could be said for R-concepts of the kind "being such that (the proposition) that P is reason-related to one's desiring that Q", but perhaps not for R-concepts of the kind "being such that (the proposition) that P is reason-related to one's intending that Q", at least not if it is held to be inconceivable that someone intends that someone else does something (as opposed to "intends to bring it about that someone else does something").

The fact that there is no conceivable world in which different individuals have the very same capacities and opportunities is of course compatible with there being both a conceivable world in which some individual has such-and-such capacities and opportunities and another conceivable world in which some other individual has the very same capacities and opportunities. But, since two such individuals may nonetheless fail to be motivationally indiscernible, it follows that R-concepts of the kind "being such that (the proposition) that P is reason-related to one's doing X" do not SC_3-supervene on "capacity and opportunity" concepts. In other words, it is not conceptually true that if S is such that the proposition that P is reason-related to S's doing X then there is some "capacity and opportunity" concept C such that S is C and it is conceptually true that everyone who is C is such that the proposition that P is reason-related to his/her doing X.

Even so, one might be tempted to suggest that R-concepts of the kind "being such that (the proposition) that P is reason-related to one's doing X" SC_3-supervene on motivational *cum* "capacity and opportunity" concepts; i.e., that it is conceptually true that if S is such that the proposition that P is reason-related to S's doing X, then there is some motivational *cum* "capacity and opportunity" concept C such that S is C and it is conceptually true that everyone who is C is such that the proposition that P is reason-related to his/her doing X. But this will not do, for *problem two* is bound to arise as long as it is allowed that *different* individuals (in different conceivable worlds) may be indiscernible with respect to motivational *cum* "capacity and opportunity" concepts.

Here again, it seems that R-concepts of the kinds "being such that (the proposition) that P is reason-related to one's believing that Q" and "being such that (the proposition) that P is reason-related to one's desiring that Q" would fare differently in this respect. For it seems plausible to hold that they do SC_3-supervene on "motivational and capacity" concepts.

Let's now turn to R-concepts of the kind "being such that (the fact) that P is *a reason* for one to do X" which, I suggested, could be seen as being of the kind "being such that P, and (the proposition) that P is reason-related to one's doing X".

On the assumption that R-concepts of the kind "being such that (the proposition) that P is reason-related to one's doing X" do WC_3-supervene on "capacity-and-opportunity" concepts, it follows trivially that R-concepts of the kind "being such that (the fact) that P is *a reason* for one to do X" do as well. Interestingly, they also (trivially) WC_3-supervene on R-concepts of the kind "being such that (the proposition) that P is reason-related to one's doing X". This is interesting insofar as concepts of the latter kind are normative without being normative force conferring.

It should also be easy to see that R-concepts of the kind "being such that (the fact) that P is *a reason* for one to do X" do not SC_3-supervene on R-concepts of the kind "being such that (the proposition) that P is reason-related to one's doing X", nor on "capacity and opportunity" concepts or motivational *cum* "capacity and opportunity" concepts. This is perhaps unsurprising, given that R-concepts of the kind "being such that (the proposition) that P is reason-related to one's doing X" do not SC_3-supervene on concepts of any of these kinds.

But it may be worth stressing that R-concepts of the kind "being such that (the fact) that P is a reason for one to do X" would still fail to SC_3-supervene on motivational *cum* capacity and opportunity concepts even if R-concepts of the kind "being such that (the proposition) that P is reason-related to one's doing X" did SC_3-supervene on them. For, suppose there is some motivational *cum* "capacity and opportunity" concept C such that it is conceptually true that everyone who is C is also such that the proposition that P is reason-related to his/her doing X. It certainly doesn't follow from this that it is also conceptually true that everyone who is C is also such that (P and the proposition that P is reason-related to his/her doing X), nor, indeed, that there is any motivational *cum* "capacity and opportunity" concept C1 such that it is conceptually true that everyone who is C1 is also such that P and the proposition that P is reason-related to his/her doing X (i.e., such that the fact that P is a reason for him/her to do X).

This actually generalizes: it is not the case that, if K is any kind of concepts on which R-concepts of the kind "being such that (the proposition) that P is reason-related to one's doing X" SC_3-supervene then it also is a kind of concepts on which R-concepts of the kind "being such that (the fact) that P is a reason for one to do X" SC_3-supervene. Not only doesn't it follow, but in the particular case of motivational *cum* "capacity and opportunity" concepts, it is obviously false that for any proposition P, there is some motivational *cum* "capacity and opportunity" concept C such that it is conceptually true that if anyone is C then P is true. This warrants the conclusion that R-concepts of the kind "being such that (the fact) that P is a reason for one to do X" *would* (and not merely could) still fail to SC_3-supervene on motivational *cum* capacity and opportunity concepts even if R-concepts of the kind "being such that (the proposition) that P is reason-related to one's doing X" did SC_3-supervene on them.

Indeed, if any concept C is to be such that it is conceptually true that everyone who is C is also such that (P and the proposition that P is reason-related to one's doing X), it will also have to be such that it is conceptually true that nothing is C unless P is true. Given that *any* proposition whatsoever (including any normative proposition) is reason-related to someone's doing something, this means that if R-concepts of the kind "being such that (the fact) that P is a reason for one to do X" are to SC_3-supervene on concepts of any kind K, it will have to be the case that for any proposition whatsoever, there is some concept C of kind K such that it is conceptually true that if anything is C then this proposition is true.[10] But if this is right, then even if we were able to identify such a kind K, it is hard to see how it could teach us any anything very specific about normative reasons, or more precisely, about the *normativity* of R-concepts of the kind "being such that (the fact) that P is a reason for one to do X", which, it would seem, resides entirely in the fact that they involve R-concepts of the kind "being such that (the proposition) that P is reason-related to S's doing X", which, it will be recalled, are *not* normative force conferring.

On the assumption that R-concepts of the kinds "being such that (the proposition) that P is reason-related to one's believing that Q" and "being such that (the proposition) that P is reason-related to one's desiring that Q" do WC_3-supervene on "motivational and capacity" concepts, it follows trivially that R-concepts of the kinds "being such that (the fact) that P is a reason for one to believe that Q" and "being such that (the fact) that P is a *reason* for one to desire that Q" do as well. They also (trivially) WC_3-supervene, respectively, on R-concepts of the kind "being such that (the proposition) that P is reason-related to one's believing that Q" and on R-concepts of the kind "being such that (the proposition) that P is reason-related to one's desiring that Q".

I said it would be plausible to hold that R-concepts of the kinds "being such that (the proposition) that P is reason-related to one's believing that Q" and "being such that (the proposition) that P is reason-related to one's desiring that Q" SC_3-supervene on "motivational and capacity" concepts. It should now be easy to see that R-concepts of the kinds "being such that (the fact) that P is a *reason* for one to believe that Q" and "being such that (the fact) that P is a *reason* for one to desire that Q" nonetheless fail to SC_3-supervene on "motivational and capacity" concepts, for it is obviously false that for any proposition P, there is some "motivational and capacity" concept C such that it is conceptually true that if anyone is C then P is true.

It is often remarked that, as McLaughlin and Bennett (2011:23) put it, "someone who asserts a weak supervenience thesis but denies the corresponding strong

[10]The same holds for R-concepts of the kind "being such that that P is a reason for S to do it", which will briefly be considered below.

supervenience thesis must provide an explanation of why the weak supervenience thesis is true that does not entail that the relevant strong supervenience thesis is true as well". However, in this instance, it seems very easy to understand why R-concepts of the kinds "being such that (the fact) that P is a reason for one to believe that Q" and "being such that (the fact) that P is a reason for one to desire that Q" fail to SC_3-supervene on "motivational and capacity" concepts, despite the fact that they WC_3-supervene on them.

Let's now turn to R-concepts of the kind "being such that (the proposition) that P is reason-related to S's doing *it*", and ask whether there is any interesting kind of (non-normative) concepts on which they could plausibly and non-trivially WC_3-supervene.

I take it that, for any X (or any "doing X"), at least some of the propositions that are reason-related to S's doing it are propositions to the effect that *doing X* has such and such features. But let C be *any* concept that applies to doing X and which is *not* such that everything which is C is identical to doing X: it is *very* hard to see how it could then ever be the case that every Y which is C is also such that the proposition that doing X has such and such features is reason-related to S's doing *it*. But if R-concepts of the kind "being such that (the proposition) that P is reason-related to S's doing it" non-trivially WC_3-supervened on concepts of any kind, there would have to be some concept of that kind that applies to doing X (which is not such that everything to which it applies is identical to doing X) and which applies to doing Y only if the proposition that doing X has such and such features is reason-related to S's doing *Y*. It seems, then, that we here encounter a problem similar to one of the two problems that we encountered above with respect to R-concepts of the kind "being such that (the proposition) that P is reason-related to one's doing X", namely *problem two*; except that in the present case, it arises for intentional attitudes as well as for actions.

For, surely, believing that Q is such that the proposition (that believing that Q is believing something supported by the evidence available to S) is reason-related to S's doing it (i.e., to S's believing that Q). But let C be *any* concept that applies to believing that Q and which is not such that everything which is C is identical to believing that Q: it is *very* hard to see how it could then ever be the case that every doing Y which is C is also such that the proposition (that believing that Q is believing something supported by the evidence available to S) is reason-related to S's *doing it*. But if R-concepts of the kind "being such that (the proposition) that P is reason-related to S's doing it" non-trivially WC_3-supervened on concepts of any kind, there would have to be some concept of that kind that applies to believing that Q (which is not such that everything to which it applies is identical to believing that Q) and which applies to doing Y only if (that believing that Q is believing something supported by the evidence available to S) is reason-related to S's *doing Y*.

Of course, in the sort of case just alluded to, what we want to say is that if doing X is such that the proposition that doing X has such and such features is reason-related to S's doing it then there is some (non-normative) concept C such that doing X is C and every doing Y which is C is also such that the proposition that *it* has such and such features is reason-related to S's *doing it* (i.e., such that if it had such and such features, the fact that it has these features would be a reason for S to do it). The trouble, as before, is that just as not all propositions which are reason-related to S's doing X are propositions about S, not all of them are propositions about doing X either. It must be allowed, for example, that the proposition that a child is drowning is reason-related to S's plunging into the swimming pool or to S's believing that this child needs help. Since I see no general solution to this problem, I conclude that R-concepts of the kind "being such that (the proposition) that P is reason-related to S's doing it" do not non-trivially WC_3-supervene on concepts of any other kind, no matter whether they are taken to apply to actions or to attitudes. And if this is right, then neither do they non-trivially SC_3-supervene on anything, and neither do R-concepts of the kind "being such that (the fact) that P is a reason for S to do it" (non-trivially) WC_3-or-SC_3-supervene on anything.

It should also be obvious that, just as R-concepts of the kind "being such that (the fact) that P is *a reason* for one to do X" do not SC_3-supervene on R-concepts of the kind "being such that (the proposition) that P is reason-related to one's doing X", R-concepts of the kind "being such that (the fact) that P *is a reason* for S to do it" do not SC_3 – supervene on R-concepts of the kind "being such that (the proposition) that P is reason-related to S's doing it".

5 Concluding Remarks

Of all the R-concepts we have examined, the only ones which could plausibly non-trivially SC_3-supervene (or even WC_3-supervene) on concepts of some other kind are R-concepts of the (sub-) kinds "being such that that P is reason-related to one's believing that Q" and "being such that that P is reason-related to one's desiring that Q". There are several other kinds of R-concepts which I haven't considered in this paper, such as R-concepts of the kind "being such that that P is reason-related to one's doing *something*", or of the kind "being such that *some* P is reason-related to one's doing X", or of the kind "being such that that P is reason-related to someone's doing it", or of the kind "being such that some P is reason-related to S's doing it", (and similarly, *mutatis mutandis*, with "reason" substituted for "reason-related") etc. For all that I have said, it may still turn out that some of them (non-trivially) conceptually supervene on concepts of some other interesting kinds (though this perhaps now seems unlikely). However, I hope, and think, that I have said enough for it to be reasonably clear that, as far as reasons-concepts are concerned, there is simply no interesting kind of concepts on which all of them conceptually and non-trivially supervene; *a fortiori* there is no interesting kind of concepts on which *all* normative concepts conceptually and non-trivially supervene.[11]

[11]Substantial parts of this paper have been read at a workshop on supervenience and normativity which has been held at the University of Montreal on February 28 and March 1 2014. I wish to thank all the participants in this workshop, and specially Carla Bagnoli, Josée Brunet, Gerald Harrison, Brian McLaughlin and Antonino Rotolo.

List of the Main Propositions

(DF1) That P is a reason for S to do X $=_{df}$ P and that P is reason-related to S's doing X.

(DF2) That P is reason-related to S's doing X $=_{df}$ if P then that P is a reason for S to do X.

(P1) If all properties of kind B are designated by some concept, then properties of kind A MOW-supervene (MOS-supervene, WC_2-supervene, SC_2-supervene) on properties of kind B only if the concepts which designate some property of kind A WC_1-supervene (SC_1-supervene, WC_3-supervene, SC_3-supervene) on the concepts which designate some property of kind B.

(P2) If all concepts of kind B* designate some property, then concepts of kind A* WC_1-supervene (SC_1-supervene, WC_3-supervene, SC_3-supervene) on concepts of kind B* only if the properties which are designated by some concept of kind A* MOW-supervene (MOS-supervene, WC_2-supervene, SC_2-supervene) on the properties which are designated by some concept of kind B*.

(P3) MOW-supervenience (MOS-supervenience, WC_1-supervenience, SC_1-supervenience) doesn't entail WC_2-supervenience (SC_2-supervenience, WC_3-supervenience, SC_3-supervenience).

(P4) WC_2-supervenience (SC_2-supervenience, WC_3-supervenience, SC_3-supervenience) doesn't entail MOW-supervenience (MOS-supervenience, WC_1-supervenience, SC_1-supervenience).

(P5) On the assumption that there is no conceivable world in which different individuals have the very same capacities and opportunities, both R-concepts of the kind "being such that (the proposition) that P is reason-related to one's doing X" and R-concepts of the kind "being such that (the fact) that P is a reason for one to do X" trivially WC_3-supervene on "capacity and opportunity" concepts, but neither SC_3-supervene on them.

(P6) Both R-concepts of the kind "being such that (the proposition) that P is reason-related to one's believing (desiring) that Q" and R-concepts of the kind "being such that (the fact) that P is a reason for one to believe (desire) that Q" WC_3-supervene on "motivational and capacity" concepts, but only the first also SC_3-supervene on them.

(P7) If R-concepts of the kind "being such that (the fact) that P is a reason for one to do X", or of the kind "being such that (the fact) that P is a reason for one to believe (desire) that Q", or of the kind "being such that (the fact) that P is a reason for S to do it" SC_3-supervene on concepts of any kind K then for any proposition whatsoever, there is some concept C of kind K such that it is conceptually true that if anything is C then this proposition is true.

(P8) R-concepts of the kind "being such that (the proposition) that P is reason-related to S's doing it" do not non-trivially WC_3-supervene on concepts of any kind.

References

Dancy, Jonathan (2009) Reasons and Rationality, Robertson *ed.* (2009) 93–112
Laurier, Daniel (2011) Intentional Normativism Meets Normative Supervenience and the Because Constraint, *Dialogue* 50, 315–331
Leuenberger, Stephan (2008) Supervenience in Metaphysics, *Philosophy Compass* 3/4, 749–762
McLaughlin, Brian and Karen Bennett (2011) "Supervenience", *Stanford Encyclopedia of Philosophy*, http://plato.stanford.edu/archives/win2011/entries/supervenience/
Parfit, Derek (2011) *On What Matters*, Oxford, Oxford U. Press
Robertson, Simon ed. (2009) *Spheres of Reason*, Oxford, Oxford U. Press
Scanlon, Timothy M. (1998) *What We Owe to Each Other*, Cambridge (Mass.), Harvard U. Press
Scanlon, Timothy M. (2014) *Being Realistic about Reasons*, Oxford, Oxford U. Press
Schroeder, Mark (2007) *Slaves of the Passions*, Oxford, Oxford U. Press
Shafer-Landau, Russ ed. (2009) *Oxford Studies in Metaethics 4*, Oxford, Oxford U. Press
Shagrir, Oron (2013) Concepts of Supervenience Revisited, *Erkenntnis* 78, 469–485
Skorupski, John (2010) *The Domain of Reasons*, Oxford, Oxford U. Press
Smith, Michael (1994) *The Moral Problem*, Oxford, Blackwell
Sturgeon, Nicholas L. (2009) "Doubts about the Supervenience of the Evaluative", Shafer-Landau *ed.* (2009) 53–90
Thomson, Judith Jarvis (2008) *Normativity*, La Salle, Open Court

The Dubious Moral Supervenience Thesis

Gerald K. Harrison

Abstract Non-reductionist moral realist views are supposed to have trouble explaining the truth of the moral supervenience thesis. In this paper I argue that the non-reductionist has nothing to worry about on this front. The positive case for the global moral supervenience thesis is flawed. I identify three considerations commonly cited in support of the thesis: the grounding concern, the horrendous deeds concern, and the normative authority concern. I argue that each one is based on mistakes, dubious assumptions and/or a question begging assumption of meta-ethical reductionism. I go on to argue that given reliable epistemic access to moral reality (something most moral realists will want to grant), the differential considered moral judgements of competent moral judges at different times and in different places is prima facie evidence that the moral landscape, like the physical landscape, is not uniform across time and space. This is incompatible with the local (non-trivial) moral supervenience thesis, according to which the subvening base excludes spatio-temporal location, thus fixing moral properties across time and space. I then argue that if the local (non-trivial) moral supervenience thesis is false there is no reason to think the global moral supervenience thesis is true. I conclude that short of a prior commitment to reductionism there is no good reason to think the global moral supervenience thesis is true.

I would like to thank the participants at the GRIN workshop on Supervenience and Normativity held at the University of Montreal in March 2014, with a special thanks to Carla Bognoli, Daniel Laurier, Brian McLaughlin and Antonino Rotolo. I would also like to thank Bartosz Brożek and Antonino Rotolo for inviting me to write this piece, and Julia K. Tanner who read and commented on an earlier draft.

G.K. Harrison (✉)
Massey University, Manawatu, New Zealand
e-mail: G.K.Harrison@massey.ac.nz

B. Brożek et al. (eds.), *Supervenience and Normativity*, Law and Philosophy Library 120, DOI 10.1007/978-3-319-61046-7_5

1 Introduction

The version of the moral supervenience thesis I will be considering here is this one:

> If two situations or actions are identical in all of their natural properties (and include mental properties if you do not consider mental properties to be natural properties), they must be identical in any moral properties they may have as well.

However, supervenience theses can be global or local. The global version claims that no two possible worlds can differ morally without also differing naturally. The local version says that no two numerically distinct acts in one and the same world can differ morally without differing naturally. But as Ridge puts it "one problem for local supervenience claims is that if the subvening base is widened far enough – say, to include spatio-temporal location – then supervenience may be trivially true for the reason that no numerically distinct things can be precisely the same in all of the subvening respects" (2007, p. 332). I will have more to say about this later, but in the meantime I should be understood to be talking about the global version unless otherwise stated. The global supervenience thesis is considered a non-negotiable truth about morality by virtually everyone (see Smith 1994, p. 21). This is not a problem for naturalist reductionist moral realists (just 'reductionists' hereafter). If moral properties reduce to natural properties it is trivially true that there cannot be a difference in moral properties without a difference in natural properties and thus reductionist views explain the truth of the moral supervenience thesis. Not so for non-reductioniststs views about moral properties, or reductionist supernaturalist views of morality (Blackburn 1993, pp. 114–119; Mackie 1977; McNaughton, Rawling and Lovibond 2003, p. 24; Brink 1989, p. 22). If, as non-reductionists maintain, moral properties are sui generis it is hard to see how to rule out the metaphysically possibility of a naturalistically identical world in which moral properties are differently arranged. Similarly, if one reduces moral properties to something like the commands and favourings of a god of some sort, then it is hard to see how to rule out the metaphysical possibility of a naturalistically identical world in which the god commands and favours different things. Either way moral properties seem to have come unmoored from their natural base.

There are three strategies available to the non-reductionist and reductionist supernaturalist (for ease I will mainly focus on the non-reductionist hereafter). She might accept the truth of the moral supervenience thesis, but deny that she needs to explain it (see Zangwill 2005). She might accept the truth of the moral supervenience thesis and argue that she can explain it (Shafer-Landau 2003, p. 77). Or she might deny the truth of the moral supervenience thesis. Here I recommend the third option. I argue first that the positive case for thinking the moral supervenience thesis is a non-negotiable truth is based on a combination of mistakes and dubious assumptions or else simply assumes the truth of reductionism about moral properties.[1] I then argue that on the assumption of moral realism and reliable

[1] See also my 2013 article, although the case I make there is different from the one I will be making here (Harrison 2013).

epistemic access to moral truths there is likely to be prima facie evidence that the non-trivial version of the local moral supervenience thesis is false. If the non-trivial local version is false, then there seems no reason to think the global version is true short of a prior commitment to reductionism.

The structure of the paper is as follows. I will begin by considering three reasons for thinking the moral supervenience thesis must be true. I call the first the grounding concern. The second I call the horrendous deeds concern. The third I call the normative authority concern. I will argue that the first and second rest on mistakes or make very dubious assumptions. The third rests on a combination of the same mistakes and/or a question begging assumption of reductionism. I will then turn my attention to the local (non-trivial) moral supervenience thesis. I will then argue that there is evidence the local (non-trivial) moral supervenience thesis is false and consequently no reason to think the global moral supervenience thesis is true.

2 The Grounding Concern

If an act is wrong it is wrong due to its natural features. The wrongness is not some free-floating extra. Many think this entails the truth of the moral supervenience thesis. For if an act is wrong because of its natural features then surely two naturalistically identical acts just must be morally identical as well (Ridge 2007, pp. 335–336).

However, reflection on the following sorts of case suggests this is a mistake. Florence is trying to make a decision about what to drink at a café and faces a conflict in her will between competing motivations. On the one hand she has a health-based motivation – P1 – to choose a low-fat tea, but she also has a gustatory motivation – P2 – to choose a tasty milkshake. Imagine it is indeterministic which set of motivational factors will win-out in the actual sequence (as many libertarians about free will would maintain).[2] So, in some possible worlds she goes for tea, and in others she goes for milkshake, holding all past states fixed. Nevertheless, it seems true to say that in those possible worlds in which she makes the decision to go for tea, her decision was caused by those motivations of hers that favoured it, namely P1. And in those possible worlds in which she decides to go for the milkshake, her decision was caused by those motivations of hers that favoured it, namely P2. It was indeterministic which motivation would cause her decision, but it does not follow from this that her resulting decision was uncaused. In the actual sequence she chose tea because of those motivations of hers that favoured it – because of P1. P1 produced her decision.

[2]See Kane (2003) for a more detailed description if a case of this kind.

We can now draw an analogy with a moral case possessing features with conflicting moral valences (and I am going to assume some form of non-reductionism about moral properties, but that seems dialectically appropriate given non-reductionist views are supposed to be those in trouble on this front). For instance Xing in circumstances S will prevent some suffering. This is a feature that, in this context, has a positive moral valence. Call it P1. However, Xing in circumstances S will also break a promise. This is a feature that, in this context, has a negative moral valence. Call it P2. Few, I think, will deny that there are cases like this and where the competing moral valences are roughly matched. So now imagine that this is just such a case and that it is indeterministic whether feature P1's positive moral valence will win out and make Xing right overall or whether feature P2's negative moral valence will win out and make Xing wrong overall.[3] So we now have possible worlds in which Xing is wrong, and others in which Xing is right, holding fixed all natural features. This contravenes the moral supervenience thesis. So, if the grounding concern is legitimate it should be the case that the wrongness of Xing has come unmoored from its natural features such that we can no longer say that Xing is wrong due to P2. But we can still say this. If in the actual world Xing in circumstances S is wrong, it is wrong due to P2. That is, it is wrong because it violates a promise. And in those naturalistically identical possible worlds in which it is right, it is right because it prevents some suffering. To think otherwise is, it seems to me, as confused as thinking that Florence's decision to go for tea in the actual world had nothing to do with those motivations of hers that favoured it simply because there is a possible world in which she decides otherwise. Florence's motivation to go for tea did not have to necessitate her decision before it can have been said to have caused it. Similarly, an act's natural features do not have to necessitate its morality before they can be said to have caused it to have the morality it had, as we have just seen. The grounding concern is misguided, then.[4] There can be a naturalistically identical

[3]I am speaking of moral valences as having causal powers. Some may object on the ground that there cannot be causation by supervenient properties. I see no good reason to hold such a view and some others agree (see for Shafer-Landau 2012, esp. pp. 27–29). But anyway, note that the moral valences are producing the overall action's moral property of rightness or wrongness (or permissibility) and so we do not have causation across different metaphysical kinds (not that I consider there to be any problem even if we did, but I know that some do).

[4]I am assuming the coherence of indeterminsitic causation, of course. Realist accounts of causation take the causal relation to be basic and maintain that one event causes another just in case the relation of causation obtains between them. On this kind of view there is nothing unintelligible in the idea of indeterministic causation. Causation just is the obtaining of a causal relation, and it can be indeterministic whether A will cause B, for it can be indeterministic whether this causal relation will obtain. If it does, then its obtaining just is A's causing of B. One might reject realist accounts in favour of Reductionist accounts of causation that seek to analyse causation in terms of constant conjunction or counterfactual dependence, or the modalities of necessity and sufficiency. But these accounts have some serious problems and strike many, myself included, as fundamentally misguided insofar as it seems more natural to understand counterfactual dependence in terms of the existence of causal relations rather than the other way around (on this see Bigelow and Pargetter 1990).

world to this one in which the morality of Xing differs (it is morally right there, but wrong here) yet it remains the case that Xing is morally right here due to its having certain natural features.

The same applies the moral valences of the features themselves. For an analogy, I used to dislike the taste of beer. Now I like it. But it is not that beer tastes different to me. It tastes the same, it is just that it now causes in me a positive attitude, whereas before it caused a negative attitude. Imagine that whenever I drink some beer there is a certain objective probability that it will cause in me a negative attitude rather than a positive one. In the actual world I take a sip and the taste non-waywardly causes in me a positive attitude. I can surely say truthfully that "I am enjoying this beer due to its taste" even though some negative attitudes might have occurred instead. So, if it is indeterministic what moral valences an act's natural properties will have this will not, in and of itself, prevent us from being able to say that the moral properties have been produced by the natural properties.

A divine command theory can help illustrate the point. Assume that the property of being morally wrong reduces to the property of being commanded not to be done by a god of a particular kind. Imagine this god is deliberating about whether to command Xing in circumstances S to be done or not to be done and is torn between competing motivations. This is because Xing in circumstances S will break a promise, a natural feature of the situation that is causing her to favour commanding Xing not to be done. But Xing in circumstances S will also save someone some suffering, and this is a natural feature of the situation that is causing her to favour commanding Xing to be done. Imagine it is indeterministic which set of motivational factors will win-out in the actual sequence. So, in some possible worlds she commands Xing to be done and in others she commands Xing not to be done. In the actual world she commands Xing not to be done. Xing got to have its 'not to be doneness' in the actual world due to it having the natural feature of breaking a promise, for it was on the basis of this feature that the god was motivated to command Xing not to be done, and that motivation produced her command in the actual sequence. Yet there are naturalistically identical possible worlds in which Xing has to be doneness instead, and got to have it due to the fact it prevents some suffering.

Alternatively imagine that sometimes feature P1 of Xing in circumstances S (the fact it breaks a promise) causes the god of morality to disapprove of Xing in those circumstances, and sometimes it causes her to approve of Xing in those circumstances and it is indeterministic which it will cause. In the actual world feature P1 causes her to disapprove of Xing. Xing is wrong, then, due to its possession of feature P1. The fact there is a naturalistically identical world in which Xing is right due to its possession of P1 is neither here nor there where grounding is concerned. She – morality – disfavours us Xing in circumstances S because it breaks a promise.

Of course, the possibility of it turning out to be indeterministic what morality some deeds have, and indeterministic what moral valence a natural feature will have in any/some situations opens up the prospect of morality being messy, unpredictable, uncodifiable. But this is a prospect already taken seriously and defended by moral particularists. True, all moral particularists that I know of affirm the moral supervenience thesis. They do this by maintaining that while it is possible for the moral valence of any natural feature to alter, any such alteration will be due to other natural differences between the situations in which it is featuring. But all this does is show that the moral supervenience thesis is entirely compatible with morality being messy, unpredictable, uncodifiable and so can hardly be viewed as a bulwark against such possibilities.[5]

3 Horrendous Deeds

Deny the moral supervenience thesis and supposedly you must allow that it is metaphysically possible for the most horrific of deeds to be morally right and praiseworthy. This is held to be absurd (see Coons 2011, p. 92; Ridge 2007, pp. 334–335 for just some examples of this common criticism).

However, the moral supervenience thesis is neither necessary nor sufficient to rule out the metaphysical possibility of horrific acts being morally right. The moral supervenience thesis is not necessary to rule out such possibilities because as I showed in the previous section one could hold that it is indeterministic whether Xing in circumstances S is morally right/wrong due to the competing moral valences of some of its features. This is incompatible with the moral supervenience thesis, but it is compatible with holding that some deeds are always wrong. There may be deeds that have natural features possessing invariant negative moral valences and no features possessing positive moral valences. Such deeds would always be wrong. The same applies to cases that have features with competing moral valences but where the negative moral valences of some far outweigh the positive moral valences of others. Again, such deeds may always be wrong, for perhaps it is only when competing moral valences are balanced – or roughly balanced – that it becomes indeterministic what morality the deed will have, just as analogously many libertarians about free will maintain that it is only when we are torn about what to do that it becomes indeterministic which way we will decide (see Kane 2003; Clarke 2003 for defences of libertarian views of this kind).

[5]I should add that though the moral supervenience thesis is compatible with moral particularism, it does seem to me to be against the spirit of moral particularism to defend it. For the moral particularist makes it his/her business to challenge the idea that the moral valence of a natural feature – or bundle of natural features – is invariant. But a moral particularist who affirms the moral supervenience thesis has to claim that the moral valence of a natural feature is invariant across naturalistically identical situations. That is a form of invariantism too.

Note also that the moral supervenience thesis is not sufficient to rule out the metaphysical possibility of horrendous acts being morally right. For the moral supervenience thesis is not a thesis about which acts are right and which ones wrong. It is entirely silent on that matter. In order to rule out the metaphysical possibility of horrendous acts being morally right the moral supervenience thesis needs supplementing with the claim that horrendous acts are morally wrong here (a very plausible claim, of course). Now consider that those who consider the metaphysical possibility of horrific acts being morally right to be absurd presumably have a very clear and distinct impression such acts are actually wrong, such that they find it inconceivable that the impression could be false. But it seems to me that that is all that is needed to preclude the metaphysical possibility of such acts being morally right in a naturalistically identical world. We might draw comparison with our clear and distinct impression of our own mind's existence. I am currently getting the impression a mind – my own – exists. There is, I think, no possible world in which there exists an impression of this clarity and distinction without there being something corresponding to it. But we might say the same about certain moral impressions as well. So clear and distinct are our impressions of the wrongness of horrendous deeds that there is no possible world in which there exist impressions of that clarity and distinction without there being something corresponding to them; without, in other words, such acts actually being wrong. This does not preclude the metaphysical possibility of horrendous deeds being morally right in some possible world. However, given that impressions are mental states and mental states are natural properties (we are considering them as such, anyway) what it does do is rule out the possibility of there being a naturalistically identical world to this one in which horrific acts had a different morality from that which they so clearly and distinctly appear to have here. The fact we have very clear and distinct intuitions about the morality of such deeds seems sufficient to preclude the metaphysical possibility of such deeds being morally right in some naturalistically identical possible world.

Some might object that our clear and distinct intuitions about horrendous deeds do not guarantee that such deeds are actually morally wrong. But surely someone who thinks this cannot be among those who maintain that there is something absurd in the metaphysical possibility of such acts being morally right in a naturalistically identical possible world? For admit that it is epistemically possible that horrendous acts might be morally right in the actual world and one accepts that it is possible for very clear and distinct moral intuitions to fail to track moral reality. If one accepts that, then what exactly is absurd about a naturalistically identical possible world in which our clear and distinct moral intuitions are failing to track moral reality? When it comes to the horrendous deeds concern we need only address those who think there is a problem here. And those who think there is a problem are going to be those who think it utterly inconceivable that moral intuitions of the degree of clarity and distinctiveness that those about horrendous deeds possess could fail to have something corresponding to them.

I recognise that what I have said above requires more detailed defence than I can provide here. It is a sketch of how one might deal with the horrendous deeds concern, rather than a fully worked out response. However, what I do hope to have shown is that one cannot just breezily insist that denying the moral supervenience thesis means having to accept the metaphysical possibility of horrendous deeds being morally right in naturalistically identical possible worlds. For the simple fact is that the moral supervenience thesis is neither necessary nor sufficient to rule this out.

4 Normative Authority

A final reason why the moral supervenience thesis is considered a non-negotiable truth by many has to do with morality's normative authority. Many consider it a conceptual truth that we have normative reason to refrain from doing what is wrong. Moral norms have the authority of practical reason, in other words. Following Vogelstein I will refer to this as the normativity thesis (2013, p. 1083). Not all agree with it (see, for example Tresan 2010). But it is widely held, I hold it, and it will be assumed hereafter. Now consider these remarks from Coons:

> To illustrate why we need the global supervenience and non-arbitrariness constraints to preserve morality's authority, suppose that those constraints are false and yet the normative authority of morality persists. Thus, there can be two counterpart worlds, W1 and W2, with identical non-normative histories, with an act that is wrong in W1, but not wrong in W2. In this case, being wrong must independently explain why you ought not to perform the act in W1. But this seems absurd. (2011, p. 92)

We have two naturalistically identical possible worlds. It is wrong for Tim to X in circumtances S in W1, but right for Tim's identical counterpart – Tim2 – to X in circumstances S in W2. This, it is held, is impossible because this would mean that Tim has normative reason not to X in circumstances S, whereas Tim2 has normative reason to S. Why think this impossible?

Here is one reason. By hypothesis, there is no difference between Tim and Tim2 in terms of their motivational sets. So, if what we have reason to do is necessarily determined by our motivational sets it seems impossible for Tim and Tim2 to have reasons to do different things. This doesn't straightforwardly follow, as even if a reason to P requires some motivation to P, it may be that Tim and Tim2 have multiple motivations, such that it would be possible for Tim and Tim2 to have reasons to do different things, consistent with those reasons presupposing motivations to do the things in question. But if same motivations = same reasons, then it would follow. However, to reach this conclusion would seem require having to assume a form of internalism, (what Darwall calls existence-internalism 1983).[6] It is a

[6]The term 'internalism' should be understood here to refer to *existence* internalism and not *judgement* internalism.

controversial view and so the moral supervenience thesis can hardly be considered beyond negotiation if it presupposes it. More damningly this kind of internalism seems incompatible with the kind of categorical normative authority moral norms appear (to many of us) to possess. Imagine Tim desires to hurt others for fun and lacks in his motivational set any desire not to. On this view Tim (and Tim2 of course) lacks any reason not to hurt others for fun. Yet it seems clear to most that nevertheless it is wrong for Tim to hurt others for fun and that he does have reason not to do so, irrespective of his desire to do otherwise.[7]

There are other ways to understand the normative concern. Many of us who subscribe to the normativity thesis would say that certain natural features of an action confer reasons, but they are not reducible to each other (either synthetically or analytically). Call this non-reductionism about normative reasons. Nevertheless, it might be thought that if natural features confer reasons then two naturalistically identical situations must confer the same reasons. If it is due to S's possession of feature P1 that Tim has reason not to X in circumstances S, then it must be the case that Tim2 has reason not to X in circumstances S in world2 as by hypothesis S possess feature P1 there as well. Unless one says this the reasons have floated free from their natural base. Hence presumably why Coons concludes that if one allows this then "being wrong must independently explain" (my stress) why Tim has reason not to X whereas Tim2 does not.

However, this is now just the grounding objection in a different guise. It may be indeterministic whether P1 in circumstances S will give rise to a normative reason to X or not. But it does not follow from this that if in the actual sequence it gives rise to a normative reason to X, it did not really do so. In answer to the question "why does Tim have reason not to X in circumstances S" one can truthfully answer that he has reason not to do so due to feature P1. So, if we assume non-reductionism about normative reasons then the normative authority concern turns into a version of the flawed grounding objection.

What if rather than natural properties somehow giving rise to normative reasons natural properties just are normative reasons? If P1 just is the reason not to X, then given S has P1 in both W1 and W2, there is reason not to X in both worlds. Well this, combined with the normativity thesis, does indeed entail the moral supervenience thesis. No doubt some will see this as a vindication of reductionism about normative reasons. But at this point in the discussion what we have discovered is that short of a prior commitment to reductionism about normative reasons there is no good reason to think the moral supervenience thesis is true. The other reasons commonly

[7]It might be objected that there are some motivations found necessarily in all agents. Moral norms just are those norms of practical reason that we all, qua agents, have reason to do/refrain from doing (see Rosati 2003). It is contentious whether there are motivations that all agents necessarily have (see Joyce 2006, pp. 196–199). But even in the event that there are motivations that we must all, qua agents, possess, and that these give rise to norms of practical reason that accord with our pre-theoretical moral judgements (again, questionable) it remains doubtful this will provide what is needed. There is no space to elaborate, but in common with other moral realists I find constitutivist views of normativity unpersuasive (see Enoch 2006).

given for thinking it needs to be true – that unless one affirms it the moral will not be grounded in the natural, and that unless one affirms it one will have to allow for the metaphysical possibility of horrendous deeds being right – have been shown to be misguided or highly questionable. And the concern about normative authority either collapses into a form of the flawed grounding concern or else just assumes reductionism about normative reasons. This does not show the global moral supervenience thesis to be false. However, it does show that absent some antecedent reason to think reductionism is true, there does not seem to be any special reason to think the global moral supervenience thesis is true. And thus the reductionist can no longer claim any advantage over non-reductionism where the global moral supervenience thesis is concerned.

In the next section I will turn attention to the local moral supervenience thesis. I will argue that there is likely to be considerable evidence that any non-trivial version of the local moral supervenience thesis is false. If the non-trivial version of the local moral supervenience thesis is false this serves to underscore that there is no antecedent reason to think the global moral supervenience thesis is true.

5 An Evidential Case Against the Local (Non-trivial) Moral Supervenience Thesis

I distinguished at the outset between the local and global versions of the moral supervenience thesis. I now want to focus on the local version. It has been noted by others that when it comes to this version of the thesis a mere difference in an act's temporal or spatial location cannot be allowed to make a moral difference in and of itself. Doing so would render the local moral supervenience thesis trivially true for the simple reason that it would now be impossible for there to be two naturalistically identical acts (Dancy 1993, p. 79; see Ridge 2007, pp. 332–333).[8] Nobody has any trouble explaining why one and the same token act has the same moral properties. So, insofar as the local moral supervenience thesis is taken to be a non-trivial thesis that non-reducionists and supernaturalist reductionists

[8]This point is, I think, more significant than it at first appears. As already noted, it is standardly seen as a virtue of reductionist views that they can *explain* the moral supervenience thesis (whereas non-reductionists cannot). However, the supervenience thesis in question cannot be one that includes under the umbrella of natural properties an act's time and place. For as just noted, *that* version of the moral supervenience is trivially true and nobody has any difficulty explaining it. So, the version of the moral supervenience thesis that the reductionist can supposedly explain is the rather narrower, but substantial one that does not include temporal or spatial properties. Yet what justifies the exclusion of such properties? Reductionism in and of itself does not explain. Perhaps the reductionist could appeal to the fact our best normative moral theories do not allow time or place to make a difference. But our best normative moral theories are those that achieve the best fit with our considered moral intuitions. The evidence – I am going to suggest – is that these have altered over time. To discount the moral intuitions of competent moral judges from a previous time is to insist that time and place are morally irrelevant, rather than to show them to be.

have trouble explaining, temporal and spatial properties need to be excluded. So, according to a non-trivial version of the local moral supervenience thesis, if Xing in circumstances S is something it would be wrong to do today, it cannot be right to do it tomorrow, other things being equal. And if Xing in circumstances S is something it is wrong to do here, it cannot be right to do it over there other things being equal.

Now note it does not seem to be any part of the objectivity of morality that it be uniform and unchanging. The physical landscape is objective. Yet it is neither uniform nor unchanging. It is no less objective for that. When it comes to the moral landscape it is the local non-trivial moral supervenience thesis (just moral supervenience thesis hereafter) that fixes and flattens it across time and space. As such if there is evidence suggesting the moral landscape changes over time and/or is not uniform across space, this would be prima facie evidence that the moral supervenience thesis is false.

I think moral realists of all kinds will want to say that moral truths are epistemically accessible to us. Other things being equal, our considered moral judgements fairly reliably reflect the moral landscape.[9] On that assumption there would be evidence that the moral landscape has altered if the considered moral judgements of those in different temporal and spatial locations are found to vary, and if there is no antecedent reason to think such judgements any less reliable than our own. For example, at the moment most people of moral sensibility judge it to be unjustifiable to push a fat man off a bridge so that his bulk may stop an out of control trolley from hitting and killing five innocent people further along its path. Imagine we find that surveys had been done in the 1900s clearly showing that people whose moral judgements we have no antecedent reason to think any less reliable than our own deemed it justifiable to push the fat man off the bridge. This would be prima facie evidence that the moral landscape has changed. Not a proof, of course. The assumption of reliable epistemic access is not an assumption of infallibility. But other things being equal it would give us some reason to think the moral landscape had changed over time and thus provide us with some reason to think the moral supervenience thesis – the non-trivial version – is false.

If one is committed to the truth of the moral supervenience thesis such differential judgements present something of a problem. They need to be explained away. Of course, it is possible that one group (or both) were/are suffering some cognitive deficiency. As Capps, Lynch and Massey put it "some moral facts, the realist must contend, are simply inaccessible to some unfortunate souls" (2009, p. 414). But press this point too hard and moral scepticism looms.

---

[9]A commitment to moral truths does not entail the epistemological commitment, but without it moral realism is unattractive. As Enoch puts it:

> If the best way out {in response to one version of the argument from disagreement] for the realist is to concede that moral beliefs – hers included, of course – do not reflect the moral facts, then she may perhaps have her realism, but only at the price of the most radical of skepticisms. A radically inaccessible realm of moral facts is, I think, a very small comfort for the realist. (2009, p. 22)

However, if we are open minded about the truth of the moral supervenience thesis then another option presents itself: take the divergent considered moral judgements at face value and conclude that the moral landscape has altered. It is not that we have achieved a rapport with the moral landscape that those in the 1900s lacked. Nor is it that those in the 1900s had achieved a rapport that we now lack. Nor is it that one group is right and one group wrong with there being no way of discovering which is which. Rather, both groups were right at the time. Rather than explaining away the divergence by appeal to cognitive shortcomings we explain it 'faultlessly' by appeal to a changing moral landscape.[10]

My example was imaginary. Is there any actual evidence of divergent considered moral judgements across time and space? A confident answer would require considerable empirical research. I have not done that research so what I say here is speculative. But all those divergent moral judgements traditionally considered to raise problems for moral realists, now become candidates. Anything previously thought to threaten epistemic access, becomes prima facie evidence of a change in the moral landscape. For instance Huemer, a moral realist, thinks that our moral intuitions about sexual morality exhibit multiple signs of unreliability. In support of this he notes that the "attitudes toward prostitution, homosexuality, and polygamy in contemporary America are much harsher than those prevalent, respectively, in modern Japan, ancient Greece, or Imperial China – suggesting that most Americans' attitudes toward these practices are determined more by the time and place in which they happened to be born than by any objective ethical truths" (2008, p. 388). However, Huemer is conflating the objectivity of morality with the fixity of morality. What we actually seem to have here is prima facie evidence that objective morality varies across time and place.

I stress that this would require far more detailed empirical investigation and I am certainly not ruling out alternative explanations. Perhaps where sexual matters are concerned these are hard to come by. However, it would not be enough confidently to dismiss such differential judgements as being due to the distorting effects of different psychological, sociological, and political factors at play in these different communities. For while that remains a possibility, we must not discount that such differential factors might be the result of a different moral landscape: that is, they may be symptom, rather than cause. And note it is not as if we live in a psychological, sociological and political vacuum. So once again, diffuse differential moral judgements by citing differential psychological, social and political environments and the moral landscape starts increasingly to be placed out of our sight. A moral realist cannot afford to make our moral vision too suggestible.

There are a range of moral judgments it is harder to convict of being unconsidered or a result of social conditioning: those of moral philosophers themselves. It is commonplace to note that the ancient Greek moral philosophers placed far more moral significance on character than we tend to today. Their normative moral

[10] I borrow the term 'faultless' from Capps, Lynch and Massey (2009, p. 414). They too offer a faultless explanation, though one that is very different from mine.

theories seem best characterised as virtue-ethical. On the assumption that the ancient Greek philosophers were competent moral judges we here seem to have some prima facie evidence that character may just have counted for more back then. Later, equally competent moral judges seemed fairly uniformly to have deemed morality to have a more deontological character, whereas today something altogether more messy seems to be true. Rather than a history of fairly arbitrary changes in focus driven partly by the fashion and tastes of the age and partly by the pioneering work of particular individuals with their break-through arguments and insights, we may have something else. Namely, a history of earthquakes and creaking shifts in the moral landscape that the fashions and judgements were merely reflecting. Natural features that at one time were morally significant, ceased to be so, or became differently morally significant. We can start to take seriously that a Kant transported to ancient Athens would have been a virtue ethicist. Not because he would have succumbed to the psychological, sociological and political pressures of the time, but rather because it would have seemed to him – as to others – that something best characterised as a virtue ethics was true at that time.

What about evidence of moral variation across space? Consider this from Peng, Doris, Nichols, and Stich and described in Doris and Plakias (2007). American subjects and Chinese subjects living in the People's Republic of China – were asked to imagine the following:

> An unidentified member of an ethnic group is known to be responsible for a murder that occurred in a town . . . Because the town has a history of severe ethnic conflict and rioting, the town's Police Chief and Judge know that if they do not immediately identify and punish a culprit, the townspeople will start anti-ethnic rioting that will cause real damage to property owned by members of the ethnic group, and a considerable number of serious injuries and deaths in the ethnic population. . . . The Police Chief and Judge are faced with a dilemma. They can falsely accuse, convict, and imprison Mr. Smith, an innocent member of the ethnic group, in order to prevent the riots. Or they can continue hunting for the guilt man, thereby allowing the anti-ethnic riots to occur, and do the best they can to combat the riots until the guilty man is apprehended . . . .the Police Chief and Judge decide to falsely accuse, convict, and imprison Mr. Smith, the innocent member of the ethnic group, in order to prevent the riots. They do so, thereby preventing the riots and preventing a considerable number of ethnic group deaths and serious injuries. (Doris and Plakias 2007)

Interestingly the American participants tended to judge that it was wrong to imprison Mr. Smith, whereas the Chinese participants did not. This does not seem to have been due to different assumptions about the non-moral features of the case.

> They asked participants whether the false imprisonment would cause the scapegoat and his intimates to suffer, and they asked whether the riots, if they occurred, would cause members of the ethnic group to suffer. They did not find significant differences in these items, suggesting that the differences are not readily to be attributed to differences in conceptions of the nonmoral facts. (Doris and Plakias 2007, p. 324)

What about differences in background beliefs? As has been noted by others, in China people have a more collectivist conception of the self (Doris and Plakias 2007, p. 325). Surely this explains why the Chinese participants were more inclined to give the answer they did? The problem is that the background beliefs may just be symptomatic of the different moral landscape there, just as the more individualistic concept possessed by the Americans may be reflective of theirs. We should take seriously that the moral landscape just looks a little different to the Chinese subjects in China to how it looks to the American subjects in America.

One might point out that this thesis could easily be tested by simply transporting the Chinese participants to America and the American participants to China and seeing if the change in location brings about a change in moral judgements. Let us imagine we do conduct such experiments and find that the moral judgements of our American and Chinese participants remain the same. What now? Do we have to conclude that the moral landscape is uniform after all and thus that either the original Chinese participants or the American participants (or both) are just not very reliably hooked up to it? Hardly. For we can just remember that the moral landscape is difficult to see clearly and that we are suggestible creatures. We need time to tune-into the moral landscape, so to speak, and one needs to maintain an open mind while doing so. Seeing the moral landscape in China would require some period of acclimatisation. And even then this might not work for the open mindedness needed to see it clearly might be extraordinarily hard (perhaps impossible) to achieve if one already has a certain moral landscape burned into the back of one's retina. This may explain why – to the extent that this is true, anyway – Chinese/American people who have been living in America/China for some time may nevertheless continue to make moral judgements that echo those of the people still residing in their respective homelands.

If I am right above, then there is evidence of differential moral judgments across time and space and these constitute prima facie evidence that the local non-trivial moral supervenience thesis is false. This does not show reductionism to be false, however, for nothing prevents the reductionist from accepting that spatio-temporal properties are morally relevant. In other words, the reductionist can endorse just the trivial version of the local supervenience thesis. However, as neither non-reductionists nor supernaturalists have any difficulty explaining that version of the local thesis, the reductionist has lost any advantage over those rival views on this front.

Nevertheless, it might be objected that the reductionist can still explain the global version of the supervenience thesis. After all, just because the local non-trivial version of the moral supervenience thesis is false, this does not show that the global version is false. True enough. However, if the local non-trivial moral supervenience thesis is false, then there seems no good reason to think the global version is true. For consider: if the non-trivial local superenience thesis is false, then there might be in some far flung corner of the galaxy a world mirroring this one in all natural respects but in which slightly different acts are right and wrong. Let us just imagine that this is so. What reason is there now to deny that there is a possible world, identical to this one in all of its natural properties, in which different acts are right and wrong? Short of the misguided concerns mentioned earlier, or some antecedent reason to think reductionism is true, I cannot think of one.

6 Conclusion

The moral supervenience thesis is held to be a conceptual truth about morality. This poses a problem for non-reductionist metaethical views and supernaturalist metaethical views as both seem incapable of satisfactorily explaining why two naturalistically identical acts must be morally identical as well. What I have tried to do above is show first that short of an antecedent commitment to some form of naturalist reductionism there is no very good reason to consider the moral supervenience thesis a non-negotiable truth. I then went on to suggest that the apparently divergent considered moral judgements of people of moral sensibility across time and place is evidence that the moral landscape is more like the physical landscape than has previously been thought. It is not just objective, it is creaking and changing. If true this would show that the local non-trivial moral supervenience thesis is false. And if the local non-trivial moral supervenience thesis is false, there seems no good reason to think the global moral supervenience thesis must be true. Although none of this demonstrates reductionism to be false, it does mean that reductionism offers no advantage over non-reductionism or supernaturalism where moral supervenience is concerned. Nobody has any difficulty explaining why the trivial local moral supervenience thesis is true, and where the global thesis is concerned all the reductionist can do is explain the truth of a thesis that we have no special reason to think is true unless reductionism is true.

References

Bigelow, J and Pargettter, R. 1990: "Metaphysics of causation," Erkenntnis, 33, pp. 89–119

Blackburn, S. 1993: Essays in quasi-realism. Oxford: Oxford University Press.

Brink, D.1989: Moral Realism and the Foundations of Ethics. (Cambridge: Cambridge University Press).

Capps, D & Lynch, M & Massey, D 2009: "A coherent moral relativism." Synthese, 166, pp. 413–430.

Clarke, R. 2003: "Toward a credible agent-causal account of free will," in Watson, G. (ed) Free Will. Oxford: Oxford University Press.

Coons, C. 2011: "How to prove that some acts are wrong (without using substantive moral premises)." Philosophical Studies, 155, no. 1, pp. 83–98

Dancy, J. 1993: Moral Reasons. Oxford: Oxford University Press

Darwall, S. 1983: Impartial Reason. Ithaca and London: Cornell University Press.

Doris, J. M., and Plakias, A. 2007."How to Argue about Disagreement: Evaluative Diversity and Moral Realism." In W. Sinnott-Armstrong (ed.), Moral Psychology, Volume 2: The Cognitive Science of Morality. Cambridge, MA: MIT Press.

Enoch, D. 2006: "Agency, Shmagency: Why Normativity Won't Come From What is Constitutive of Agency," Philosophical Review. 115, pp. 169–198.

Enoch, D. 2009: "How is moral disagreement a problem for realism?" Ethics, 13, pp. 15–50.

Harrison, G. 2013: "The moral supervenience thesis is not a conceptual truth" Analysis 73.1, pp. 62–68.

Huemer, M. 2008: "Revisionary intuitionism," Social Philosophy and Policy, 25 (1), pp. 368–392.

Joyce, R. 2006: The Evolution of Morality. Cambridge, Mass.: MIT Press.

Kane, R. 2003: “Responsibility, luck, and chance,” in Watson, G. (ed) Free Will. Oxford: Oxford University Press.
Korsgaard, C. 1996: The Sources of Normativity, Cambridge: Cambridge University Press
Mackie, J.L. 1977:Ethics: Inventing right and wrong. Harmondsworth: Penguin
McNaughton, D. and Rawling, P. and Lovibond, S. 2003: “Naturalism and Normativity,” Aristotelian Society Supplementary. Volume 77, 1, pp. 23–45.
Ridge, M. 2007: “Anti-Reductionism and Supervenience,” Journal of Moral Philosophy, Vol. 4 (3), pp. 33–348.
Rosati, C. 2003: “Agency and the open question argument.” Ethics 113, pp. 490–527.
Ross, S. 2012: “The Natural and the Normative: Supervenience and Counterfactuals,” The Philosophical Forum. pp. 197–2014
Shafer-Landau, R. 2003: *Moral Realism: A Defence*. Oxford: Oxford University Press.
Shafer-Landau 2012: “Evolutionary debunking, moral realism and moral knowledge,” Journal of ethics and social philosophy, vol. 7, no. 1.pp. 1–37
Smith, M. 1994: The Moral Problem. Oxford: Blackwell Publishers.
Tresan, J. 2010: “Question authority: in defence of moral naturalism without clout” Philosophical Studies 150, pp. 221–238.
Vogelstein, E. 2013: “Moral normativity,” Philosophical Studies 165, pp. 1083–1095
Zangwill, N. 2005: “Moore, morality, supervenience, essence, epistemology,” American Philosophical Quarterly, 42, pp. 125–130.

The Supervenience Dilemma Explained Away

Carla Bagnoli

Abstract According to an anti-realist argument, realist accounts of supervenience face the following dilemma: either they accept naturalistic reduction, an ontological claim about the nature of normative properties that is incoherent with their defining agenda, or they recognize that their agenda is based on a queer ontology, which is at risk of being unintelligible. In a recent defense of robust moral realism, David Enoch recognizes that this is a serious challenge but argues that it is not a conclusive argument against to moral realism because queerness is after all tolerable. His strategy is to minimize the costs of admitting queerness by focusing on the explanatory role of moral principles, in analogy with law. This is a promising approach to the problem of supervenience, but it is doubtful as strategy. I will show that in favor of moral realism. In fact, if all the explanatory work is done by normative principles, there is nothing for the realist account of supervenience to do.

In this paper, I argue that this debate about normative supervenience rests on a misunderstanding of the role of normative principles. As an alternative, I offer a constructivist explication of the epistemic and ontological role of normative principles, which proves the notion of supervenience to be redundant. The advantage of this constructivist approach to supervenience is that it directly addresses a legitimate demand for an explanation of the function of normative discourse, which is often kept in the background. In providing a response to this demand, this constructivist argument also shows – *pace* Enoch and others – that an account of practical reasoning is not only pertinent but also essential to successfully address the meta-ethical issue of supervenience.

1 Reduction or Queerness?

Supervenience names alleged normative relations of various strengths between normative properties and natural properties. In what follows I will be concerned with *strong individual supervenience*, which is the claim that it is impossible for

C. Bagnoli (✉)
University of Oslo, Modena, Italy
e-mail: carla.bagnoli@unimore.it

B. Brożek et al. (eds.), *Supervenience and Normativity*, Law and Philosophy Library 120, DOI 10.1007/978-3-319-61046-7_6

there to be two things that are indistinguishable in their natural properties, but differ in their normative ones.[1]

According to a mainstream position, either normative supervenience involves reduction of normative properties to natural properties or it is ontologically queer. According to anti-realists, this dilemma rules out moral realism as a plausible meta-ethical theory, pointing out that its ontological and epistemological agenda is marred. From an ontological point of view, by admitting of queer properties moral realism violates the principle of ontological parsimony, according to which we should admit only of properties that serve some purpose in the account of phenomena. From an epistemological point of view, moral realism faces the problem of explaining how such queer properties are made available to us. Originally, J.L. Mackie directs this argument against G.E. Moore's understanding of supervenience as an a priori and synthetic normative relation, hence different from causal and logical relations. Mackie objects that Moore's normative relation raises the epistemological issues of how we come to know such extravagant entities.[2] Partly, these issues arise because of Moore's peculiar definition of normative properties as non-natural ones. In addition, the problem is framed from a non-cognitivist perspective, in which ethical judgments are necessarily action-guiding, whence the question how to think of properties that are part of the fabric of the world and at the same time necessarily and directly action-guiding. Such properties would indeed be queer. Along these lines, Simon Blackburn has subsequently argued that supervenience calls for an explanation, and that moral realism fails to provide a plausible one because it is committed to the claim that there are irreducibly normative facts (Blackburn 1971, 1984, 1985: 415; see Dreier 1992). But it is neither obvious nor agreed that in order to perform their practical function normative properties need to be intrinsically and directly action-guiding. The latter claim is phrased in terms that make concessions to the non-cognitivist meta-ethics.

These considerations may seem to suggest that the dilemma arises only for intuitionist meta-ethics such as Moore's, and it is damaging only from a non-cognitivist standpoint. However, in recent debates the same objection of queerness has been extended to any theory that admits of non-reductive normative relations. More recently, Nadeem Hussain and Nishitan Shah have argued that also Kantian constructivism is vulnerable to the objection of queerness because it defends the production of moral facts *ex nihilo* (Hussain and Shah 2006: 293; 2013).

---

[1]See Enoch (2011). I deploy Enoch's formulation because the ensuing discussion revolves around his account. A different formulation takes the subvenient bases to be descriptive properties, namely, properties picked out in purely descriptive terms. As Ridge observes this formulation does not beg any questions against descriptivists, unlike the formulation in terms of the (Moore 1998, Ridge 2007). The descriptivist agrees that the normative supervenes on the descriptive since he holds that the normative just is the descriptive.

[2]"The wrongness – Mackie writes – must somehow be consequential or supervenient. [An action] is wrong *because* it is a piece of deliberate cruelty. But just what in the world is signified by this 'because'? And how do we know the relation that it signifies?" (Moore 1988: 38).

2 The Nature of the Issue at Stake

It is noteworthy that the real challenge behind the objection of metaphysical queerness is ultimately epistemological, rather than vice versa. The argument is that the phenomena associated with supervenience require an explanation, and that a plausible explanation ought to be in naturalistic terms. On this ground, either the explication of supervenience ultimately commits one to naturalistic reduction, or such phenomena remain mysterious, or at least unexplained. This line of argumentation is based on the presumption that the only kind of explanation acceptable for the relation between supervenient properties and their natural bases is naturalistic reduction. This is because the explication is sought at the ontological level. In other words, ontology is called to answer an epistemological question, that is, the request of intelligibility of the alleged between normative properties and their natural bases.

Interestingly, the strategy of answering the epistemological questions about the intelligibility of normative supervenience via ontological claims is at work in many anti-realist arguments against supervenience. The anti-realist argument against moral realism is the following. Moral realism is committed to supervenience. Supervenience must be explained in order for it to identify an intelligible phenomenon. The only acceptable explanation involves naturalistic reduction. Therefore, in order to explain supervenience, moral realism must accept the naturalistic reduction of normative properties, but this is incoherent with the defining features of moral realism. Choosing the other horn of the dilemma does not make realism incoherent, but queer.

There are two ways of capturing the significance and impact of the objection of queerness. First, queerness indicates that moral realism lacks adequate explanatory power. This is a weak claim. A second, stronger claim is that moral realism stands in violation of the principle of ontological parsimony, because it introduces "queer properties", irreducible normative properties that are unnecessary in a naturalistic conception of supervenience. These two claims are intertwined in the literature, but it is important to keep them separate. Arguably, the second strong claim begs the question against moral realism, insofar as it implies that irreducible normative properties are unnecessary to explicate the phenomena associated with supervenience. Moral realists urge that naturalistic reduction imposes a serious loss in terms of the explanatory powers of the theory (Sturgeon 1986). Whether we need a distinctively normative ontology for understanding the basic functions of normative concepts is indeed the question at stake (Sturgeon 2006). In contrast to reductive naturalists, realists insist that such normative ontology is not dispensable. Thus the real issue at stake is whether and to what extent the realist construal of supervenience undermines or warrants its own explanatory powers, given that it exposes the theory to queerness.

Early debates focus almost exclusively on the ontological commitments underlying normative supervenience. More recently, however, the focus of the debate has shifted onto issues that it would be misleading to characterize solely in terms of ontology (Ridge 2007, cp. Enoch 2010). My working hypothesis is that the questions about the status and explanatory power of normative supervenience belong somewhere in the middle between practical reasoning, social ontology and moral epistemology. One major difficulty in defending and explicating supervenience is that it is a claim situated at the interface between the ontology and (social) epistemology a claim concerning the function of normative discourse. This hypothesis allows us to face upfront a fundamental question: when the function of normative discourse is fully explicated, is there still room for the concept of supervenience to play any philosophical role? The key philosophical problem is not whether normative supervenience best fits in the realist rather than the anti-realist agenda, but whether we need such a concept at all.

3 Enoch's Strategy of Damage Containment

In his recent defence of robust moral realism, David Enoch takes normative supervenience to be a central and fundamental claim which robust moral realism cannot afford to deny. The rejection of normative supervenience would be "a devastating loss of plausibility points" (Enoch 2011: 141–142). Nonetheless, Enoch recognizes that because of this commitment to normative supervenience, his moral theory faces the same old dilemma about queerness that previous realist accounts have faced. He chooses to avoid incoherence by admitting of moral queerness (Enoch 2011: 135–136); and, repeating Mark Platts' words, he insists that the world is indeed a queer place (Platts 1979: 82). In acknowledging that the dilemma above is genuine, Enoch also recognizes that the anti-realist argument potentially undermines the prospects of robust moral realism, which "does lose some plausibility points merely for not being naturalist" (Enoch 2011: 135). This venue is preferable to naturalistic reduction and, he thinks, sustainable. His conclusion is that the anti-realist argument based on queerness does not succeed in ruling out moral realism.

At the ontological level, there is not much interesting to say about this dispute. Naturalists hold that supervenience entails reductive naturalism via the identity of necessarily co-extensive properties. By contrast, Enoch holds that normative properties are necessarily coextensive with natural ones, but not identical. "Intuitively", he thinks, normative and natural properties are distinct. Regarding the ontological implications of supervenience, and the anti-realist claim that there cannot be necessary relations between distinct existences, Enoch's position is straightforward, but explicitly unargued: "I do not have an answer to this question, but I do not feel the need to give one" (Enoch 2011: 147). As he presents the case, his failure to give an answer is affordable because it is "merely theoretical".

This way out of the dilemma may sound way too quick to be effective, but we should be careful about the alleged impact of the queerness problem. As I clarified above, by defending the stronger claim about the ontological reductivist commitment of explanation, one begs the question about normativity. To adequately and fairly assess the prospects of non-reductive meta-ethics, such as moral realism or Kantian constructivism, it is best to assess the explanatory powers of such theories on their own terms. Enoch admits that his move is simply a dialectical (or rhetorical) move, but he also remarks that in this dialectic the impasse between naturalists and realists is not neutral. Since the naturalist argument about supervenience is meant to be an argument against moral realism, it is the naturalists who bear the burden of proof. From the receiving end (i.e. the moral realist standpoint), it is enough defense to show that the alleged argument is not conclusive (Enoch 2011: 139). Enoch's reasoning is recognizably modeled on the forensic argument of the burden of proof according to which one is innocent until proven guilty. Analogously, moral realism is viable until definitely proved flawed. On the basis of these considerations he concludes that putting the anti-realist claim aside is costless and shows that "progress has been made" (Enoch 2011: 139).

I am willing to grant that some progress is made insofar as the argument shifts the focus of the dispute from the ontological to the epistemological level. This is a more promising way to address the problem of normative supervenience; but I will argue that once the shift from ontology to epistemology is effected, robust moral realism can be shown to lack adequate explanatory powers.

4 A Second Dilemma: Queerness or Redundancy

Normative supervenience is indispensable for robust moral realism. But what exactly does the realist understanding of normative supervenience warrant that naturalistic reduction lacks? To properly address this question, we should take notice of Enoch's distinction between specific and general normative supervenience.

General normative supervenience is a conceptual claim stating that normative properties supervene on whatever natural properties. Since this claim is conceptual, evaluators denying general supervenience prove themselves not to be fully competent users of normative terms. Insofar as this claim is defended as a matter of conceptual necessity, Enoch says that it does not require any justification at all (Enoch 2011: 149). It is taken to govern the logical behaviour of normative concepts.

Specific normative supervenience, instead, is the claim that some normative properties (e.g. wrong) supervene upon some natural properties (e.g. fail to maximize utility). Specific supervenience is stronger than general supervenience insofar as it anchors some normative properties onto some specific natural properties, but it is also weaker because unlike general supervenience it cannot be taken as a conceptual claim. Specific supervenience is a normative claim that identifies a normative relation between normative and non-normative properties from within a normative theory. For instance, utilitarianism establishes a normative relation between the normative concept of wrongness and the non-normative property of failure to maximize utility. Specific supervenience thus stands in need of an explanation and it appears that such an explanation should be formulated in normative terms.

It is to this effect that Enoch proposes a legal analogy: Within a given jurisdiction J, there can be no difference in legal status (e.g. concerning prohibition of drinking alcohol) without a difference in natural properties (e.g. age). The difference in age results in the different juridical status of drinking alcohol and it does so in a principled manner, e.g. because of the law that relates the two terms. As it appears, the proposal of a naturalistic reduction is implausible in the legal case. According to Enoch, there are three important lessons to draw. First, at least sometimes, normative supervenience is more plausible without reduction. That is, at least for some normative properties such as legal properties, the prospect of naturalistic reduction cannot be taken seriously. Second, sometimes, that is, at least for the domain of legal properties specified above, specific normative supervenience does not even significantly count in favour of naturalistic reductionist. Third, and most importantly, what explains the supervenience of legal drinking status (normative property) upon age (natural property) in the legal case is simply the content of the relevant legal norms. This explanation does not commit one to any naturalistic reduction. In fact, it excludes such a reduction as implausible. Enoch's proposal is to extend this account to moral properties by invoking a sort of "moral legislation".

According to Enoch, in order to explain and justify strong specific supervenience all robust realist has to do is to point at the content of the basic fundamental normative principle. But this is a self-defeating move for moral realism. By explaining supervenience in terms of normative principles, the realist concedes that such a relation is not primarily ontological but normative. The explanatory work is not done by the ontological relation between the two orders of properties as one would expect in a realist approach, but by the normative principles that *establish* such a relation. This is to say that in order to minimize the appearance of queerness, the robust moral realist is forced to move away from the ontological commitments that are distinctive of his own theory, and toward debates that investigate the nature of normativity, that is, theories of practical reason or more broadly, to social and moral epistemology. Thus, if progress has been made in approaching supervenience, it hardly counts in favour of robust moral realism. In fact, the argument that hinges on the explanatory work of normative principles also shows that moral realism is at a clear disadvantage vis à vis other robustly cognitivist theories of normativity, such as Kantian and Aristotelian theories (Engstrom 2002, 2013; Bagnoli 2011, 2017a, b). This is because to avoid naturalistic reduction, moral realism has to abandon its distinctive and defining claim, i.e. its primitive moral ontology. Moral ontology contributes nothing to the explanation of the phenomena of supervenience. In other words, robust moral realism does not provide an explanation that differs from other non-reductive strategies for explaining supervenience. The features of the explanation of specific supervenience which minimize queerness depend on the specific normative theory that realism adopts in order to account for the contents of the normative principles by which normative properties are related to natural properties. But there is nothing distinctively realistic or ontologically robust about this strategy.

Furthermore, by pursuing the strategy modeled on the legal analogy, the robust realist faces another serious challenge, which is that of arbitrariness. This is because *any* normative principle relating normative and normative properties would suffice to explain supervenience. To justify the choice and avoid the charge of arbitrariness, robust realism must engage even further in normative theorizing. This is a perfectly legitimate move, but the point is that the robust moral realism cannot accomplish this task in virtue of its distinctive meta-ethical or ontological commitments. The conclusion of this discussion is that the realist conception of supervenience is redundant. It does not play any role at all in accounting for the normative phenomena associated with supervenience.

5 The Worry About Redundancy

I have argued that robust moral realism avoids the dangers of queerness by explaining it away in terms of normative principles, and that this explanation makes supervenience redundant. Redundancy may seem to be a less worrisome problem than incoherence, but it is equally damaging. If the robust realist explanation is redundant, then there is nothing distinctive about the ontological features of robust realism that uniquely explains supervenience vis à vis other metaethical views. Non-cognitivist meta-ethics such as Richard M. Hare's universal prescriptivism explains supervenience in terms of universal prescriptions (Hare 1952, 1984). Moral realism might reply that these strategies do not refer to the cognitive content of moral principles. The strategy avoids the charge of incoherence, but fails to vindicate robust realism as an interesting and fecund meta-ethical theory. Thus, this is not a good strategy for the robust realist to contain the damage inflicted by the anti-realist argument.

One may respond that this is due to the fact that there are further steps to take for the justification of the contents of the explanatory principles. But this is to admit that moral realism must engage in practical reasoning, after all. As Enoch briefly conjectures, he intends to backtrack practical syllogism to the major premises, until we reach some major premise that it is not in itself the conclusion of the practical syllogism.

This move is not as simple as Enoch makes it seem to be, however. It amounts to saying that in explicating supervenience one needs to embark in "the search for the unconditional", until one finds a norm that is not grounded on any other more basic norms. Furthermore, backtracking is a move within a theory of practical reasoning, and it should be defended as such. This defensive strategy requires further argument, especially in relation to some disputable assumptions about the form that practical reasoning should take. Enoch's explication assumes that practical reasoning takes the form of a syllogism where there are practical laws serving as major premises, but which are they, and how are they available to us? These questions remind us of those pressed by Mackie against Moore (Mackie 1977: 38), and prompt us to compare robust realism with other theories of norms and practical reasoning available. In particular, once the discussion of supervenience is brought to bear at the level of the practical laws of practical reasoning, there is an (obvious) direct competitor for robust realism. This is Kantian constructivism.

6 A Constructivist Appeal to Moral Legislation

In commenting the power of the analogy between the legal and the practical case, Enoch remarks that: "the analogy is extremely close (perhaps to the point of making it misleading to describe it as an analogy)" (Enoch 2011: 145). The suggestion is that legal and moral norms share the very same structure: They are norms with a modal-maximal jurisdiction form. While Enoch does not make reference to any previous work, the comparison between principles of positive jurisdiction and practical laws is a well-traveled path in the history of moral theory as well as in the more recent theories of practical reasoning. By Kantian lights, Enoch is right: moral legislation is not a metaphor but a strict analogy to positive legislation.[3] In the remaining part of the essay, I argue that Kantian constructivism makes a better case for moral legislation, which explains away any worry about normative supervenience.

To begin, Kantian Constructivism does not simply exploit the analogy between positive and practical legislation as rhetorical strategy. Rather, it defines reasoning as the legislative activity of reason which is designed to account for the objectivity and authority of moral obligations. "Construction" is a technical term that stands for rational justification; and its constitutive norm takes the form of a law. Reasoning by principles is an activity distinctive of "practical subjects", that is, evaluators endowed with the specific cognitive and practical requisites for the exercise of rational agency. Humans qualify as practical subjects insofar as they are equipped with reason, and thus they are reflective enough to question the appropriateness of their actual interests and cognitive claims. Such practical subjects exhibit other features that prove important for the exercise of rational agency. First, they are interested in pursuing their goals and satisfying their particular needs and desires, but they are also capable of acting independently of the urgency of their current desires and needs. Second, they are mutually dependent, and this means that their desires are shaped socially and often satisfied only by engaging through cooperative activities. Third, they are finite, act in time, and under conditions of epistemic uncertainty or ignorance, but they are also capable of pursuing distant rather than present goals and, more importantly, they are capable of making long term plans. While human agents are vulnerable to various kinds of limitations, both epistemic and practical, they also exhibit distinctive resources that enables them to solve problems that arise in their situation. Such resources can be grouped under the label of practical rationality. Constructivism accounts for the exercize of practical rationality in terms of universal normative principles. Such normative principles are the result of the activity that such finite and mutually dependent evaluators could fruitfully undertake in order to deal with their practical problems. When

[3]There are also important disanalogies between positive laws and practical laws, which are the focus of much investigation in Kantian literature; but for the present argument, similarities are more relevant. On the forensic analogy see Bagnoli 2013, 2016b, O'Neill 1989: 3–28, 1992, 1996.

such evaluators succeed in reasoning together it is because they construct normative principles exerting universal authority. This is where the idea of moral legislation proves crucial.

Moral legislation names the specific form that reasoning should take in order to its conclusion to exhibit universal validity and unrestricted authority. By engaging in reasoning one legislates for oneself, but legislating requires that one aims at producing laws that are authoritative to all relevant others. The class of "relevant others" serve as a deliberative constraint on the deliberative process that produces laws. This feature ensures that one relates to relevant others as co-legislators. To put it otherwise, and more perspicuously, this is to say that when one legislates for oneself, one is legislating also and at the same time as standing in relation of mutual recognition with others. The criteria of relevance matter for determining the sort of universality and authority we are after. Presumably, in the case of the positive laws, relevant others are fellow citizens. In the case of laws regulating membership of a golf club, the criteria of relevance are more restrictive. But in the case of morality, moral laws are not restrictive at all, otherwise the products of the deliberative process would lose genuine moral authority.

Strict universality is a structural requirement, in that it lays the ground for further questions about the specific normative principles establishing the relations between normative properties on the one hand and natural properties on the other hand. Moral legislation and positive legislation differ as to the structural requirements, not because of their contents. In particular, contrary to the core claim of robust moral realism, moral and positive laws do not differ as to their origin. There are no primitive contents of the moral law that legislation merely ratifies. By contrast, both in the moral and in the positive legal case, the content of the law is the result of the proper activity of legislation. There are no contents of the law prior to such an activity, either in the moral or in the positive case. There are decisive differences between the moral and the positive contexts, but they have not to do with the primitive character of the moral content of the moral law. Rather, they have to do with the nature and normative justification of the structural constraints that are in place in the respective form of legislation, and consequently the scope of the respective laws. In the moral case, legislation should respect the structural norm of strict universality, while in the positive case legislation concerns a narrower scope. In the following sections I show that there are some significant explanatory advantages in adopting the Kantian constructivist approach to this difference.

7 Autonomy and Co-Legislation

According to Kantian constructivism, autonomy is a feature of rational agency. The demand for rational justification is deeply associated with rational agency. Rational agents are both capable and entitled to question the legitimacy of *any* prescriptive or cognitive claim. Insofar as they are rational they can address any such claim and consider whether it withstands rational scrutiny and, consequently, bears authority on them. This sort of examination is a measure of autonomy, and it is protected by the very idea of self-legislation. In the following three sections, I consider some objections, with a view to further clarifying the conception of moral legislation at the core of Kantian constructivism.

A first objection to the Kantian view of autonomy is that the very idea of making laws for oneself involves a contradiction. The criticism is based on the presumption that law exerts genuine authority only if its source is different than its target, and hence external to it; but if the source of authority is external, autonomy is vacuous. As I have argued at length elsewhere, the objection rests on a misleading account of the analogy with law, which in fact does not assume the collapse of the distinction between the legislator and the subject of the law (Bagnoli 2013, 2016b). The point of the analogy with law is just the opposite: It distinguishes and keeps different functions separate. When the agent legislates for herself, she legislates as a co-legislator in a community of equals (Bagnoli 2013, 2016b). In virtue of this feature, the moral law carries genuine authority, i.e. it binds the deliberator as well as all other agents with the same normative status who enter the deliberative field as co-legislators. The only source of authority is the legislating activity and explained in terms of co-legislation, which appears to be a shared activity.

In order to be universally authoritative, laws must be justifiable and intelligible to the universal audience of subjects having equal normative status. To accomplish this task, moral legislation importantly presupposes that the agents entering the legislative activity are capable of mutual respect and recognition, which is to say that they are naturally endowed with a generic sort of moral sensibility. The role of this moral sensibility is not cognitive, that is, such embodied rational agents do not become acquainted with moral truths because they discern them in virtue of their sensibility. By contrast, an appropriate moral sensibility is a requirement for entering moral legislation as construed above, as an activity of co-legislation.

8 A Moralized View of Reasoning?

A second objection to the Kantian approach to moral legislation is that it imposes a "moralized" view of practical reasoning. Respect and attention to others as equals may seem to introduce heavy moral constraints on practical reasoning. Indeed, some recent accounts of Kantian constructivism do recognize the value and dignity of others as a necessary presumption of practical reasoning. Critics have objected that to take the value of others as a starting point compromises the constructivist account of rational justification, which ultimately appears to build on a realist foundation.[4] I share the view that practical reasoning should not start off with a specific moral

[4] See, for instance, Korsgaard 1996. For this objection of moralization, see Copp 2013, Street 2010.

grounding, but I also think that these complaints against Kantian constructivism are exaggerated and rest on a misunderstanding of the term "moral".

To begin with, Kantian constructivism as I understand it does not accord special weight to any specific interests or intentions predefined as "moral". In fact, it does not even identify any special moral perspective or point of view. This is an advantage in comparison to ethical theories that draw a sharp line between natural interests and moral claims, and consequently divide practical rationality into two domains of instrumental principles and moral principles. Such views typically mischaracterize the place that moral obligations have in our life, not only because they miscalculate the normative force of the claims of others but also because they misunderstand the nature of subjective moral concerns. This is a serious normative problem, which affects the epistemological prospects of such theories. In particular, they are at loss in explaining how moral requirements can be rationally authoritative if they are cut off from all other concerns finite rational agents naturally have.[5]

By contrast, constructivism starts with a definition of practical subjects as "animals endowed with reason". The definition singles out the animal root of our rational agency, emphasizing the features of embodiment, mutual dependence, and finitude. This definition suits the account of reasoning as a practical device for tackling practical problems. If reasoning is a shared activity in which rational agents partake, the rationale for the constitutive requirement of co-legislation becomes clear. Insofar as they are endowed with the capacities for reasoning, embodied evaluators can engage in deliberation taking others as co-legislators. Among these capacities there is a very general disposition to respect others as having equal standing. This is both a cognitive and emotional capacity, which enables us to think dialogically, as it happens in co-legislation. The capacity for respect can be characterized as a practical capacity, but it neither identifies a moral point of view nor does it fix the starting points of practical reasoning; it is not a source of moral knowledge and does not determine specific moral duties. Respect should be considered as a placeholder for a large and diversified network of emotions and cognitive dispositions that allow us to relate to other subjects as co-legislators.

Finally, in responding to the objection of moralization, I should notice that the constructivist strategy marks a departure from Kant's ethics. In Kant's writings, as well as in some contemporary Kantian theories, co-legislation is warranted by the presumption of moral equality, which is based on a metaphysical account of its moral basis. Moral equality is an important moral premise which rests on a metaphysical argument, and the constructivist proposal is to do without it. In the place of such a presumption of moral equality, I propose that we consider the capacities and dispositions for respect and recognition of equals as a constitutive part of the competences necessary for practical reasoning (Bagnoli 2013, 2016b).

---

[5]This is Williams' well known objection to Kantian ethics, Williams 1985. Understood as a form of practical cognitivism, constructivism is not immediately vulnerable to this objection. On the contrary, it is sensitive to Williams' worry against realist interpretations of Kant's ethics, see e.g. Engstrom 2002, 2013, and Bagnoli 2013, 2017c.

This strategy differs from treating formal qualifications or equal computational abilities as input conditions for reasoning. It also differs from other current definitions of parity because it does not imply that two peers always perform equally well; nor does it imply that they have equal access to the same epistemic resources or to the same domain of epistemic objects.

Finally, the network of emotional skills and dispositions that allows us to stand in relations of mutual respect and recognition with others cannot be described solely as a network of enabling dispositions. An important feature of Kantian constructivism is that recognition of others serves as a deliberative constraint of practical deliberation. Recognition and respect for others is the counterpart of autonomy. There is no genuine autonomy (of reasoning) without the recognition of others as having equal standing. This is because for reasoning to be genuinely authoritative it must have the form of a law: this ensures that its claims have unrestricted authority insofar as they do not depend and are not conditional on anything particular such as the individual own stance. In the practice of rational deliberation this is equivalent to saying that the recognition of oneself in relation to other co-legislator is the source of constraints. But respect does not fix the starting points of practical reasoning. On the constructivist view, it is exactly the freestanding character of reasoning that guarantees the rational authority and unrestricted efficacy of its claims. Nothing said about moral sensibility as a constitutive or qualifying aspect of co-legislation undermines the freestanding character of practical reasoning.

9 Queerness, Again?

In virtue of its legislative structure, constructivism can coherently affirm that there are moral facts and objects, even though they are not discovered by observation or discerned by intellectual insight. These facts are genuine because they are not produced from the projection of our sentiments, nor are they the end point of a hypothetical or ideal agreement. They are the results of the proper activity of reasoning.

According to some critics this claim makes constructivism vulnerable to the objection of queerness much in the same way as robust moral realism is. If so then there is no advantage to register in favour of constructivism. Along these lines, Hussain and Shah object: "once the normative facts are created they could be just like the substantive realist's normative facts. It is not obvious that the different ontogeny entails different ontology" (Hussain and Shah 2006: 293). Hussain and Shah think that "the mysteriousness of such acts of creation *ex-nihilo* seems to be of the same order as the ontological and epistemic mysteries of the non-reductive realist's intrinsically normative entities and our supposed intuitive access of them" (Hussain and Shah 2006: 292).[6]

[6]For a different debate about the problem of supervenience in Kantian ethics, see Forschler 2012.

In responding to this third objection, it is important to say that Hussain and Shah identify Kantian constructivism with the view that "normative facts are *created* by correct procedures" (Hussain and Shah 2006: 292). Their target is the so-called proceduralist version of constructivism. This objection misses the point in the case of Kantian constructivism I defend, since the distinctive feature of this cognitivist variety takes the structural constraints on rational construction to be such that the activity of construction is hardly reducible to the arbitrary and gratuitous process of creation (Bagnoli 2013, 2017a).

Contrary to what Hussain and Shah presume, the activity in virtue of which moral facts are produced, hence the distinctive ontogeny advocated here is key in explicating the difference between robust moral realism and Kantian constructivism. Constrictive ontogeny is crucial in several respects. First, for the difference in ontogeny is crucial to establish how knowledge of what there is reason to do becomes effective, that is, it explains the practical significance of rational cognitions. This is in a nutshell the constructivist complaint against moral realism: insofar as moral realism cannot account for how moral ontology came about, it cannot show that it has any bearing on us. It is precisely the difference in terms of ontogeny that makes moral realism unable to account for the normativity of rational cognitions. The tragic result is that the realist findings about primitive values have no normative authority for practical subjects, hence exert no influence on action. I take this to be Christine M. Korsgaard's argument against moral realism, which (at least partly) tracks Kant's own argument against perfectionism (Korsgaard 1996; see Bagnoli 2017b: 2.1).

Even if the argument does not rule out robust moral realism, it suffices to show that the issue of ontogeny is decisive in order to assess the comparative merits and prospects of realist and constructivist metaethical theories. The difference between Kantian constructivism and moral realism concerning ontogeny cannot be disregarded without seriously misunderstanding the respective agenda of such theories. Moral realism takes practical reason to track moral truths which are there to be tracked. Moral truths lack any history; they stand there prior and independently of practical reasoning, and this is the proof that they are real and objective. By contrast, Kantian constructivism claims that in representing moral truths as the realist does, we undermine their normative authority, and hence also their objectivity. On this picture, losing sense of the practical significance of moral truths means to be at loss with justifying compellingly moral obligations. The Kantian proposal is that the authority of moral obligation can be vindicated by showing that it is a rational requirement, rather than by grounding it on a primitive moral value. The normative authority of morality ultimately amounts to rational authority, and this is why it unrestrictedly binds all beings endowed with reason. In other words, the ontogeny of moral facts crucially matters for establishing ethical objectivity. In this regard, there is a genuine and unresolvable disagreement between robust moral realism and Kantian constructivism, which cannot be comprehended without taking into account their respective ontogeny.

This disagreement about ontogeny is the root of other important disagreements. Constructivism rejects the realist thesis that moral judgments are truth-apt because they describe some portion of reality. It shares the view that ethical judgments are truth-apt, but holds that their truth-makers are formal rather than factual. Ethical judgments are true if they conform to a law. Since all rational cognitions as such are law-like, a significant part of the constructivist agenda is devoted to explaining the difference between theoretical and practical cognitions (Engstrom 2002, 2013). Such a difference does not depend on their respective subject matter, as we are led to assume when we start off with a fixed moral ontology. On the contrary, whether there is a distinctive "subject matter" of practical knowledge identified by a fixed domain of facts is precisely what is under dispute between realism and constructivism. Realism holds that such facts are truth-makers, while constructivism holds that the practical domain is not a pre-defined domain of objects and properties, but the result of the activity of practical reasoning.

For all these reasons, *pace* Hussain and Shah, Kantian constructivism is not vulnerable to the objection of queerness in the same way robust moral realism is. On the contrary, it makes the relation between normative and descriptive properties a perfectly intelligible phenomenon: it is the upshot of rational justification. This is not a decisive merit in favour of constructivism, since it is shared by other non reductivist yet naturalist views; but there are other advantages in endorsing constructivism which current debates have not yet noticed.

10 The Barrier Against Arbitrariness

In addition to escaping the queerness objection, Kantian constructivism promises other advantages which are less apparent but more significant. In short, it offers a general practical justification for the normative principles, which works both at the normative and at the meta-normative level. The nature and significance of this feature may be best elucidated by comparison with Enoch's view that general and specific supervenience are sharply separated.

Recall that for Enoch general supervenience is a conceptual claim, which has nothing to do with normative theory; and specific supervenience is compatible with any normative principles. The problem arises for Enoch as to how to pick the normative theory by which strong individual specific supervenience becomes credible and intelligible. General and specific supervenience are logically independent claims, but the explanation that robust moral realism affords for specific supervenience work out with *any* normative account of the content of principles. As an example, he takes Utilitarianism, and thus talks of the range of legislation in terms of maximality, but there is no interesting relation between this specific normative theory and the general claim of supervenience. The meta-ethical account of supervenience is independent of and severed from the very normative theory that accounts for its explication. This is not an advantage for Enoch, because his meta-ethics is not free-standing with regard to normative theory. By his own lights, supervenience requires an account and defense of the content of normative principles that only a normative theory can afford. These are issues that Enoch does not touch on at this point in the argument. The danger lying ahead is that of a perilous schizophrenia of ethical theory, whose metaphysical and semantic concerns are cut off from practical and normative concerns, despite the commitment to take morality seriously.

By contrast, Kantian constructivism avoids this difficulty altogether because it does not address supervenience as a theoretical problem. The importance of considering the relation between normative and descriptive properties as principled is not primarily metaphysical, but practical. It is rooted in the preoccupation about legitimacy and serves to guard against arbitrariness, special pleading, and bias. As constructivism treats it, this is a problem that calls into question the practical use of reason, rather than a specifically moral problem. The task is to investigate the nature of reason, through the study of its proper activity. Our cognitive and practical claims are genuinely authoritative insofar as they are rationally valid.

The realist response to the problem of arbitrariness is to anchor normative properties onto natural properties, via universal normative principles that work as their foundations. As noticed above, any normative principles can do the anchoring. By contrast, in the constructivist account, universal principles work as constraints which select considerations that count as objective reasons for acting. In its practical function, reason does not presume that there is an object of knowledge that exists prior to and independently of the activity of knowing; hence, practical knowledge is not knowledge of something external to the practice of moral judgment. This is where the constructivist interpretation of the relation of supervenience eludes the objection of queerness and proves better than robust realism. Furthermore, differently than in Enoch's view, not just any universal normative principles would do. The constructivist notion of moral legislation has a richer and higher significance than it does in the realist account. Legislation sets a standard that is the same for all practical subjects. The dependence of normative properties on other natural properties is stable across evaluators. This is what grants the possibility of objective moral knowledge.

These remarks point out that normative principles are not merely *ex post* theoretical devices such that they sustain the aspiration to structural integrity, systematization, integration, coherence, and completeness. The crucial function of normative principles is to be registered at the level of organizing subjective experience, and transforming it into practical knowledge. Practical knowledge is both objective and authoritative because it is constituted by principles. The Kantian view is that practical reasoning provides genuine knowledge not because it gives access to a special domain of objects, but because it is principled.

11 Constructivism as Practical Cognitivism

Since the moral law is an idea of reason, which is binding for rational agents as such, it is legitimate to ask how it can be of any relevance for human agents, whose condition is heavily marked by vulnerability. The answer is that for human agents, animals endowed with reason, the moral law is binding through the constraints of the categorical imperative. Constructivists generally adopt a procedural rendering of this claim as a heuristic device to bracket metaphysical issues.[7] In recent debates, however, critics have taken this proceduralist aspect of constructivism not as a heuristic device, but as the defining ontological claim of constructivism. Consequently, they have classified constructivism as an anti-realist theory. Under this classification, the purported merit and the distinctive mark of Kantian constructivism is a weak conception of objectivity, which grants the advantages of realism (e.g. standards of correctness) without sharing the disadvantages of its robust ontology (i.e. vulnerability to the objection of queerness). Understood as a merely proceduralist view of practical reason, constructivism appears to weaken the standard of objectivity by reinterpreting it as inter-subjective agreement under ideal conditions (Hussain and Shah 2006; Enoch 2009). It is this definition that generates the appearance of queerness, because the categorical imperative is expected to function as a mechanic device for the derivation of duties or creation of normative facts.

As John Rawls has clarified "it is a serious misconception to think of the CI-procedure as an algorithm intended to yield, more or less mechanically, a correct judgment. There is no such algorithm. It is equally a misconception to think of this procedure as a set of debating rules that can trap liars and cheats, scoundrels and cynics, into exposing their hand. There are no such rules", (Rawls 2000: 166). This misconception amounts to a confusion between practical knowledge and applied knowledge. More precisely, it perpetrates a misunderstanding concerning the practical significance of normative discourse. That is, it presumes that practical knowledge must be knowledge of some external objects, and that its practical significance must be decided on the basis of its action-guidingness. The two claims are shared by realists and anti-realists, even though they disagree about whether normative discourse has a cognitive or a non-cognitive function.

On the Kantian view, practical knowledge is knowledge of what to do which is importantly grounded on knowledge of oneself as a practical subject. The efficacy and normativity of moral obligations should be understood from the perspective of subjects capable of being bound by principles that they have legislated.

12 Concluding Remarks

In have argued that Kantian constructivism contributes to clarify and better understand the phenomena associated with supervenience. I would like to conclude this chapter by drawing some more general lessons from this discussion. In the

[7]For an overview see Bagnoli 2017b. Rawls proposes the procedural representation of the categorical imperative as a heuristic device, see Rawls 1971: 21, Rawls 1993: 26. For a detailed argument is support of a robust characterization of construction, see Bagnoli 2017a.

last thirty years, there has been a resurgence of interest in meta-ethics. Kantian constructivism faced serious obstacles to enter such debates. A view that is more often heard than argued is that Kantian constructivism does contribute meaningfully to meta-ethics because it is a normative theory of practical reason, not well equipped to provide conceptual analysis.

Problems such as that of normative supervenience arise because of our need for regulation and our sensitivity to normative principles. We should expect that our philosophical investigation of these problems profit both from conceptual analyses and theories of normativity. It is at this juncture that current theories of normative supervenience should be compared. I have shown that robust moral realism as well as constructivism make reference to normative principles in explaining supervenience. My argument has been that the comparative merits of Kantian constructivism are significant. I suggest that this finding calls for a larger reflection about the alleged boundaries of the meta-ethical inquiry and its distinctive means of investigation. I want to conclude by saying that to draw a sharp line between the conceptual and normative aspects of the philosophical inquiry is futile and sometimes detrimental to our perspicuous understanding of our normative practices and, ultimately, of our selves.

References

Bagnoli C. (2013) "Constructivism about Practical Knowledge", in *Constructivism in Ethics,* Bagnoli ed., Cambridge University Press, 2013, 153–182.

Bagnoli C. (2017a) "Constructivism and the Moral Problem", *Philosophia* 44/4: 1229–1246.

Bagnoli C. (2017b) "Constructivism in Meta-ethics", *Stanford Encyclopedia of Philosophy,* Edward N. Zalta ed.

Bagnoli C. (2017c) "Kant in Metaethics: The Paradox of Moral Autonomy, Solved by Publicity", *Kant Handbook*, Matthew Altman ed., London: Palgrave-Macmillan, chapter 14.

Blackburn, Simon (1971). Moral realism. In John Casey (ed.), *Morality and Moral Reasoning*. Methuen.

Blackburn, Simon W. (1984). Supervenience revisited. In Ian Hacking (ed.), *Exercises in Analysis: Essays by Students of Casimir Lewy*. Cambridge University Press, 59–74.

Blackburn, Simon (1985). "Errors and the Phenomenology of Value". In Ted Honderich (ed.), *Morality and Objectivity*. Routledge & Kegan Paul.

Copp, David (2013) Is constructivism an alternative to moral realism? in *Constructivism in Ethics,* Bagnoli ed., Cambridge University Press, 2013, 108-132.

Dreier, James (1992). The supervenience argument against moral realism. *Southern Journal of Philosophy* 30 (3):13–38.

Engstrom, S. (2002) "Kant's Distinction Between Theoretical and Practical Knowledge", *The Harvard Review of Philosophy* 10 (1): 49–63.

Engstrom, S. (2013) Constructivism and practical cognitivism, in C. Bagnoli ed., *Constructivism in ethics*, Cambridge University Press, 133–152.

Enoch, D. (2009) "Can There Be a Global, Interesting, Coherent Constructivism about Practical Reason?" *Philosophical Explorations* 12: 319–39.

Enoch, David (2010). The epistemological challenge to metanormative realism: how best to understand it, and how to cope with it. *Philosophical Studies* 148 (3): 413–438.

Enoch, David (2011). *Taking Morality Seriously: A Defense of Robust Realism.* Oxford University Press.
Forschler, Scott (2012). From Supervenience to "Universal Law": How Kantian Ethics Become Heteronomous. In Dietmar Heidemann (ed.), *Kant and Contemporary Moral Philosophy*. De Gruyter.
Hussain, N., Shah, N. (2013) "Meta-Ethics And Its Discontents: A Case Study Of Korsgaard", in *Constructivism in Ethics,* Bagnoli ed., Cambridge University Press.
Hare, R. M. (1952) *The Language of Morals*, Oxford: Clarendon Press. doi:10.1093/0198810776.001.0001
Hare, R. M. (1984). "Supervenience". *Proceedings of the Aristotelian Society* 58:1–16.
Hussain, Nadeem J. Z. & Nishi Shah, (2006) "*Misunderstanding Metaethics: Korsgaard's Rejection of Realism*". *Oxford Studies in Metaethics*, 1: 265–294.
Korsgaard, C. M. (1996) *The Sources of Normativity*. Ed. O. O'Neill. Cambridge: Cambridge University Press.
Mackie, J. L. (1977). *Ethics: Inventing Right and Wrong*. London: Penguin.
Moore, G. E. (1998). The Conception of Intrinsic Value. In James Rachels (ed.), *Philosophical Studies*. Oxford University Press.
O'Neill, O. (1989) *Constructions of Reason: Exploration of Kant's Practical Philosophy.* Cambridge: Cambridge University Press.
O'Neill, O. (1992) "Vindicating Reason," in *The Cambridge Companion to Kant*, P. Guyer (ed.), Cambridge: Cambridge University Press, pp. 280–308.
O'Neill, O. (1996) *Toward Justice and Virtue. A constructive account of practical reasoning.* Cambridge: Cambridge University Press.
Platts, Mark (1979). *Ways of Meaning: An Introduction to a Phiosophy of Language*. MIT Press.
Rawls John (1971) *A Theory of Justice*, 2nd edition 1999, Cambridge, MA: Harvard University Press.
Rawls John (1993) *Political Liberalism*, New York: Columbia University Press.
Rawls, J. (2000) *Lectures on the History of Moral Philosophy*, Ed. B. Herman and C. M. Korsgaard. Cambridge, MA: Harvard University Press.
Ridge, Michael (2007). Anti-reductionism and supervenience. *Journal of Moral Philosophy* 4 (3):330–348.
Street (2010) "What is Constructivism in Ethics and Metaethics?", *Philosophy Compass*, 5(5): 363–384. doi:10.1111/j.1747-9991.2009.00280.x
Sturgeon, Nicholas L. (1986). Harman on moral explanations of natural facts. *Southern Journal of Philosophy* 24 (S1):69–78.
Sturgeon, Nicholas L. (2006). Moral Explanations Defended. In James Dreier (ed.), *Contemporary Debates in Moral Theory*. Blackwell 241–262.
Williams, B. (1985). *Ethics and the Limits of Philosophy*. Cambridge University Press.

Law, Normativity, and Supervenience

Bartosz Brożek

Abstract In this chapter I argue that the relation of supervenience is insufficient to account for the normative dimension of the law. I begin by analyzing in some detail the traditional ways of relating normative (especially legal) and non-normative (natural) facts or properties: separation and reduction. Having identified their flaws, I consider the possibility of rendering the relationship in question with the use of the concept of supervenience. It transpires, however, that the claim that legal facts (properties) supervene on natural facts (properties) has limitations of its own. In particular, it cannot explain the normative character of legal rules, but rather presupposes it. Therefore, supervenience turns out to be insufficient when it comes to providing a full account of the normativity of law.

1 Introduction

The main goal of this chapter is to consider what it means that the law supervenes on facts (henceforth: the supervenience thesis). However, before I sketch my answer to this question, I will attempt to uncover the motivation behind the claim that the law is a supervenient entity. I will argue that the search for a more nuanced account of the relationship between legal rules and facts stems from the failure of two quite straightforward ways of conceptualizing it, which I call separation and reduction. Since legal rules can neither be fully separated from facts, nor reduced to them, the way is wide open to consider other accounts of the link between the law and psychological and/or sociological phenomena. It transpires, however – or so I will argue – that the alternative supplied by the supervenience thesis has its own limitations. In particular, while it provides a satisfactory account of the normative character of legal properties, it fails to do the same in the case of legal rules.

B. Brożek (✉)
Jagiellonian University, Kraków, Poland
e-mail: bartosz.brozek@uj.edu.pl

B. Brożek et al. (eds.), *Supervenience and Normativity*, Law and Philosophy Library 120, DOI 10.1007/978-3-319-61046-7_7

2 Separation

The first view regarding the relationship between legal rules and facts may be deemed *separation*: there exists a gap between what is and what ought to be such that there is no identifiable relation between facts and norms. In legal philosophy, the doctrine which explicitly embraces separation seems to be Hans Kelsen's conception of law. Kelsen's *idee fixe* is best encapsulated by the title of his major work: he sets out to develop a pure theory of law. What does it mean, however, that legal theory should be "pure"? Kelsen explains it in the following way:

> [T]he purity of the theory or – amounting to the same thing – the independence of the law as an object of scientific cognition is what I am striving to secure, specifically in two directions. The purity of the theory is to be secured against the claims of a so-called 'sociological' point of view, which employs causal, scientific methods to appropriate the law as a part of natural reality. And it is to be secured against the natural law theory, which, by ignoring the fundamental referent found exclusively in the positive law, takes legal theory out of the realm of positive legal norms and into that of ethico-political postulates (Kelsen 1911: 3–4).

Thus, Kelsen's goal is to make sure that law is independent of both axiological considerations and sociological and psychological facts. Because of that, Kelsen takes the law to be a system of ideally existing norms, i.e. norms belonging to the sphere of pure ought (*Sollen*). Such an understanding of legal norms and legal duties makes it possible to construe the validity of law as independent of any facts. However, this "purity" comes with a price, which is easy to spot once we consider the Kelsenian view of the legal system. He believes that the law is a dynamic system of norms, where norms are connected through a formal competence relation: a higher norm establishes a competence to issue a lower norm. The closure of such a system is provided by the so-called Basic Norm (*die Grundnorm*). But what is the *Grundnorm*? It is difficult to answer this question, particularly since Kelsen himself refers to it, *inter alia*, as the presupposed norm, presupposition, a norm included in a supposition, juristic hypothesis, ultimate hypothesis of positivism, ultimate ground of the validity of the legal system, thought norm, genuine fiction, judicio-logical constitution, constitution in the transcendental-logical sense, transcendental-logical concept, or transcendental-logical condition of the interpretation in legal sciences (Bindreiter 2002: 17–18). These descriptions – as differentiated as they are – uncover two crucial aspects of the Kelsenian understanding of the Basic Norm. First, it is an assumption or a hypothesis, which makes it possible to "close" the legal order and separate it from other normative and factual orders. Second, the *Grundnorm* is a certain fiction; Kelsen realizes that morality, economy or politics do influence legal practice and the shape of the existing law. However, he insists that a lawyer – who considers a matter at hand *as a lawyer* – should act *as if* there were no such influences. Kelsen observes also that such a strategy is by no means revolutionary, since it.

> merely makes conscious what most legal scientists do, at least unconsciously, when they understand [legal] facts not as causally determined, but instead interpret their subjective meaning as objectively valid norms, that is, as a normative legal order, without basing the validity of this order upon a higher, meta-legal norm, that is, upon a norm enacted by an

> authority superior to the legal authority (. . .). The theory of the basic norm is merely the result of an analysis of the procedure which a positivistic science of law has always applied (Kelsen 1967: 204–205).

Given all this, it may seem that on Kelsen's view the law has nothing to do with facts. In other words, legal norms stand in no relation to the statements of facts. The price we have to pay for this autonomy is a kind of fiction – the assumption that legal order is based on a merely "thought" or "fake" Basic Norm.

However, things get more complicated once we consider Kelsen's analysis of the relationship between the concepts of law's validity and effectiveness. Here are the definitions of them both:

> By "validity" we mean the specific existence of norms. To say that a norm is valid, is to say that we assume its existence or – what amounts to the same thing – we assume that it has "binding force" for those whose behavior it regulates.
>
> Efficacy of law means that men actually behave as, according to the legal norms, they ought to behave, that the norms are actually applied and obeyed (Kelsen 1949: 30, 39).

Importantly, "although validity and efficacy are two entirely different concepts, there is nevertheless a very important relationship between the two. A norm is considered to be valid only on the condition that it belongs to a system of norms, to an order which, on the whole, is efficacious. Thus, efficacy is a condition of validity; a condition, not the reason of validity. A norm is not valid *because* it is efficacious; it is valid *if* the order to which it belongs is, on the whole, efficacious" (Kelsen 1949: 41–42). Thus, Kelsen considers the following sentences:

(*LO*) The legal order is valid.
(*BN*) The Basic Norm is valid.
(*E*) The norms of the legal order are, on the whole, efficacious, i.e. they are actually applied and obeyed.

What are the relationships between those sentences? Let us consider formalizing them in modal logic. The first relation would be:

(1) $\Box\,(LO \rightarrow E)$

(we use the necessity operator $\Box$ in order to stress that the relationship between validity and effectiveness is of a conceptual nature, i.e. it obtains in every possible world). The sentence (1) says that, necessarily, if a legal order is valid then it is efficient. In other words, it is impossible that the norms of a legal order are valid and the order, as a whole, is not efficacious; however, it is possible that the norms are efficacious (*E* is true), but one cannot say that a legal order exists (or, which amounts to the same thing, is valid). Kelsen explicitly allows such a possibility as when he says that an absolutely efficacious norm can be considered invalid if it is not treated as a legal norm at all (Kelsen 1949: 39). Let us observe, however, that Kelsen posits also the existence of a strict relationship between the validity of the assumed Basic Norm and the validity of the entire legal order, which is best encapsulated as:

(2) $\Box\,(BN \rightarrow LO)$.

(This sentence captures the intuition that the norms of the positive legal order are valid because the fundamental rule which established the competence to issue them, i.e. the Basic Norm, is valid). However, if both (1) and (2) obtain, it is also true (on the basis of the transitivity of the material implication) that:

(3) $\Box\,(BN \rightarrow E)$.

This formulation is problematic, since Kelsen does not claim that whenever a merely thought Basic Norm is valid, the legal order is efficacious. It shows that the Kelsenian intuitions cannot be formalized in the standard modal logic.

This leaves us with no other option but to look for non-standard formal techniques. One such option is to use defeasible logic (cf. Prakken 1997), which enables the following rendering of the relationship between the validity of the Basic Norm and the entire legal order on the one hand, and its effectiveness on the other:

(4) $BN \Rightarrow LO$
(5) $\sim E \rightarrow \sim LO$

The sentence (4) contains the so-called defeasible implication ($\Rightarrow$), which enables the derivation of its consequence (*LO*) whenever its antecedent (*BN*) is true, unless it is otherwise established that such a derivation would lead to inconsistency. In other words, the sentence (4) says that if the assumed Basic Norm is valid, then, given no evidence to the contrary, we are entitled to conclude that the entire legal order is valid. The sentence (5), on the other hand, which takes advantage of the classical material implication ($\rightarrow$), states that if the legal order as a whole is not efficacious, then it is not valid. This formalization captures the following intuition: as long as we are not in a position to say – according to (5) – that the legal order is invalid, we should assume (on the basis of (4)) that if the Basic Norm is valid, then the entire order is valid. It seems that this reconstruction is faithful to Kelsen's intentions. First, the relationship between the validity of the Basic Norm and of the legal order is much stronger than the connection between the validity of the legal order and its effectiveness: *BN* is a constitutive reason for *LO*, which is not the case with *E*. Second, the sentences (4) and (5) do not lead to the conclusion that there exists a logical relationship between the validity of the basic norm (*BN*) and the effectiveness of the legal order as a whole (*E*), which was the problematic aspect of the formalization carried out in the standard modal logic.

The soundness of the formalization using defeasible logic uncovers a certain weakness of the conceptual construction developed by Kelsen. Let us observe that his defense of the law's autonomy comes with the price of accepting a fictitious or "merely thought" Basic Norm, which constitutes the foundation of the validity (and existence) of the entire legal order. However, it turns out that a lawyer cannot escape facts altogether – an inefficacious legal order cannot be deemed valid. At the same time, Kelsen must insist that effectiveness is not a constitutive condition or a reason for validity; otherwise, it would be difficult to speak of law's autonomy. Therefore, he is forced to propose a complicated conceptual scheme, where effectiveness, whereas it influences validity, does not give rise to it; the Basic Norm remains the only foundation of law's validity.

As I have tried to show, this conceptual construction can be formalized in a defeasible logic. The problem is that defeasible logic is based on certain epistemological assumptions: it models a cognitive situation of an imperfect agent, i.e. an agent who does not have full access to the relevant information. The defeasible implication (of the form '$A \Rightarrow B$') is a useful tool as it may serve to reconstruct those aspects of our knowledge, which are used to draw conclusions in situations, when information is limited. For example, sometimes one reasons on the basis of a conditional such as "If *x* is a bird, then *x* flies", although one is aware that there exists flightless birds. The mechanism of the defeasible implication makes it possible to see how such arguments work, but also what happens if the argument is defeated (e.g., the conclusion "*x* flies" is withdrawn once we establish that *x* is a penguin or a hen). Thus, defeasible implication of the form '$A \Rightarrow B$' may be used when the cognitive situation one models involves (potential) incomplete factual knowledge (cf. Brożek 2004). Whenever *A* obtains, one is entitled to conclude that *B*, although there may arise (predictable or unpredictable) exceptions which will force one to reject *B*.

Meanwhile, the sentence (4) $BN \Rightarrow LO$ is neither open to unpredictable exceptions, nor describes a cognitive situation of an imperfect agent. Kelsen explicitly states that there exists only one set of circumstances which may "defeat" the conclusion that a legal order based on an assumed Basic Norm is valid – it is when the legal order in question, as a whole, ceases to be efficacious. Therefore, the formalization of the Kelsenian view of law's validity and effectiveness encapsulated in the sentences (4) and (5) is *pragmatically equivalent* to the following classical formalization:

(6) $(BN \wedge E) \rightarrow LO.$

On this view, both the validity of the Basic Norm as well as the effectiveness of the legal order have the same logical status – they are necessary constitutive conditions of the validity of the order.

What this exercise in the formalization of Kelsen's doctrine shows is that it is difficult to imagine a purely "separationist" view of legal rules. Once we admit that a lawyer cannot dismiss with facts and is forced to include law's effectiveness in the equation establishing legal validity, the way is wide open for factual claims to "invade" the legal realm. Of course, the above analysis is confined to one – even if highly characteristic – example. It is quite possible that a different formal approach may weaken the conclusion we reached. However, I cannot see the way to escape the conclusion altogether, unless one claims that the effectiveness of the legal system does not influence the existence and validity of legal orders. But in such a case one would simply remain in the fictitious realm funded by the "merely thought" Basic Norm.

3 Reduction

The second view regarding the relationship between legal norms and facts is reductionism. It is best encapsulated in the doctrines of legal realists such as Oliver Wendell Holmes or Leon Petrażycki. In *The Path of the Law* Holmes famously claims that "the prophecies of what the courts will do in fact, and nothing more pretentious, are what I mean by the law" (Holmes 1897: 393). Thus, on Holmes's view, to say that there exists a legal duty or a legal rule is equivalent to a certain prediction regarding the behavior of the courts. In other words, the norm:

(N) One should not harm other people.

is equivalent to the statement:

(H) If a person x harms a person y, the court will order x to redress the harm.

Another example of the reduction of norms to facts can be found in the writings of Leon Petrażycki, the preeminent Polish legal philosopher, who believed that legal phenomena (norms and duties) are complex mental states, involving a specific kind of imperative-attributive emotions.[1] Within the Petrażyckian framework, the norm (N) would become:

(P) Whenever a person x imagines harming a person y, in x's mind there emerges an imperative-attributive emotion, which motivates x not to harm y.[2]

These two examples illustrate what reductionism amounts to: it assumes that any legal norm (or duty) is logically equivalent to the description of some facts. This ontology of law can be criticized in a number of ways. The first objection it brings to the fore may be deemed the intuitive argument, and boils down to the thesis that – from the perspective of the basic linguistic and common sense intuitions – the norm (N) simply is not equivalent to (H) or (P); these are sentences conveying different information. Moreover, the intuitive argument can be extended as to show some paradoxical consequences of reductionism. In *The Concept of Law* Herbert Hart observes:

> If it were true that the statement that a person had an obligation meant that he was likely to suffer in the event of disobedience, it would be a contradiction to say that he had an obligation, e.g. to report for military service but that, owing to the fact that he had escaped from the jurisdiction, or had successfully bribed the police or the court, there was not the slightest chance of his being caught or made to suffer. In fact, there is no contradiction in saying this, and such statements are often made and understood (Hart 1994: 84).

However, the intuitive argument does not suffice as grounds for rejecting reductionism. The very fact that such equivalences as (N)$\Leftrightarrow$(H) or (N)$\Leftrightarrow$(P) contradict our linguistic intuition or lead to some consequences which are considered paradoxical, is exactly the truth about the law and legal practice that the proponents

[1]For a more detailed exposition of Petrażycki's legal philosophy see Brożek 2014.

[2]Cf. Petrażycki 1985. In both cases – of Holmes and Petrażycki – the reconstructions I present are quite simplified.

of reductionism aim to uncover. Holmes and Petrażycki are perfectly aware of how the law is usually understood, and it is this understanding they are trying to undermine. The intuitive argument may be sufficient for someone who – like Hart – assumes that the analysis of the workings of the ordinary language may cast some light on – if not determine – the nature of law and other social phenomena. Without this assumption, however, the intuitive argument loses its appeal, and may even become counterproductive: when one is looking for the "scientific foundations" of law, the common sense approach is by definition inadmissible.

The second argument against reductionism may be called the argument from methodological schizophrenia. Let us come back to the predictive theory of law. As Holmes observes: "if you want to know the law and nothing else, you must look at it as a bad man, who cares only for the material consequences which such knowledge enables him to predict" (Holmes 1897: 458). Therefore, it transpires that the reduction of legal norms and duties to the prediction of court's behavior is not a merely theoretical maneuver, but has a practical goal: only precise predictions of this kind will enable "the bad man" to correctly assess the consequences of his actions (Holmes 1897: 462).

But why does "the bad man" care about such consequences? The only coherent answer is that "the bad man" is someone who from among the possible courses of action always chooses the one which is the most profitable. To put it in a different way – he is instrumentally rational. The model of instrumental rationality can be understood in two ways: descriptively (when we claim that people actually act as if they maximized their utility functions) or normatively (when we believe that they should act in such a manner). If the Holmesian model of "the bad man" was normative, it would lead to a kind of "methodological schizophrenia", since one would be forced to say that legal norms and duties are mere predictions, which are used by "the bad man" to act in the way he ought to act, i.e. in a way which is the most profitable. In other words, one would reduce legal duty to a description of some facts only to show how it is possible to fulfill another, extra-legal (prudential) duty. Of course, under such circumstances an explanation would be needed what is it that distinguishes legal and prudential duties so that only the latter are genuine, while the former are "facts in disguise".

It may be argued, however, that "the bad man" simply acts in such a way that he maximizes his utility function; on this reading the claim that we always chose those courses of action that bring us the most profit is a description of our actual actions. Thus, Holmes could defend his position against the argument from methodological schizophrenia by insisting that prudential duty – just like legal duty – may be reduced to facts. There is one aspect of Holmes's theory, however, which makes this strategy useless. "Even if it is plausible to think that a working attorney advising his client the Bad Man is trying to predict what a judge would decide, it seems ludicrous to suppose that this is what the judge himself is doing" (Haack 2005: 86). Holmes admits so much, at least indirectly, as when he says:

> I think that the judges themselves have failed adequately to recognize their duty of weighing considerations of social advantage. The duty is inevitable, and the result of the often

> proclaimed judicial aversion to deal with such considerations is simply to leave the very ground and foundation of judgments inarticulate, and often unconscious (Holmes 1897: 472).

Thus, Holmes openly says that the duty of a judge is to act in a way which maximizes social welfare. It is debatable whether this duty is legal or moral; however, there is no doubt that it cannot be reduced to any prediction, and this only reinforces the argument from methodological schizophrenia. Holmes owes us an explanation why some duties (of the addressees of the law) are actually "hidden predictions", why other duties – e.g., the judge's duty to issue such rulings which maximize social utility – is a genuine duty, irreducible to facts.

It may be added that Petrażycki faces similar problems when he considers the role of the legislator. In this context, he observes:

> The essence of the legal policy problems boils down to scientifically justified prediction of the effects of enacting legal provisions. Legal policy aims at developing such principles, which – introduced into the legal system or in some other way – would yield the required effects (Petrażycki 1985: 13–14).

Thus, it transpires that the legislator does not act as a mere mortal motivated by emotions, but in an instrumentally rational way: by establishing goals and choosing the best means to achieve them (cf. Motyka 2007: 48–49). The legislator's actions cannot be explained within the same framework which serves to account for the behavior of the addressees of the law, which leads to a different kind of methodological schizophrenia: legal duties are reducible to complex emotional states, but the duties of the legislator have an altogether different nature, being independent of the emotional mechanisms.

To put it more generally: the argument from methodological schizophrenia boils down to the thesis that the reduction of legal norms and duties to the descriptions of certain facts is always only partial. Even when we establish the equivalence between such sentences as (N) and (H) or (N) and (P), there must be a norm (whether legal or extra-legal), which is not reducible to facts. On Holmes's view, it is the judge's duty to maximize social utility, whereas in Petrażycki's theory – the rules of instrumental rationality followed by the legislator. In both cases theoretical problems follow, since one can ask, what is the purpose of reducing legal norms and duties to the descriptions of facts when one is forced to admit that – ultimately – there exist some norms and duties which are immune to any reductions.

Under such circumstances, a defender of reductionism has one last option: to become a heroic reductionist and claim that all kinds of rules and duties – legal, moral, prudential, conventional, linguistic, and so on – are reducible to facts. Heroic reductionism is usually formulated against the backdrop of Saul Kripke's interpretation of Wittgenstein's *Philosophical Investigations* (cf. Kripke 2007). Kripke's reading leads to rule-skepticism – the thesis that there exist no rules of conduct, duties or normative standards. Arguably, this radical stance is justified by the fact that Wittgenstein rejects three different conceptions of rules, understood as dispositions to act in a certain way, mental pictures, and platonic objects (cf. Brożek 2013: 27–33). If rules belong to neither of those categories, we are left with but one option: it is possible to speak of rule-following or being obliged to do something only because there exists a certain convergence in social interactions – for instance, is someone fails to keep his promise, uses a linguistic expression incorrectly or commits a crime, he will suffer a more or less severe negative social reaction. In other words, there are no rules of conduct or duties, but once we adopt the communal perspective it is possible to grasp the roots of the way of speaking which suggests that we actually follow rules or fulfill obligations. Kripke further observes that the Wittgensteinian problem of rule-following is similar to the Humean puzzle of causality. Hume claimed that we have no grounds for believing in the real existence (or inexistence) of causal relation; however, our mental habits, shaped by the repeated observations of one kind of events following another, makes it clear how the category of causality emerged and why it is used. Thus, Hume is a skeptic in relation to the existence of causal relations, just like Wittgenstein is skeptical with regard to rules: one cannot say that rules exist, but only that there exist the relevant social reactions.

Leaving aside the fact that Kripke's interpretation is not necessarily concurrent with Wittgenstein's intentions (cf. Brożek 2013), it leads directly to some controversial, if not paradoxical consequences. They are nicely summarized by Susan Hurley:

> [I]t is not an adequate answer to say that the solution [to the problem of rule-following] practices provide is a skeptical one, that nothing underwrites content and we just, contingently, happen to agree in doing this rather than that. (...) [T]he full force of the skeptical view dissolves our capacities for intentional action, for trying and choice, however arbitrary, as much as for perception and thought. It takes the ground out from under the feet of pragmatism and conventionalism, as much as Platonism and psychologism. It rules out appeals by the skeptic to our intentional responses, our attributions, our constructions, our investigations, our procedures of verification or ratification, etc. (Hurley 1995: 234).

Thus, Hurley stresses that the rejection of the existence of rules, duties and normative criteria results in the questioning of the reality of such fundamental phenomena as intentional action, choice or justification. From this point of view, heroic reductionism is *extremely counterintuitive.*

Moreover, heroic reductionism is not only counterintuitive, but also inconsistent, or – more precisely – it leads to a performative contradiction. Since what is that the heroic skeptic does? He says that from such and such premises it follows that there exist no rules of behavior. Thus, using some rules (of justification) he argues that there are no rules. The only way to avoid this paradox is to insist that it is not a paradox at all – that one does not have to worry about contradictions, since a heroic skeptic recognizes no normative standards. This line of defense is, of course, admissible, but it also makes the skeptical view an irrefutable, and hence theoretically uninteresting one.

All in all, reductionism faces one of two objections: it either only partially accounts for the normative sphere or else becomes a dogma that cannot be discussed, since there are no – and there cannot be any – criteria for comparing and rejecting theories. In light of this conclusion, as well as the problems inherent in separationism, it seems only reasonable to seek for the "third way" of determining the relation between legal rules and facts.

4 Between Scylla and Charybdis

The question I would like to address now is to how to steer between Scylla of separation and Charybdis of reduction. The natural option is to claim that the law supervenes on facts. The relation of supervenience – while much weaker than material equivalence – does establish a formal link between the factual and the normative spheres. Much ink has been spilled over the proper understanding of supervenience (cf. Kim 1993). Below, I will not delve into any details pertaining to this debate. Instead, I will adopt a very general definition thereof; at the same time, I believe that the conclusions I reach are applicable, *mutatis mutandis*, to any concrete conception of supervenience. I shall understand supervenience as a relation between properties which obtains when there can be no change at the supervenient level without a change at the subvenient level. Thus, if legal properties – such as being legally obliged to do something, being entitled to do something, being under a contract – supervene on facts, it is impossible for the law to change without a modification at the factual level. It also follows that – given two factually identical worlds – they must also be identical from the legal point of view; at the same time, it is possible that two factually different words are legally evaluated in the same way. Thus, the following holds:

(SUP_1) For any possible worlds w_i and w_j, if w_i and w_j are factually identical, then w_i and w_j are legally identical.
(SUP_2) For any possible worlds w_i and w_j, if w_i and w_j are legally identical, w_i and w_j are not necessarily factually identical.

Let us consider those statements in some detail. My first observation is that the conditions (SUP_1) and (SUP_2) show that supervenience is weaker than material equivalence; speaking loosely, on this account the implication between facts and norms holds only in one direction (i.e., some particular constellation of facts implies some particular constellation of norms, but not *vice versa*).

It seems, moreover, that some serious theoretical problems are connected with the concepts of "factual identity" and "normative identity". Let us begin with the former. What does it mean that two worlds, w_i and w_j, are "factually identical"? Of course, no two different possible worlds are identical – if it were so, it would be one and the same world. But (SUP_1) and (SUP_2) are not intended to mean that the constellation of *all* facts in any possible world determines the normative level. It should be possible to say that the normative level remains unchanged despite *some* changes at the factual level. "Factual identity" must refer to some set of descriptive or natural properties, and not to any such property; norms and duties cannot change without an *appropriate* change at the factual level. The problem is that every possible world is infinitely characterizable, i.e. for every world there are infinitely many properties which are truly or falsely predicated of the individuals in those worlds. Thus, any two possible worlds, w_i and w_j, share an infinite number of similarities, but also differ in an infinite number of ways. It follows that no two different worlds would be "factually identical" if the identity in question were determined by taking into account all the properties. This, in turn, leads to the claim that "factual identity" – as used in (SUP_1) and (SUP_2) – is a relation which holds between some finite subsets of the properties instantiated in the possible worlds under consideration. Let us reformulate both conditions so as to include this insight:

(SUP_1)* For any possible worlds w_i and w_j, if w_i and w_j have the same distribution of the natural properties $P_1, \ldots, P_x$, then w_i and w_j are legally identical.

(SUP_2)* For any possible worlds w_i and w_j, if w_i and w_j are legally identical, w_i and w_j do not necessarily have the same distribution of the natural properties $P_1, \ldots, P_x$.

By "the same distribution of properties" I mean the existence of an isomorphism **I**, which preserves the P-properties and which is defined in the following way:

> An isomorphism **I** between the inhabitants of worlds w_i and w_j preserves P-properties if and only if for any x in w_i, x has a P-property P_y in w_i just in case the image of x under **I** (the individual to which **I** maps x) has P_y in w_j (McLaughlin and Bennett 2014).

This new formulation underscores a serious problem with the thesis that the law supervenes on facts: there must exist an *external criterion* for determining which are the facts constituting the subvenient level of the legal phenomena. Of course, the question what are the natural properties $P_1, \ldots, P_x$ is a matter decided by a chosen ontology of law. For example, it is possible to interpret Herbert L.A. Hart's conception of social rules as involving supervenience. Hart believes that in order to speak of the existence of social rules one must take into account two different points of view: external and internal:

> It is possible to be concerned with the rules, either merely as an observer who does not himself accept them, or as a member of the group which accepts and uses them as guides to conduct. We may call these respectively the 'external' and the 'internal points of view' (Hart 1994: 89).

Leaving aside the controversy of what exactly is the "internal point of view" (cf. Holton 1998; Shapiro 2006), it transpires that for Hart a social rule exists only if it is commonly followed as well as accepted as a standard of conduct within the given community. To put it differently: when one wishes to know whether some social (including legal) rules exist, one needs to establish a sociological fact (i.e., that a certain pattern of conduct is in fact followed in the given community) and a psychological one (that the pattern in question is accepted as binding). Thus, Hart does not believe that social rules are strictly reducible to the observed sociological and/or psychological regularities, but at the same time he sees some connection between the two phenomena. Were it impossible to establish (with adequate sociological and psychological methods) that certain facts obtain, there would be no grounds for the thesis that certain social rules are in force. However, Hart does not claim that the sociological and psychological facts in question exhaust what we mean by saying that a social rule exists. At the same time, Hart does not seem to suggest that each particular constellation of psychological (assessed from the internal point of view) and sociological (assessed from the external point of view) facts determine a *unique* set of social rules. He would rather say – or so I argue – that sufficiently similar constellations of such facts yield identical normative systems. For example, let us imagine two societies, S_1 and S_2, of one million individuals each. Let us further assume that the societies consist of the same individuals among which there is Jones and Smith. Both societies generally follow the rule R: "The tax return should be filed by April 30 each year". Moreover, the rule R is generally considered binding. I said "generally", because in S_1 Jones does not follow the rule and does not consider it binding, while in S_2 it is Smith that represents the anarchistic wing of the society (at least in connection to filing tax returns). According to Hart's conception, the shape of the legal system in both S_1 and S_2 is the same – in both societies the rule R is valid. This shows that a given constellation of (psychological and sociological) facts determines the form of a social normative system (e.g., the law), but not uniquely. Therefore, it seems only natural to say that according to Hart social normative orders (including the law) supervene on psychological and sociological facts.

However, Hart's view is not the only possible conception of legal (and, more generally, social) rules which arguably embraces the supervenience thesis. *Prima facie* at least, it is possible to develop alternative accounts, which would also posit that the law supervenes on facts. For example, one can insists – along the lines of a modified Holmes's theory – that the subvenient level of the legal phenomena consists solely in the regularities of social behavior; or – by adapting Petrażycki's theory – it may be claimed that the law supervenes on psychological facts only. Of course, such theories would probably be less persuasive than the Hartian conception of law, or at the very least it would be easier to put forward arguments undermining them. This is, however, inessential with regard to the understanding of the supervenience thesis: it transpires that the conditions (SUP_1) and (SUP_2) are compatible with a number of different conceptions of law. On the other hand, the supervenience thesis is not trivial, since it excludes an entire class of the definitions of law, and in particular those embracing reduction or separation.

The second problem connected to the claim that the law supervenes on facts is how to determine when two different possible worlds are "legally identical". It is tempting to say – like we did in the case of "factual identity" – that given two possible worlds, w_i and w_j, they are legally identical if they have the same distribution of the "legal properties", $L_1, \ldots, L_y$. What are, however, "legal properties"? *Prima facie*, one can list a number of obvious examples: "being a legal person", "being entitled to sue someone", "being obliged to pay X the damages in the amount of USD 3.000", "being fired by the company Y", "being married to *Z*", "being the owner of a concrete exemplar of a 1982 Pontiac Firebird", etc. It follows that two possible worlds, w_i and w_j, are legally identical if all the legal properties $L_1, \ldots, L_y$ in w_i and w_j have the same extensions.

This leads, however, to a troublesome consequence. Let us imagine two possible worlds, w_1 and w_2, which are identical but with one exception: in w_1 Peter is married to Janet, while in w_2 they both remain unmarried. According to the definition we consider, the two worlds are not legally identical, since the distribution of the legal properties differs from world to world (the extensions of the predicates "is married to Peter" and "is married to Janet" are different in w_1 and w_2). But this is problematic. Let us observe that the legal rules in both w_1 and w_2 are the same, and so – at least according to a persuasive interpretation – they *are* legally identical. When we read Hart as saying that the law supervenes on sociological and psychological facts, the claim we defend is that the shape of the legal system, i.e. the kinds of rules it is built of, cannot change unless there are some specific changes in the patterns of social behavior and the attitudes people have towards them. In other words, what we want to say is that it is legal rules which constitute the supervenient level, not (or not only) legal properties.

5 Do Legal Rules Supervene?

There seems to be no easy way out of the problem identified at the end of the previous section. Where – in the framework determined by the conditions (SUP_1) and (SUP_2) – is the place for legal rules? One possibility is to treat legal rules as *derivative* of legal properties. Let us consider a set of three possible worlds, in all of which the domain consists of three individuals: *a*, *b*, and *c*. Moreover, our language has three predicates standing for natural properties (*killed with cruelty*, *caused damage to*, *is six feet tall*), as well as two predicates representing legal properties (*ought to pay compensation to*, *being sentenced to life imprisonment*). The semantic interpretation **I** of those predicates in each of the three worlds is as follows:

w_1:
I(*ought to pay compensation to*) = {(*a*,*b*)}.
I(*being sentenced to life imprisonment*) = {*a*}.
I(*killed with cruelty*) = {*a*}.
I(*caused damage to*) = {(*a*,*b*)}.
I(*is six feet tall*) = {*a*}.

w_2:
I(*ought to pay compensation to*) = {(*a*,*c*)}.
I(*being sentenced to life imprisonment*) = {*a*}.
I(*killed with cruelty*) = {*a*}.
I(*caused damage to*) = {(*a*,*c*)}.
I(*is six feet tall*) = {*b*}.

w_3:
I(*ought to pay compensation to*) = {(*a*,*b*)}.
I(*being sentenced to life imprisonment*) = {*b*,*c*}.
I(*killed with cruelty*) = {*b*,*c*}.
I(*caused damage to*) = {(*a*,*b*)}.
I(*is six feet tall*) = {*c*}.

When we are working under the assumption that legal properties supervene on natural properties, it is easy to establish that the only candidates for the argument of the supervenience relation are the following pairs of properties: *ought to pay compensation to* supervenes on *caused damage to*, and *being sentenced to life imprisonment* – on *killed with cruelty*. Moreover, the natural property *is six feet tall* is in no supervenience relation. Now, once we spot such regularities, we are entitled to say that – in our example – there are two legal rules:

(1) If *caused damage to* (*x*,*y*), then *ought to pay compensation to* (*x*,*y*).
(2) If *killed with cruelty* (*x*), then *being sentenced to life imprisonment* (*x*).

Both rules are *derivative* of the legal properties since they are mere descriptions of the patterns supervenience takes across possible worlds. In other words, while one cannot say that legal rules supervene on facts, they are intimately linked to an existing supervenience relation. Let us also observe that our theoretical maneuver is made possible by the fact that we *know beforehand* which properties are legal, and which are natural. Therefore, on the current interpretation, the claim that legal properties supervene on natural properties is *relative* to the accepted definition of what is legal and what is natural.

The second way of incorporating legal rules into the picture we contemplate is to assume that the rules *constitute* the supervenience relation. Legal properties do not just *happen* to supervene on natural properties; they do so *because* such a relation is determined by a set of legal rules. In our example, the fact that the rules (1) and (2) are in force is what makes *ought to pay compensation to* supervene on *caused damage to* and *being sentenced to life imprisonment* – on *killed with cruelty*.

The contrast between the two views of legal rules – as *derivative* or *constitutive* of legal properties – is quite similar to the understanding of individual identity in different possible worlds. On the first view one treats possible worlds as "given" and looks at them "from above", trying to establish which individuals from different worlds are their respective counterparts. This, of course, requires some complex patter-finding. Let us have a look at an example: in the actual world Barack Obama is the President of the United States. The question is, which individual is Obama's counterpart in a possible world in which Hilary Clinton is the President. Does he have to be a politician of the Democratic Party? Does he have to be married to Michelle? Does he have to be black? Can he have a twin brother? Does he have to be human at all? It is easy to realize that the problem boils down to identifying some set of properties which are definitional of Obama across possible worlds. The second view is that – when contemplating possible worlds – one begins with one particular such world (e.g., the actual one) and then takes a particular (set of) individual(s) or properties(s) and constructs a possible world around it (them). For example, if we begin with the actual world, we take an individual – Barack Obama – and assume that in another possible world Obama is not the President of the United States (since Hilary Clinton is), and that he has a twin brother, etc. Therefore, on the first view, individual identity across possible worlds is *derivative* of the (distribution of) properties individuals have in the respective worlds, while on the second view the identity in question is *constituted* by what Jaakko Hintikka calls "trans world lines", i.e. links between individuals in different worlds.

It transpires, therefore, that the supervenience thesis (i.e. that legal properties supervene on natural properties) is compatible with two different ontologies of legal rules. On the one hand, legal rules may be regarded as superficial entities derivative of legal properties; importantly, on this view one also needs an independent criterion for identifying legal properties: they do not come "labelled" and hence cannot be easily distinguished from moral, prudential or some other normative properties (the same holds, of course, for natural properties). Only after establishing – through the utilization of *some* definition of law – the class of legal properties, can one attempt to discern some patterns or regularities in the relationship between natural and legal properties and thus determine the set of legal rules. On the other hand, one can place legal rules at the center of one's ontology of law and regard them as constitutive of the legal reality. From this perspective, rules are what links together natural and legal properties and – in this way – generates the supervenience relation. Crucially, on both conceptions legal rules are *not* supervenient entities – this role is, in both cases, reserved for legal properties.

One can argue that the above conclusion is just an artifact of the way the relation of supervenience is defined. The definition is provided in the framework of the possible world semantics, and hence it is not surprising that the supervenient level is composed of legal *properties*, not rules. However, it seems *prima facie* possible to develop a generalized theory of supervenience where both the subvenient and the supervenient levels are any structures. In such a case, it should be possible to find a suitable formal expression of the thesis that legal rules supervene on some facts.[3] Be that as it may, my claim that legal rules are not supervenient entities, but are either *derivative* or *constitutive* of legal properties, remains valid within the current paradigm of the supervenience theory.

The most significant conclusion to be drawn from the above considerations is that the supervenience thesis fails to fully account for the existence of the normative sphere. When legal rules are treated as derivative of legal properties, one requires an external normative criterion for establishing which properties counts as legal, and which do not. Importantly, the criterion is not determined by the supervenience thesis but is logically prior to it. When legal rules are considered constitutive of legal properties, they are normative themselves, and – again – their normative character is not accounted for by the supervenience thesis, but precedes it. Thus, on both interpretations of the thesis, there remains some normative sphere which does not supervene on facts.

***

In this essay I have argued that the utilization of the theory of supervenience in legal philosophy is a natural consequence of the failure of two contrasting conceptions of legal rules: separation and reductionism. The proponents of separation claim that there is no relationship between legal rules and natural properties such as mental states or regularities in social behavior. It transpires, however, that separation fails as soon as one admits that any legal order must be, by and large, efficacious. The formal attempts to capture this intuition lead to the conclusion that some facts

[3] I have described this idea informally in Brożek 2012.

must be constitutive of any legal order. Reductionists, on the other hand, believe that legal rules are "hidden descriptions": they are logically equivalent to statements of some facts (psychological and/or sociological). But reductionism also fails, as it is unable to account for the normative dimension of social practices. Those two failures fuel the search for an alternative explication of the relationship between legal and natural phenomena. One such alternative is the utilization of the concept of supervenience. It turns out, however, that the supervenience thesis does not provide a fully satisfactory account of the link between norms and facts, as it "pushes" legal rules out of the picture. Only legal properties are supervenient entities, and rules are either mere descriptions of the formal links between natural and legal properties or they constitute the supervenience relation. In both cases, there is a normative dimension (some chosen definition of law in the former, and legal rules in the latter), which is not accounted for by the supervenience thesis.

References

Bindreiter, Uta. 2002. Why Grundnorm? Dordrecht: Kluwer.
Brożek, Bartosz. 2004. Defeasibility of Legal Reasoning. Kraków: Zakamycze.
Brożek, Bartosz. 2012. Normatywność prawa [The Normativity of Law]. Warszawa: Wolters Kluwer.
Brożek, Bartosz. 2013. Rule-Following. From Imitation to the Normative Mind, Kraków: Copernicus Center Press.
Brożek, Bartosz. 2014. The Emotional Foundations of Law: on Petrażycki's Legal Theory. Rivista di filosofia del diritto 2, 279–288.
Haack, Susan. 2005. On Legal Pragmatism. Where Does 'The Path of the Law' Lead Us?. American Journal of Jurisprudence 50.
Hart, H.L.A. 1994. The Concept of Law. 2nd ed. Oxford: Clarendon Press.
Holmes, O.W. 1897. The Path of the Law. 10 Harvard Law Review 457 (1897).
Holton, R. 1998. Positivism and the Internal Point of View. Law and Philosophy 17, 597–625.
Hurley, Susan. 1995. Natural Reasons. Oxford: Oxford University Press: Oxford.
Kelsen, Hans. 1911. Hauptprobleme der Staatslehre. Tubingen: JBC Mohr.
Kelsen, Hans. 1949. General Theory of Law and State. Trans. A. Wedberg. Cambridge, MA: Harvard University Press.
Kelsen, Hans. 1967. Pure Theory of Law. Berkeley: University of California Press.
Kim, J. 1993. Supervenience and Mind: Selected Philosophical Essays. Cambridge: Cambridge University Press.
Kripke, Saul. 2007. Wittgenstein on Rules and Private Language. Cambridge, MA: Harvard University Press.
McLaughlin, B. and K. Bennett. 2014. Supervenience. The Stanford Encyclopedia of Philosophy, Edward N. Zalta (ed.). URL = <http://plato.stanford.edu/archives/spr2014/entries/supervenience/>.
Motyka, Krzysztof. 2007. .Leon Petrażycki's Challenge to Legal Orthodoxy. Lublin.
Petrażycki, Leon. 1985. Wstęp do nauki prawa i moralności [Introduction to the Science of Law and Morality]. Warszawa: PWN.
Prakken, Henry. 1997. Logical Tools for Modelling Legal Argument. Dordrecht: Kluwer Academic Publishers.
Shapiro, S. 2006. What is the Internal Point of View?. Faculty Scholarship Series. Paper 1336. http://digitalcommons.law.yale.edu/fss_papers/1336.

The Metaphysics of Law: From Supervenience to Rational Justification

George Pavlakos

Abstract The paper challenges the view that the metaphysical grounding of the law - in contrast to other domains - requires a special legal grounding relation, which involves the condition of rational determination. It is argued that rational determination ought to be extended to all metaphysical grounding, for otherwise general metaphysical grounding would easily deteriorate to supervenience, which has already been rejected as a plausible basis of the grounding relation by many a contemporary metaphysician. What is special about the metaphysics of law is not the general framework of grounding through rational determination, but the engagement in a rational reconstruction of legal facts in terms of their capacity to generate normative reasons for action.

1 Conspectus

The positivist thesis according to which only social facts need to feature in explanations of legal facts sits comfortably with a *leger* requirement of metaphysical determination of legal facts. Under such a requirement all that is asked is showing that a modal relation between social facts and legal norms obtains along the lines of a supervenience relation. Recent challenges to this view have pointed out that metaphysical determination must become more demanding if it is to offer deep

I would like to thank Sam Chilovi, Tria Gkouvas and Alexi Patsaouras for providing detailed comments on an earlier draft. Research for the paper was supported partially by the long-term strategic development financing of the Institute of State and Law of the Academy of Sciences of the Czech Republic (RVO: 68378122).

G. Pavlakos (✉)
University of Glasgow, Glasgow, Scotland, UK
e-mail: Georgios.Pavlakos@glasgow.ac.uk

B. Brożek et al. (eds.), *Supervenience and Normativity*, Law and Philosophy Library 120, DOI 10.1007/978-3-319-61046-7_8

explanations of (legal) phenomena. In becoming so demanding, it ends up engaging more substantive moral facts in the explanation of legal phenomena.[1]

The said argument consists of two parts: The general part challenges in principle the adequacy of supervenience to generate deep metaphysical explanations. The special part argues that law poses an additional challenge: namely that in order for social facts to generate 'in virtue of' or grounding explanations of legal facts, a further condition must be met: social facts about legal practices need to be made sense of as *rationally contributing* to the truth of the relevant legal propositions (Rational Determination Condition). Thus it would follow that in the legal domain metaphysical grounding is special in a further sense: not only is supervenience inadequate for capturing the grounding relation (as is in the general case) but in addition there exists a special legal grounding relation (Grounding-Leg), which involves the condition of rational determination. Finally, the view proceeds to show that the only plausible candidate facts for discharging the requirement of rational determination are moral facts.

The paper will aim to dispel exceptionalism about the law, if only to point out what is really special about the legal domain. Here are the two main points that will be explored: rational determination cannot be limited only to Grounding-Leg but ought to be extended to all metaphysical grounding; Second, what makes law (and, more generally, any action-guiding domain) 'special' is not any requirement of rational determination, but rather whatever turns out to count as appropriate rational determination within action-guiding or practical domains.

However, and this is the rub, what turns out to count as appropriate rational determination within action-guiding domains is generated by the practical nature of those domains. To put it differently, when we ask the question about law's grounds in terms of rational determination, then we engage in a rational reconstruction of legal facts in terms of their capacity to generate normative reasons for action. In this context, we are not so much constrained by rational determination *simpliciter* but rather by an *open question* concerning the irreducibility of normative reasons to social facts.

2 Background Remarks

The debate between positivism and non-positivism can be usefully rephrased in the parlor of the grounds of legal propositions.[2] While the positivist denies that moral facts necessarily feature amongst the grounds of legal propositions, the

[1] I should guard against understanding my claim as implying that positivism does not consider the relation between non-legal and legal facts as explanatory in any robust sense. Rather the reason why positivism does not regard that relation to be posing any special demand is because it holds legal facts to be non-normative and as such amenable to direct explanations by other non-normative facts (such as e.g. social facts). It is for that reason that mere supervenience suffices for robust explanation. I thank Tria Gkouvas for pressing this point.

[2] Following a common understanding of facts as true propositions, I shall use interchangeably 'legal facts' and 'true legal propositions' or, for simplicity, 'legal propositions'.

non-positivist holds the negation of this claim to be true. Dworkin was the one to draw our attention to this dimension, notably through his distinction between propositions of law and grounds of law (Dworkin 1986: 4–7; Shapiro 2011: 284n).

Further Dworkin spelled out the importance of this distinction by reference to the idea of theoretical disagreement: that is disagreement not merely about whether the one or other agreed ground obtains, but also disagreement about the kinds of items that can play the role of the ground of legal propositions.

The distinction of Dworkin notwithstanding, there is nothing to suggest that one must opt for the positivist exclusion of normative truths from the grounds of the law or, alternatively, for the non-positivist inclusion of moral truth into the grounds of propositions of law. Indeed Scott Shapiro in *Legality* presents Dworkin's insights on the grounds of law and the idea of theoretical disagreement as useful meta-theoretical devices for accommodating the possibility of meaningful disagreement about the grounds of the law (cf. Shapiro 2011). Arguably, however, Dworkin's point was not merely to accommodate that possibility but also to suggest that one particular type of ground (moral fact) possesses special explanatory power in accounting for the truth of propositions of law.

In recent years none other has done more work in investigating the role played by facts (normative and non-normative alike) in the grounding of propositions of law than Mark Greenberg. Early on, in his seminal 'How Facts Make Law', Greenberg states:

> Understanding and resolving the debate between positivists and antipositivists requires understanding the nature of the relevant determination relation—the relation between determinants of legal content and legal content. The debate, as noted, concerns whether law practices are the sole determinants of legal content. It is difficult to see how one can systematically address the question of whether A facts are the sole determinants of B facts without understanding what kind of determination is at stake. But the positivist/antipositivist debate has so far been conducted with almost no attention to this crucial issue (Greenberg 2004: 158).

In particular Greenberg wishes to capture the role of facts about law practices in explaining the obtaining of propositions of law as one that purports to demonstrate how those *make* the content of the law what it is. Instructively he takes that relation between contributing practice-based facts and the relevant domain of legal propositions as a metaphysical or constitutive relation, or in the parlor of metaphysics as one of metaphysical determination:

> A preliminary point is that the determination relation with which we are concerned is primarily a metaphysical, or constitutive, one, and only secondarily an epistemic one: the law-determining practices *make* the content of the law what it is. To put it another way, facts about the content of the law ("legal-content facts") obtain *in virtue of* the law-determining practices. It is only because of this underlying metaphysical relation that we ascertain what the law is by consulting those practices (Greenberg 2004: 158).

Taking on board the debate on metaphysical determination contributes to a significant clarification of the debate on the grounds of law. For a start it imports into legal philosophy the more stringent standards which that debate has established within metaphysics. Once the question about the grounds of law is re-stated in terms of the debate on metaphysical determination, we can apprehend which kind of metaphysical relation is apt for the legal domain.

3 Metaphysical Determination as Supervenience

An apparent candidate for stating the relation between grounds of the law and propositions of law is in terms of a modal relation. Supervenience relations are apt in this context:

> One common way of explaining what the notion involves is as follows: one set of facts (the Z facts) supervenes on another set (the Y facts) when no two possible situations are the same with respect to their Y facts while differing in their Z facts. To take a common example, it is likely the case that the biological facts supervene on the physical facts in the following sense: two situations that are the same with respect to the physical facts are also the same with respect to the biological facts. As this example illustrates, supervenience is the name for a type of relationship that holds between facts (Plunkett 2012: 150).

Supervenience may works well for vindicating the positivist thesis about social facts being the ultimate[3] determinants of propositions of law, without excluding the involvement of moral facts (or truths) from law's determination. The argument runs somewhat like this: Assuming that moral truths are necessary (that is, they obtain in all possible situations or, in the parlor of metaphysics, worlds) then they remain constant across situations. Therefore what 'explains' fluctuations in the supervening level of legal facts are those items in the supervenience base, which vary from situation to situation: namely, social descriptive facts about law practices. In Greenberg's words:

> Even if the value facts are relevant to the content of the law, it is still true that the content of the law could not be different from what it is without the descriptive facts being different (since it is impossible for the value facts, being necessary, to be different from what they are). Necessary truths cannot be a nonredundant element of a supervenience base. Hence both positivists and antipositivists can agree that descriptive facts alone metaphysically determine the content of the law (Greenberg 2004: 159).

To that extent supervenience relations do not appropriately redeem the role of moral truths in the determination of legal propositions: because moral truths are arguably necessary, that is to say true in all possible worlds, there is little they can do to shed light on the determination relation obtaining between facts that feature in the supervenience base (more fundamental facts about legal practice) and those items (legal facts) that appear in the supervening level. Even though that occurrence might present the non-positivist camp with a problem about accommodating the role of moral truths in the determination of the content of the law, it should not

[3]Notwithstanding the use of language in the Greenberg - Plunkett debate, social facts can never be 'ultimate' since they arguably are in turn grounded in other more basic facts (mental, biological and – ultimately – physical). All the positivist thesis requires in order to be vindicated is that social facts be the *sole immediate* grounds. I thank Sam Chilovi for drawing my attention to this point.

be deemed a problem simply on that basis: namely, if supervenience can explain the determination of legal content simply by pointing at the social, descriptive facts of law practices there would exist no legitimate concern about finding a role for moral facts. Accordingly the next question to ask is: 'has supervenience the resources to offer a complete explanation of the facts obtaining in target domain of explanation?'

Arguably not: there is widespread consensus that the relation captured by supervenience is hardly an explanation, for supervenience maps the relation between two levels of sets of fact (or other item) as it were from 'the outside', without explaining its obtaining: it captures the pattern in which the two levels of fact interact with one another, but fails to explain why the supervenience base stands in the relation is does to the supervening level. In Kim's instructive words:

> [...] supervenience itself is not an explanatory relation. It is not a 'deep' metaphysical relation; rather, it is a 'surface' relation that reports a pattern [...] suggesting the presence of an interesting dependency relation that might explain it (Kim 1993: 167).

Notice that this shortcoming of the supervenience relation is not one restricted to law. If it were, one might have been inclined to explore other types of fact, which in conjunction with facts of law practices, would be capable of determining the content of the law.[4] But, so it seems, the problematic aspect of supervenience lies in its structure, or in the kind of determination relation it envisages. It is a relation that falls short of a deep metaphysical relation, such as the one that is required for a full-blooded explanation of the truth of legal propositions as envisaged by Dworkin. Assuming that for any X to be part of the nature of any Y, an explanation of Y 'in virtue of' X must obtain (grounding relation), then the premises of a general objection to supervenience may be reconstructed as follows: (1) Modal relations fail in principle the test of a grounding relation. (2) Supervenience falls short of a grounding relation.

Moving on from a more impressionistic understanding of the shortcomings of supervenience – in terms of 'surface mapping' or 'mapping from the outside' – we should now turn to specify those elements in metaphysical determination that make it more demanding than any supervenience relation could be. Instructively, in an effort to redeem the relevant depth of the metaphysical relation between practice facts and propositions of law, Greenberg imposes a further constraint that the relation needs to satisfy. In his vocabulary the relation must be capable of offering an explanation of how facts make law, in the sense of making it *intelligible* how practice facts contribute to the content of propositions of law in order for the latter to have the content they have. The constraint of intelligibility can generate full or deep explanations about how descriptive facts generate legal content. The result is

---

[4]As alternative elements of the supervenience base could be envisaged conceptual truths. Indeed some argue that facts of law practice plus some conceptual truths (i.e. truths amounting from conceptual analysis – e.g. a rule of recognition) would suffice for generating the requisite determination relation. Yet, if the argument presented above is sound, this option would not be available.

that Greenberg reconstructs the metaphysical determination that is required in law's case as being of a special, deeper, kind: it is, in his words, metaphysical *rational* determination. He says so much:

> I maintain that the relevant kind of determination is not bare metaphysical determination but what we can call *rational determination*. The A facts rationally determine the B facts just in case the A facts metaphysically determine the B facts *and* the obtaining of the A facts makes intelligible or rationally explains the B facts' obtaining. Thus, [the thesis that the Law-determining practices partly determine the content of the law] is the conjunction of two doctrines, a *metaphysical-determination doctrine* and a *rational-relation doctrine* (Greenberg 2004: 163).

While the metaphysical-determination doctrine may comfortably accommodate the modal relation between law practices and propositions of law, law practices on their own could not have amounted to a deeper explanation. That would be different if we were looking at a case of bare or brute metaphysical relation:

> The *metaphysical-determination doctrine* is that these more basic facts that determine the content of the law non-redundantly include law practices [...] Metaphysical determination can be brute. If the A facts are more basic facts that metaphysically determine the B facts, there is a sense in which the A facts explain the B facts, for the A facts are more basic facts, the obtaining of which entails that the B facts obtain. But there need be no explanation of why the obtaining of particular A facts has the consequence that it does for the B facts. To dramatize the point, even a perfectly rational being may not be able to see why it is that particular A facts make particular B facts obtain (Greenberg 2004: 164).

But Greenberg argues that in the case of the law brute metaphysical determination cannot offer the requisite deep explanation but that a further relation ought to be envisaged:

> The metaphysical-determination doctrine is not enough to capture our ordinary understanding [···] of the nature of the determination relation between the law practices and the content of the law. We also need *the rational-relation doctrine*, which holds that the relation between the determinants of legal content and legal content is reason-based. In the relevant sense, a reason is a consideration that makes the relevant explanandum intelligible. Here is one way to put the point. There are indefinitely many possible mappings, from complete sets of law practices to legal content (to complete sets of legal propositions). As far as the metaphysical- determination doctrine goes, it could simply be arbitrary which mapping is the legally correct one. In other words, the connection between a difference in the practices and a consequent difference in the content of the law could be brute [...] By contrast, according to the rational-relation doctrine, the correct mapping must be such that there are reasons why law practices have the consequences they do for the content of the law (Greenberg 2004: 164).

Thus to meet the constraint of intelligibility one needs to include amongst the grounds of propositions of law not merely facts about law practices but also such facts that make it rationally intelligible how facts of practice contribute to the content of the law.[5] The opposite is the case with aesthetic facts (Greenberg 2004: 160): in contrast to aesthetic facts, whose grounding through facts about the distribution of

[5] A more fine-grained distinction is called for in this context: normative facts may operate either as concurrent grounds of legal facts (alongside with social facts) or as iterative grounds, in the sense

colour over the surface of a painting is unmediated by reasons, i.e. *non-rational*, law-facts cannot be metaphysically explained without reference to reasons that make it intelligible (or epistemically justify) why particular law practices have the consequences they do for the content of the law. To that extent Greenberg submits that the law presents us with a *sui generis* case of metaphysical relation which involves an epistemic dimension:

> Rational determination is an interesting and unusual metaphysical relation because it involves the notion of a reason, which may well be best understood as an epistemic notion. If so, we have an epistemic notion playing a role in a metaphysical relation [...] For this reason, I believe that the rational-determination relation is of independent philosophical interest (Greenberg 2004: 160).

In other words, the case of the law points us in the direction of a special kind of metaphysical relation which is different both from simple modal relations (supervenience) but most notably, also from what Greenberg calls brute or non-rational metaphysical determination.

Greenberg juxtaposes rational determination to two instances of brute or non-rational metaphysical determination (Greenberg 2004: 170–171): the first includes cases in which the relation between the grounding facts and the grounded facts is opaque; such is the relation between microphysical facts and facts about water, the weather or conscious experience. The second case includes instances in which the relation between the facts of the two levels (i.e. the grounding level and the grounded level) is unmediated or direct. Such is the relation between facts about the distribution of color over a surface and aesthetic facts; or between facts about what was said and done and humor-facts; or even facts about the use of words and facts of linguistic meaning. Strictly speaking Greenberg envisages only the former instance as one of brute/non-rational determination. Arguably, however, both instances exemplify relations of non-rational determination because the grounding relation obtains 'directly or through some other route' (Greenberg 2004: 170) which does not require any rational transition between grounding and grounded facts.[6]

---

that they explain the obtaining of a grounding relation between legal and social facts. For further discussion see Plunkett 2012; and Gkouvas 2015: 261–263.

[6]For want of a more fine-grained differentiation of the two instances, I will treat them as cases of non-rational determination in Greenberg's sense, be it on grounds of opacity (as in the case of water) or unmediated intelligibility (as in the case of aesthetics or humor). Notice further that the case of opacity can be easily unpacked as an instance of brute grounding, on a par with the aesthetic case: if what determines (metaphysically) the content of, say, facts about water does not need to be rationally intelligible to us, then the fact that we might completely ignore the facts on the microphysical level (because they are opaque, as in: 'beyond our powers of discrimination') does not affect the grounding relation between those facts and the facts about water. Notably, in both the case of facts about water and aesthetic facts, we can have thoughts about such higher-level facts irrespective of whether the grounding facts or the determination relation are transparent to our thoughts. In a series of more recent articles Greenberg seems to subscribe to the externalist programme of, amongst others, Kripke, Putnam and Burge, according to which one may have thoughts about facts in a domain without being aware of the facts that ground the facts that feature in one's thoughts. See Greenberg 2014a, b.

Ultimately, Greenberg submits, owing to the epistemic constraint introduced by rational determination it is moral truths (or facts), which make it intelligible how descriptive social facts make (as in: contribute to the content of) the law.[7] I think there is little to disagree with Greenberg about the importance of clarifying the metaphysical relation holding between grounds and propositions of law. Further the requirement of intelligibility and the attendant rational determination condition seem apposite for that task.

4 Metaphysical Grounding

In this section I will turn to discuss in more detail the rational determination condition as one that enables a full-blooded metaphysical determination, which is often discussed in the literature[8] as *metaphysical grounding*.[9] In doing so, I will suggest a number of modifications on Greenberg's picture. While my intervention is more of a 'friendly comment' I still think that the implications of what I will propose are important, mainly in two respects: first they offer a more unified picture of metaphysical grounding which avoids rendering law an exceptional instance of metaphysical grounding. Second, my picture suggests a more plausible understanding of moral truth as the ultimate determinant of legal content. While the details of that understanding need to be postponed for another occasion, I will offer some signposting to back my claim.

Greenberg's rejection of a modal relation such as supervenience seems to be in line with a general skepticism about supervenience expressed by proponents of metaphysical grounding. We read in Kit Fine:

> There would appear to be something more than a modal connection in each case. For the modal connection can hold without the connection signified by 'in virtue of' or 'because'. It is necessary, for example, that if it is snowing then $2 + 2 = 4$ (simply because it is necessary that $2 + 2 = 4$), but the fact that $2 + 2 = 4$ does not obtain in virtue of the fact that it is snowing; and it is necessary that if the ball is red and round then it is red but the fact that the ball is red does not obtain in virtue of its being red and round (Fine 2011: 38).

---

[7] A further possibility, which is not clearly settled by Greenberg, is that the grounds of law should also feature the very requirement of rational intelligibility. In an instructive but sparse footnote he remarks: 'I will not attempt to spell out the relevant notion of a reason more fully here. One possibility is that the best way to do so is in terms of idealized human reasoning ability. For example, the idea might be that practices yield a legal proposition if and only if an ideal reasoner would see that they do. The notion of a reason would hence be an epistemic notion. In that case, L would imply that the metaphysics of law involves an epistemic notion; that is, what the law *is* would depend in part on what an ideal human reasoner would find intelligible' (Greenberg 2004: 164).

[8] See instead of others Fine 2011.

[9] Accordingly I will use 'metaphysical grounding' to refer to full-blooded metaphysical determination while reserving metaphysical determination to characterize a more loose relation that can also accommodate modal relations (supervenience).

Instead, Fine submits, we should be looking for a deeper explanation which succeeds in accounting for 'in-virtue-of' relations between the explanans and the explanandum:

> In addition to the modal connection, there would also appear to be an explanatory or determinative connection – a movement, so to speak, from antecedent to consequent; and what is most distinctive about the in-virtue-of claims is this element of movement or determination (Fine 2011: 38).

Such statements of in-virtue-of explanations aim to offer 'as strict an account of the explanandum as we might hope to have':

> It is for this reason that it is natural in such cases to say that the explanans or explanantia are constitutive of the explanandum, or that the explanandum's holding consists in nothing more than the obtaining of the explanans or explanantia [...] all that is properly implied by the statement of (metaphysical) ground itself is that there is no stricter or fuller account of that in virtue of which the explandandum holds. If there is a gap between the grounds and what is grounded, then it is not an explanatory gap (Fine 2011: 39).

When we transpose these thoughts to the realm of law, two observations seem pertinent: the first concerns the explanans and explananda of metaphysical grounding. The second is about the contribution of rational intelligibility to metaphysical grounding. I shall discuss them in order:

Greenberg seems to think that a central feature of the determination relation between grounds of law and propositions of law is that the two levels display different degrees of ontological basicness:

> A [...] point, which should be uncontroversial, is that no legal-content facts are plausibly metaphysically basic or ultimate facts about the universe, facts for which there is nothing to say about what makes them the case. [...] The important implication for present purposes is that the full story of how the determinants of legal content make the law what it is cannot take any legal content as given. It will not be adequate, for example, to hold that law practices plus some very basic legal-content facts (for example, legal propositions concerning the relevance of law practices to the content of the law) together make the law what it is, for such an account fails to explain what it is in virtue of which the very basic legal-content facts obtain (Greenberg 2004: 158–159).

Greenberg seems to assume that grounding, qua metaphysical determination in terms of 'in-virtue-of' explanation, obtains between levels that display different degrees of ontological basicness. Notably, Greenberg is in agreement with Fine and others that what is required for deeper, full-blooded metaphysical determination are 'in-virtue-of' explanations. On the basis of this agreement the following stipulation is possible: let us reserve the term 'metaphysical grounding' for those cases of metaphysical relation that involve 'in-virtue-of' explanations. It would follow that while the *thinner* term 'metaphysical determination' remains neutral toward modal relations such as supervenience, metaphysical grounding purports to capture a more strict relation between explanans and explanandum, which amounts from 'in-virtue-of' explanations. Along these lines, 'metaphysical grounding' denotes a metaphysical relation that is deeper than the one captured by 'metaphysical determination'.

Greenberg, however, does not think that all in-virtue-of explanations of less fundamental facts through more fundamental facts are subject to the constraint of rational intelligibility, as is the case for law. Indeed he seems to suppose that legal facts are a special case in that they are subject to the condition of rational intelligibility (on a par with facts of other domains that require rational intelligibility). In effect, Greenberg builds a case for a differential treatment of the metaphysical grounding of the content of the law. Presumably the reason for that move is that his ultimate aim is to argue for the role of moral facts as the ultimate determinants of legal content. Here is a possible rehearsal of his argument: if rational determination is a condition for in-virtue-of explanations of higher-level legal facts and if, arguably, non-normative practice facts cannot discharge that condition, then we need to take on board normative moral truths: those must feature amongst the explanatia of the content of the law.

This is problematic in two at least ways: even though facts about legal practices may be more basic, ontologically speaking, than legal facts or – what is more important – may never be ontologically basic,[10] it is still conceivable that the moral facts that contribute to the rational determination are themselves not ontologically basic (Plunkett 2012: 147). Were the latter true a regress of explanations would occur, whereby the explanatory burden would, *ad infinitum*, be delegated to an antecedent class of descriptive, non-normative facts. But if no non-normative fact can generate rational intelligibility, as Greenberg rightly observes, then law's grounding would turn into an illusory enterprise. Later on I will have to say a bit more about the way of understanding moral facts (or truths) in a manner that avoids this conundrum.

But Greenberg's understanding is also problematic for a further reason. It introduces a distinction between brute (or non-rational) and non-brute (or rational) metaphysical grounding. The problem here is not just one about theoretical elegance or economy. It cuts deeper, because it opens up conceptual space for a type of 'shadow' grounding, i.e. non-rational grounding, which might be difficult to reconcile with standard understandings of grounding, those offered either by Greenberg himself or the grounding literature more generally. Let me demonstrate what I mean:

It would seem that both Greenberg and Fine draw a distinction between full-blooded grounding and less strict modal explanations obtaining between any two sets of explanantia and explananda. Notably, what distinguishes the former over the latter is their capacity to generate 'in-virtue-of' explanations. According to Fine an in-virtue of explanation is characterized by its strictness: that is, the highest possible proximity between explanans and explanandum. Conversely, modal connections are insufficient because they lack the requisite element of 'movement or determination'

[10] In the sense that practice-facts are already composite facts.

from the explanans to the explanandum, which delivers the requisite 'strictness' of the explanation that pertains to metaphysical grounding (Fine 2011: 38). In short, it would seem that the standard way for characterizing the distinctive contribution of metaphysical grounding is in terms of 'in-virtue-of' explanation.

Yet, Greenberg introduces further possibilities for cashing out the 'in-virtue-of' relation: a reconstruction of his view suggests that 'in-virtue-of' explanations come in two forms: they can either take the form of brute or non-rational grounding or that of rational grounding.[11] Thus in cases such as those of facts about the weather, humor or aesthetics[12] Greenberg submits that an explanation in terms of more lower-level, foundational facts (facts about hydrogen and oxygen and their combinations; or facts about what was said) can offer 'in-virtue-of' explanations without further reference to reasons that would make the explanation intelligible. Contrariwise, propositions of law cannot be intelligibly explained only on the basis of law-practices without further reference to reasons that rationally determine the contribution of law-practices to the content of the law.

In other words, and to revert to earlier formulations of the same author, while the metaphysical relation in the case of meteorology, aesthetics and humor is unmediated, law presents us with a special case in which the metaphysical relation involves an epistemic constraint (i.e. 'what makes it the case that the contribution of law-practices is *made intelligible* qua contribution to the content of the law?') Effectively the move seems to suggest that we can conceive of three broad notions of metaphysical relation: metaphysical determination *simpliciter* (which, incidentally, collapses into a modal relation that fails to capture the distinctive 'in-virtue-of' character of metaphysical explanation); metaphysical non-rational grounding (where the 'in-virtue-of' explanation is unmediated or non-rational); and metaphysical rational grounding (where the 'in-virtue-of' explanation is mediated by the epistemic notion of intelligibility).

In what follows I will ask into the reasons for arriving at the picture that emerges from Greenberg's analysis. I will then point out some of the costs involved in it; finally suggest what might be a more plausible picture by doing away with the notion of non-rational grounding and instead conceive all grounding as rational, or else as being subject to an epistemic constraint along the lines of Greenberg's rational determination condition.

---

[11] Plunkett (see Plunkett 2012) proposes 'rational grounding' as the appropriate term for capturing the fact that Greenberg's rational determination is a relation of metaphysical grounding, which places it over and above mere metaphysical determination. In addition to that, my further contention is that for Greenberg rational determination is just one of (at least) two forms that the grounding relation may assume.

[12] Greenberg submits aesthetic facts as a case of non-rational grounding but does not commit to it; see Greenberg 2004: 160.

5 Rational Grounding

Why is Greenberg committed to the idea of non-rational grounding? Early on he says to us:

> Before Saul Kripke showed that there are necessary a posteriori truths, philosophers assumed that all necessary truths were a priori. If that assumption were correct, the metaphysical-determination doctrine would imply the rational-relation doctrine. Once we grant, however, that there are necessary truths that are not a priori, the rational-relation doctrine is a further premise (Greenberg 2004:165).

In other words while facts about 'being bachelor' are metaphysically *and* rationally determined by facts about 'being an unmarried man' (for 'bachelor = unmarried man' is a *rational* truth), in the case of facts about, say, 'water' and facts about 'H2O' the rational dimension of the determination is missing. This statement is to a certain extent puzzling. At first glance, it reads as if Greenberg is diagnosing a loss in the arrival of *a posteriori* necessary truth: i.e. the loss of the link between metaphysical and rational determination. On the face of it the diagnosis provokes an expectation of a remedy for recovering the rational aspect of the explanation. Surprisingly Greenberg suggests that the remedy is called for only for *a sub-class* of *a posteriori* necessary truths: those depicting the physical microstructure of natural kinds do not need to conform to the rational determination doctrine. Contrariwise, true statements depicting the moral nature of law – them being also necessary *a posteriori* – need to satisfy the intelligibility requirement imposed by the rational determination doctrine. On what grounds is Greenberg entitled to draw a distinction between domains, claiming that in some of them (law) but not in others (natural kinds) the rational relation is redundant? One possibility is that in the latter metaphysical explanation is *ipso facto* rational determination. This is of course an option but then it would not justify the fact that Greenberg reserves the term 'non-rational determination' for characterizing the explanatory relation in the relevant domains.[13]

Perhaps a more plausible view to attribute to him is the following: intelligibility in those domains is delivered through the metaphysical relation that obtains between higher level and lower level facts (water, H2O). In such cases the metaphysical relation is free of any epistemic notion, contrary to cases about legal content. To draw an analogy with necessary *a priori* truths: cases of non-rational grounding also demonstrate that the explanatory move between explanans and explanandum requires no further 'bridge'; not because, as in the case of *a priori* truth, the bridge is already part of the explanation relation but because the move itself renders the determination relation intelligible as such.

[13] I am aware that this paragraph is merely a reconstruction of what I take to constitute Greenberg's background philosophical views on the matter. However I think that it is a charitable reconstruction, considering his expressed views in the paper under discussion. I thank Alexi Patsaouras for pressing me to clarify my exposition, although I suspect that I might still have failed to convince him.

We need to look closer: Greenberg understands grounding relations as relations between facts of different levels: pace him there is a basic level of facts that constitute the fabric of the world, which are foundational and do not admit of constitutive explanations: they are the building blocks for any constitutive explanation of higher order facts (further, any constitutive explanation of higher-order facts must take recourse to those fundamental facts) (Schroeder 2005).

It should be mentioned in passing that, there is no reason to suppose that grounding or constitutive explanations *necessarily* obtain between sets of facts belonging to different levels of fundamentality. In fact the in-virtue of relation does not require any such commitment. For example, Fine speaks of grounding explanations holding between sets of facts none of which appears to be more fundamental that the other: such is the case of the grounding explanation of facts of acceleration through facts of time and velocity (Fine 2011: 37–8). The two latter are only trivially basic, for they themselves seem to be composite facts. To that extent, the in-virtue-of relation should not be taken to entail that the explanans be ontologically more fundamental than the explananandum.

However, for the sake of argument, let it be granted that grounding explanations require a difference in levels of fundamentality. Then it would seem that in cases of non-rational grounding there is something special that generates unmediated in-virtue-of explanation. Now given that, pace Greenberg, all successful grounding should use basic facts as explanantia, what makes non-rational grounding special must be located at the level of the explanandum.[14] To put it more strikingly: what is it about humour-facts or water-facts that can generate non-rational determination as opposed to legal facts, given that both are explained by the appropriate lower-level facts? I will attempt a conjecture a little later, but for now let me adumbrate a danger from creating a dichotomy between non-rational and rational grounding.

It seems to me that cases of non-rational grounding would collapse to supervenience (a simple modal relation). There would be no reason to employ the concept of a ground, which philosophers have striven so much to bring to the fore. Here is why: if the determination of aesthetic facts through facts about the distribution of colour were direct and unmediated (or transparent), that would mean that we would be 'reading off' aesthetic-facts (or the content of aesthetic propositions) from facts

[14]There is a further, more charitable, way to understand Greenberg's requirement of different levels of facts: not as suggesting that any constitutive explanation should make ultimate reference to the most basic facts of the universe, but rather that constitutive explanations of higher-level facts in a domain should make reference to lower-level facts *of that* domain. Yet, this modification shows once again why there is less there than meets the eye in the insistence of defining the grounding relation as one that involves as explanantia fundamental facts about the environment: basic-level facts would carry a universal significance in the grounding relation (and therefore could be deemed as defining features of it) if and only if all constitutive explanations were using as explanantia facts that are located in the same level of metaphysical simplicity; but that is not the case. It would seem, instead, that the in-virtue-of relation (or the idea of explanatory strictness) is much more central to grounding and, for that reason, probably a much more helpful concept for defining grounding.

about the distribution of colour.[15] But if that were possible, then a modal relation such as supervenience would be sufficient for arriving at 'in-virtue-of' explanations of the kind needed in constitutive metaphysical grounding.

I am not going to repeat why supervenience cannot meet the demands of constitutive explanation, but merely assume that conclusion in order to point out that the cost for taking on board a dichotomy between non-rational and rational grounding might, ultimately, undermine the valuable project of metaphysical grounding. Greenberg's distinction between brute and rational determination dislodges the value of his fundamental interest in the grounding relation. For no sooner non-rational determination becomes available, than supervenience takes hold as a plausible alternative to constitutive explanations, because the pattern of facts occurring on the supervenience base would suffice for a full-blooded explanation on the supervening level. But we know that it doesn't. The problem of supervenience is not one about law only. It is more general. Law is not exceptional in the relation of determination that it requires.

What to make of this discussion:

I can only suggest but not fully develop at this juncture that what distinguishes 'in-virtue-of' explanation from other forms of explanation is the involvement of an epistemic constraint in the explanatory relation. Several notable consequences would follow from this that can be summarized under two slogans: 'fundamentality is not fundamental'; and 'grounding is a relation of propositions'.

(a). *Fundamentality is not fundamental*: should all metaphysical grounding be governed by an epistemic constraint, it would follow that grounding explanations aim, first and foremost, at *maximum rational justification*. While the fundamentality would remain a relevant feature of the grounding level, fundamentality itself would cease to play an independent role in grounding explanations. For, on the suggested reconstruction, what may count as fundamental is picked out by its capacity to deliver maximum rational justification. Indeed, on many an occasion, that which has the capacity to ground facts on some target domain may be of the same or comparable level of fundamentality as the target-domain: (grounding) facts about velocity and time are arguably as fundamental as facts about acceleration; more obviously so, moral facts are not clearly more fundamental than the social or legal facts they purport to ground. Newly a major challenge has been raised for the standard explanation of facts of knowledge as being grounded on facts about belief and truth, which until recently were uncontroversially regarded as more fundamental than the former

[15]The same, *mutatis mutandis*, would be the case with respect to facts about the weather or water. Greenberg thinks that water presents a different case than aesthetics or humour. His reason is that in the case of facts about water we rarely have access to the microphysical facts that ground them; they mostly remain opaque to us. However, if the account of grounding were to remain consistent, then opacity should not serve as a reason for drawing a distinction between the said cases.

(See Williamson 2000). Such puzzles or inversions of received understandings of degrees of fundamentality can be easier dealt with when we turn to the notion of rational justification.

(b). *Grounding is a relation of propositions*: A related consequence is that justificatory relations are, trivially, instantiated between *propositions* rather than facts or other 'ontological simpletons' (see Rosen 2010). Thus accounts of acceleration in terms of velocity and time would count as 'in-virtue of' explanations when they are embedded in propositions that stand to one another in relations of maximal rational justification. It is on the basis of the epistemic constraint of rational justification that we could pass further judgment on the degree of fundamentality of the ontological items (e.g. facts) featuring in the relevant propositions.

Finally, a caveat should be drawn: placing all grounding explanations under an epistemic constraint would far from threaten to topple the order of the universe: trivially, relations of maximal rational justification (holding between propositions) would still single out facts about the physical microstructure of the universe as constituting the most fundamental level of explanation. But, bar the obvious domains of the hard sciences, such facts would have little to offer in terms of grounding explanations within domains of higher complexity (including the social and normative ones). In such domains the most interesting (and challenging) explanations obtain between levels which are already loaded with complexity, often in a manner that makes differences in fundamentality hard to discern. It is such cases which show rational justification at its most powerful.

6 Law as a Special Case

Notwithstanding the reconstruction of metaphysical grounding in terms of rational justification, there is a lingering question about metaphysical explanations in the legal domain. For, even if law no longer appears to constitute a special case of metaphysical grounding – in terms of evoking a special constraint of rational justification – it still poses a different challenge than those other domains which, in Greenberg's parlor, seem to eschew altogether rational determination.[16] In line of what I have argued so far I wish to propose a different account of law's specialty: not one in terms of presence or absence of rational determination; but instead in terms of the content that rational determination assumes in the legal domain. To put my cards on the table, I will argue that rational justification in the legal domain operates with substantive, practical reasons as opposed to the kinds of reasons that are at work in the non-practical domains.

[16] I will, following Greenberg, include in those domains humor and aesthetics, even though I am rather skeptical that these are different from law.

In arguing toward that conclusion I shall take three steps: I will first review Greenberg's justification for the specialty of law. I will then point out that the specialty of law comes from its content, and argue that rational intelligibility in explanations of legal content is one about the intelligibility of action-guiding, moral norms. Finally I will briefly suggest that moral norms or facts are subject to the same kind of rational justification as law. I will avail myself of this latter step to strengthen my earlier claim about grounding relations being better understood as justification relations between propositions.

(a) In defending his view Greenberg writes:

> First, our only access to the content of the law is through law practices. It is not as if we can find out what the law is directly or through some other route. And the whole enterprise of lawmaking is premised on the assumption that the behavior of legislators, judges, and other law-makers will have understandable and predictable consequences for the content of the law [...] Second, we are able to work out what the law is and predict the effect on the law of changes in law practices through *reasons*, not through some nonrational human tendency to have correct law reactions to law practices (Greenberg 2004: 171).

And elsewhere:

> This paper explores the necessary conditions for law practices' making the content of the law what it is. The central argument is that descriptive facts cannot determine their own rational significance—what reasons they provide. The argument therefore depends on the claim that the descriptive facts determine the content of the law in a reason-based way. It turns out that value facts are needed to make it *intelligible* that law practices support certain legal propositions over others (Greenberg 2004: 172–173).

Earlier in the paper I demonstrated that Greenberg understands intelligibility as a constraint on the metaphysical explanation of legal facts in contrast to other domains which admit of non-rational grounding. I tried to show that the option of non-rational grounding is detrimental to the programme of metaphysical grounding not the least so because it threatens to collapse it into other less informative metaphysical relations (e.g. supervenience). To the extent to which Greenberg's reason for subjecting the grounding of the law to a constraint of intelligibility were *contrastive* they should be rejected. However, Greenberg provides an independent account of the specificity of the legal domain: Roughly put, his argument is that, given the constraint of intelligibility, more fundamental facts about law practices cannot rationally determine their own relevance/contribution to the content of legal rules. He draws on familiar considerations about rule-following more generally:

> [...] such considerations show that practices cannot determine legal content without standards independent of the practices that determine which differences are relevant and irrelevant. Hence law practices alone cannot yield determinate legal requirements. The point is a specific application of a familiar, more general point that Susan Hurley has developed. Formal requirements such as consistency are meaningful only in the light of substantive standards that limit which factors can provide reasons [...] It would be missing the point to suggest that law practices themselves can determine the appropriate standards. Without such standards, a requirement of adherence to practices is empty. In epistemic terms, we cannot derive the standards from the practices because the standards are a prerequisite for interpreting the practices (Greenberg 2004: 181).

And

> For example, the argument shows that without standards independent of the practices, no set of practices can rationally determine rules. What rules a set of practices rationally determines will depend on what aspects of the practices are relevant and how those aspects are relevant. And the practices cannot themselves resolve those issues (Greenberg 2004: 184).

His conclusion is that, given the constraint of intelligibility, in order to find out how law practices make the content of the law what it actually is, we need to take on board moral facts; hence moral facts (or value-facts, as is his favourite expression,) must feature amongst the ultimate grounds of legal propositions.[17]

Yet, if all metaphysical grounding were mediated by an epistemic notion, as I sought to suggest earlier, wherein would the specificity of law lie, if any at all? Greenberg distinguishes the metaphysical explanation of legal (and presumably other normative) facts on the basis of a constraint of intelligibility which he takes to be absent from (presumably most other) non-normative domains: law-practices cannot be the ultimate determinants of legal facts because they cannot, on their own, make it intelligible why the content of the law is as it is. Thus it might appear that if, on my reconstruction, all metaphysical explanation needs to operate under a constraint of intelligibility, then facts in the legal domain would be on a par with those in any other domain. Yet we should resist that conclusion. Even when intelligibility remains, as it should, a constraint on any type of metaphysical explanation, the kind of intelligibility required can vary depending on the domain of the explanation. In particular, metaphysical explanations of normative facts (such as legal) must satisfy a distinct form of intelligibility which is tied to the categorial difference between normative and non-normative content or, in more common terms, between the domain of 'is' and that of 'ought'.

On a familiar, well-established argument attributed to Hume, it is not possible to derive 'ought'-propositions from 'is'-propositions. In the present context, the argument would suggest that any attempt to explain normative items (facts, propositions and so on) through non-normative ones would be fallacious. In this respect metaphysical explanation is not special but shares the fate of any other explanatory relation (causation or supervenience). Because, for all we have said about a normative domain in descriptive terms, we cannot offer a constitutive explanation of anything that requires us to act (by, say, imposing duties or conferring

[17] A comment is due at this juncture: I believe that the 'indeterminacy' of the facts of a practice, which Greenberg points at, is part of the more general reason why any practice (legal or otherwise) cannot resolve the problem of its own relevance to the determination of the facts of the relevant domain. To that extent I am inclined to think that Greenberg's argument provides a reason why rational intelligibility is a constraint that applies across domains. But presumably Greenberg would want to resist the idea that any, say cognitive, practice plays a constitutive role to the facts of such domains as physics or chemistry. Granting such a response, I will assume Greenberg's argument to apply to law practices only. But even so my earlier point about metaphysical determination being subject to a constraint of rational intelligibility still holds (that is, irrespective of whether it can be supported by an argument on the indeterminacy of practices *tout court*).

powers and privileges). For the question 'why ought I to F?' will always remain open, if all one is offered by way of an explanation is some elaborate list of facts about the sayings and doings of the participants in some practice.

Rather an appropriate explanation of normative facts would need to provide normative reasons or standards determining why and how the non-normative items, which feature amongst the explanantia, contribute to the content of the relevant normative explananda. Law-practices, as the collection of non-normative facts that constitute the 'material' aspect of legal practice, remain silent as to the required reasons or standards that purport to guide action. To recall Greenberg: 'In epistemic terms, we cannot derive the standards from the practices because the standards are a prerequisite for interpreting the practices' (Greenberg 2004: 181). Instead, it is precisely the injunction to derive an 'ought' from an 'is' which explains the failure of law-practices to generate standards for determining their relevance to the content of the law, rather than any fact about the metaphysical explanation in law being subject to a *sui generis* constraint (i.e. rational intelligibility). Hence in explanations of normative facts the constraint of intelligibility (and the concomitant requirement of rational justification) take a specific form: that of contributing to the explanation of *something that is normative*. I shall label this type of intelligibility *normative intelligibility*.

This is hardly surprising. H.L.A. Hart of all legal philosophers had given an early warning against attempts to explain legal obligation based on descriptive facts of any kind. This seems to have remained an established view amongst legal positivists since he put forward his argument.[18] But it is hardly the end of the story. Acknowledging the problem contemporary positivists have tried to avoid the 'is-ought' fallacy by treating both legal facts and the facts that explain them as descriptive facts.[19] Notwithstanding its capacity to steer clear of the 'is-ought' fallacy, this strategy faces a different challenge. In depriving legal norms of their normative force, it postpones the question about law's normativity to a later stage: whether legal norms give rise to normative obligations is a further question and depends on whether they actually succeed to obligate, when they are measured up to genuine moral obligations. Short of that stage, all that legal norms can (and actually) do is to merely *claim* or *purport* to obligate (see Shapiro 2011). In this fashion the proponents of that strategy believe to have immunized the metaphysical explanation of legal facts from any reference to the domain of moral obligation.

If legal norms could be accounted for in non-normative terms, then the specificity of the metaphysical relation between legal norms and their grounds would come under pressure. Not because it would turn out that *that* relation is not subject to any

[18] Arguably Hart's own version of explaining legal obligation in terms of an 'internal point of view', which participants in the legal practice occupy, did not succeed to steer clear of the same shortcoming. This is a central element of Ronald Dworkin's criticism which has been advanced in a series of writings since the 1970s.

[19] Joseph Raz's sources thesis and Scott Shapiro's explanation of legal facts as being grounded on social facts about plans count amongst the most prominent contemporary efforts to avoid the 'is-ought' fallacy.

intelligibility requirement, but because the intelligibility at stake wouldn't be one about the explanation of *normative facts*. Notably, this observation further suggests that the requirement of intelligibility cannot, by itself, recover the link between legal facts and their obligating force, which accounts for the specificity of metaphysical explanations in law. To put it differently, it would be insufficient to argue, merely on the basis of some constraint from intelligibility, that successful metaphysical explanation of legal facts must involve genuine normative (as in: moral) facts.

But, of course, the threat posed by the said positivist strategies is genuine only if non-normative explanations of legal norms (or facts) are a real possibility. However, the chances of success of an argument along these lines seem to me to be extremely low. For a start, the proponents of the decoupling strategy are caught in a dilemma: on one hand they agree that law's authority involves the authority to impose moral rights and obligations[20] while, on the other hand, they attempt to immunize the grounds of legal facts from those moral facts that actually determine the obtaining of moral obligations. To avoid the paradoxical effect of the dilemma, they settle on the, largely unstable, position that the law – even when it fails to actually obligate – at least purports or claims to be doing so. Their hope is that by making purported or claimed obligation the actual content of the law they can hold on both to the idea that the grounds of normative facts are non-normative and the idea that legal authority can ultimately generate moral rights and obligations. However, even purported or claimed moral authority is sufficient for drawing moral facts into the grounding of the law, as I have tried to argue elsewhere (see Pavlakos and Gkouvas 2016). In particular, on closer reflection it turns out that the content of an institutional norm, which merely purports to obligate morally, cannot be determined independently of the facts of the domain to which it purports to refer (the moral domain) (see Pavlakos and Gkouvas 2016).

Proving wanting the decoupling strategy of positivism ultimately serves the purpose of showing that law is metaphysically interesting not because, in contrast to other domains, it uniquely is required to meet a constraint of intelligibility, but because the intelligibility of explanations of legal facts is *normative intelligibility*. This has been concluded from the conjunction of three theses: first, rational intelligibility marks the entire domain of metaphysical determination, not just the domain of the law; second, rational intelligibility derives its scope from the domain of facts it purports to explicate; third, the domain of facts which determine the existence of both genuine and claimed/purported obligations is that of moral or evaluative facts.

Presumably Greenberg, as anyone who is looking into relations of metaphysical constitution, would want to object that the obligating nature of the law is something to be settled *on the basis of the enquiry into what grounds the law,* and not to be assumed already at an earlier stage. In fact he seems to admit so much when he cautions us not to be misled in believing that rational determination relates to the

[20]In fact Scott Shapiro (Shapiro 2011) goes as far as to declare that there exists only one kind of obligation: moral obligation and that, conversely, there is no such thing as legal obligation.

content of the law. Which is to say, he resists the idea that the content of the law makes any difference to the kind of rational intelligibility that is called for:

> It bears emphasis that what must be rationally intelligible is not the content of the law but the relation between determinants of legal content and legal content. L holds *not* that the content of the law must be rational or reasonable but that it must be intelligible that the determinants of legal content make the content of the law what it is (Greenberg 2004: 165).

Greenberg's reason is mainly to avoid building too strong premises into his account, with an eye to engaging with the widest possible range of legal thinkers, positivists and non-positivists alike. Yet such a concession is unnecessary: as indicated, many prominent positivists are already committed to the idea that legal authority entails the authority to impose moral rights and obligations. In addition, there is sufficient evidence to suggest that their strategy to de-couple the content of the law from the obligating force of legal norms is unpromising.

Further it seems consistent with Greenberg's theory that legal facts are normative in a pre-theoretical stage, that is, before they are subjected to metaphysical scrutiny. In later work Greenberg argues that the law is the moral impact of the relevant actions of legal institutions (Greenberg 2014c: 1290). Roughly put Greenberg's argument is that legal obligations are the moral obligations that obtain through the actions of the institutional legal actors. In his view the actions of institutional actors can generate two kinds of moral obligation: obligations that are created in the legally proper way, for which the term 'legal obligation' should be reserved; In addition to those, there is a further class of moral obligations that are created paradoxically, that is, when what is legislated or pronounced by the legal actors is plainly unjust. In those cases there is no legal obligation but there might arise a moral obligation to undertake the contrary from that which institutions command. I take this to suggest that he implicitly imposes a requirement of rationality on the content of the law, in the following sense: in imposing moral rights and obligations the law opens itself up to the domain of obligation *simpliciter*. Thus, even though the rational determination condition relates to the relation between the determinants of the law and the content of the law, the content that the law has is of a particular kind: it is content about obligations and as such imposes certain constraints on the way we should rationally understand its content. To that extent, rational intelligibility is not intelligibility about 'anything' but about moral rights and obligations, in other words *normative intelligibility*.

7 How Is Morality Fundamental?

I shall conclude with some remarks on moral facts as being the ultimate determinants of legal facts. Greenberg's 'hierarchical' understanding of metaphysical grounding suggests that moral (or value-) facts are, metaphysically speaking, more fundamental that legal facts. This is not uncontroversial. Arguably moral facts are highly complex facts as a result of which they might themselves be subjected to 'in-virtue of' or grounding explanations. There is no reason to suppose that such explanations would be very different from explanations of legal facts. Most likely their grounding base would include non-normative facts about some social practice. Again unsurprisingly, those facts would not be able to provide standards for their own relevance to the constitution of moral facts. To cut a long story short, we would need anew to involve normative or ought-facts which would rationally justify the contribution of practices to the content of morality.

But short of embarking on a debilitating regress, we should not take those ought-facts as being subject to the same order of explanation. We should consider them as fundamental. However, rendering them fundamental succeeds only in an attenuated sense: lest we buy into some version of moral intuitionism, one that posits simple moral items as part of the 'fabric of the world', a more nuanced account is in order.[21] Earlier I pointed out, more in terms of a slogan that a fully argued position, that 'fundamentality is not fundamental'.[22] My point there was that what determines 'fundamentality' in the context of metaphysical explanation is the capacity to generate maximum rational justification. Further, I suggested that the epistemic constraint of rational justification pertains more appropriately to relations between propositions than between any 'ontological simpletons' such as properties, facts or objects. These remarks were offered as the upshot of an argument for rejecting the notion of brute or unmediated grounding relations and, instead, proposing to understand all grounding relations as being subject to a constraint of rational intelligibility which subjects grounding to a condition of rational justification.

These remarks lend themselves to some coarse signposting on how to conceive of fundamental ought-facts. A plausible characterization would be in terms of conceptual normative truths. Such truths can be better understood as normative propositions that derive from conceptual analysis of our most general normative concepts ('ought', 'obligation', 'right', 'duty' and so on). One way to understand the form of such propositions is to consider them as definite descriptions, which do not directly depict substantive moral reasons but instead outline a structure of justification for moral standards of conduct.[23] Being the product of conceptual analysis, such normative propositions are *a priori* true; further, in virtue of being true normative propositions they depict normative or 'ought'-facts. These 'ought'-facts are fundamental in the sense that they can generate grounding explanations of substantive moral reasons.

The proposed explication of fundamental 'ought'-facts is in line with the contours of the programme of metaphysical grounding as it has been reviewed and partially reconstructed in this chapter. First, it respects the requirement that

[21] John Mackie has issued a strong and rather effective warning in Mackie 1977.

[22] Section 5, this chapter.

[23] Classic instances is this context are: Kant's Categorical Imperative; Apel's principle of a universal communication community; and Habermas's Discourse-principle, which purports to govern the justification of all practical reasons. Recent efforts to ground moral facts in rational truths include Jackson 1998 and, arguably, Scanlon 2014. For an overview of a rationalist programme of grounding moral norms, see Pavlakos 2011 and 2015.

grounding relations be mediated by an epistemic notion of rational justification: fundamental 'ought'-facts turn out to be constructions of reason (*a priori* propositions arrived at through conceptual analysis) and as such can contribute to rational explanations of more complex normative propositions. Second, it reflects the specificity of rational explanation in normative domains (law, morality) by enabling legitimate transitions from 'is'-propositions to 'ought'-propositions: fundamental 'ought'-facts provide reasons determining how and why non-normative items, which feature amongst the explanantia of law and morality, contribute to the content of legal and moral propositions.

References

Dworkin, Ronald. 1986. Law's Empire. Cambridge, MA: Belknap Press.
Fine, Keith. 2011. 'Guide to Ground'. In F. Correia and B. Schnieder (eds). Metaphysical Grounding. Cambridge: Cambridge University Press, 37–80.
Gkouvas, T. 2015. Law's Humility: The Possibility of Meta-Jurisprudence. PhD Thesis. Antwerp University.
Greenberg, Mark. 2004. 'How Facts Make Law'. Legal Theory (10), 157–198.
Greenberg, Mark. 2014a. 'Troubles for Content I'. In A Burgess and B Sherman (eds). Metasemantics. Oxford: Oxford University Press.
Greenberg, Mark. 2014b. 'Troubles for Content II: Explaining Grounding'. In A Burgess and B Sherman (eds). Metasemantics. Oxford: Oxford University Press.
Greenberg, Mark. 2014c. 'The Moral Impact Theory of Law'. 123 Yale Law Journal, 1288–1342.
Jackson, F. 1998. From Metaphysics to Ethics. Oxford: Clarendon Press.
Kim, J. 1993. Supervenience and Mind: Selected Philosophical Essays. Cambridge: Cambridge University Press.
Mackie, John. 1977. Ethics: Inventing Right and Wrong. New York: Penguin Press.
Pavlakos, George. 2011. 'Law, Normativity and the Model of Norms'. In G. Pavlakos and S. Bertea (eds). New Essays on the Normativity of Law. Oxford: Hart Publishing, 246–280.
Pavlakos, George. 2015. 'On Second-Order Morality'. Jurisprudence (6), 276–297.
Pavlakos, G., and T. Gkouvas. 2016. 'Law's Authority: Authorizing or Obligating? A Comment on S Shapiro's Legality'. Unpublished MS.
Plunkett, D. 2012. 'A Positivist Route for Explaining How Facts Make Law'. Legal Theory (18), 139–207.
Rosen, G. 2010. 'Metaphysical dependence: Grounding and Reduction'. In Hale and Hoffman (eds.). Modality: Metaphysics, Logic and Epistemology. Oxford: Oxford University Press, 109–136.
Scanlon, T. 2014. Being Realistic About Reasons. Oxford: Oxford University Press.
Schroeder, M. 2005. 'Cudworth and Normative Explanations'. JESP 1(3), 1–27.
Shapiro, Scott. 2011. Legality. Cambridge, MA: Belknap Press.
Williamson, Timothy. 2000. Knowledge and its Limits. Oxford: Oxford University Press.

Supervenience and the Normativity of Folk Psychology in the Legal-Philosophical Context

Łukasz Kurek

Abstract Folk psychology is a normative phenomenon. When the behavior is explained from a folk psychological perspective, the explanation consists in the ascription of beliefs, desires and intentions it would be rational to have for the agent in her situation. In this chapter it will be argued that law adopts the folk-psychological model of explanation of behaviour and the legal image of the mind corresponds to the image of the mind present in folk-psychology. Both law and folk-psychology presuppose that the mind is reason-responsive, i.e. it is able to recognize reasons and to react to reasons. Furthermore, it will be argued that – at the conceptual level – reason-responsiveness is constitutively supervenient on our understanding of, *inter alia*, reasons, and the abilities to recognize and to react to reasons. On the other hand, at the cognitive level, reason-responsiveness is causally supervenient on the cognitive mechanisms which generate reasons and underlie our abilities to recognize and to react to reasons. Finally, in the last part of the chapter, some empirical challenges to reason-responsiveness will be discussed.

1 Introduction

Folk psychology conventionally means our common sense understanding of other minds. It is required to perform such features as explaining, predicting, justifying, and interpreting behavior, all of which are indispensable in the social context. However, in the recent literature, "folk psychology" is understood more broadly, to encompass other abilities which enable us to interact with others, such as recognizing their past histories, personalities, or moods, as well as their goals, emotions, and the social context of their behavior. In this chapter "folk psychology" will be understood in the narrow, conventional sense, according to which it consists in "mindreading". What is more, unless stated otherwise, we will focus on only one folk psychological ability, namely the explanation of behaviour, since it is especially relevant in the legal contexts. Despite the fact that reading off other

Ł. Kurek (✉)
Jagiellonian University, Kraków, Poland
e-mail: l.kurek@uj.edu.pl

B. Brożek et al. (eds.), *Supervenience and Normativity*, Law and Philosophy Library 120, DOI 10.1007/978-3-319-61046-7_9

people's minds may appear somewhat mysterious, it means nothing more than the everyday attribution of mental states, such as beliefs, desires or intentions.

Despite the fact that mindreading skills have received a large amount of attention from cognitive scientists, the first goal of the chapter is to argue that their main purpose is normative rather than descriptive. The descriptive goal of folk psychology consists in reconstructing how the mind actually works. Such mindreading tasks as predicting behaviour will be successful only when its assumptions about mental architecture will be, at least to a certain extent, correct. Because people engage in mindreading on a daily basis and usually it helps them to achieve their goals – e.g. our predictions of behavior on the basis of the attribution of mental states tend to be accurate – it appears that there is something right about our common sense understanding of the mechanisms of thought and their connection with action. In other words, folk psychological mental states seem to supervene on states of the person which find their place in current scientific theories in behavioural sciences. What is more, the descriptive goal of folk psychology aids its normative goal, i.e. the regulation of social behavior. Mindreading is heavily influenced by judgments about what makes sense to think or do in particular situations.

To a large extent, law adopts the folk psychological model of the mind. Lawyers and philosophers of law take special interest in the mental states, as their correct ascription is often crucial to – *inter alia* – legally classify the behavior under consideration. For instance, answer to the following question is required to classify a particular behavior as an instance of murder or manslaughter: did the defendant intent to kill the victim when he fired the fatal shot? The second goal of the chapter is to argue that the crucial assumption of legal folk psychology, which has its roots in our common sense understanding of other minds, is that people are reason-responsive. Reason-responsiveness means that people have the ability to recognize and react to reasons – understood as combinations of beliefs and desires – in their thought and behavior. Therefore, explanation of behavior for legal purposes is first and foremost a normative practice. It consists in the ascriptions of reasons it would be rational for the person to have, i.e. ascriptions of reasons according to the appropriate rules of rationality. With some minor exceptions, as it appears to be the case with psychopaths, if people are not reason-responsive, it is will not be justified to hold them legally responsible for their behavior.

The third and the last goal of the chapter is to assess the empirical challenges to reason-responsiveness based legal folk psychology. There are two types of such challenges. Challenges of the first type are aimed to undermine the very possibility of reason-responsiveness. Some authors claim that there are empirical findings which suggest that there is no coherent way to ascribe folk psychological mental states. If this is the case, then there is no coherent way to ascribe reasons and the legal folk psychology is false. Challenges of the second type are connected with the fact that reason-responsiveness is conceptualized as a unified ability, i.e. an ability which is realized by cognitive processes of a single type. However, according to the influential, scientific conception of the mind, it consists in at least two cognitive systems, which may be described as "intuitive" and "analytic". The relevant research suggests, the former system plays a dominant role in reasoning and decision making, but only the latter may underlie reason-responsiveness.

2 The Normativity of Folk Psychology

One of the folk psychological assumptions pertaining to the nature of the mind is that it is normative. For instance, it seems that one ought to believe that the ball is in the box if the ball is in the box, and when one believes that the ball is in the box one ought not believe that the ball is not in the box. At first glance it is self-evident that such common sense rules of belief formation hold. Indeed, it would be hard to imagine how a person could explain, understand, predict, justify, or coordinate behavior in everyday situations, if there were not only no rules governing how we think about thinking, but also no rules governing how the mind actually works, and no correspondence between these two sets of rules.

Despite the fact that there seems to be some correspondence between our everyday understanding of the mind and the way it actually operates, it seems that what folk psychology proposes should be viewed as a *model* of the psychology of the person whose behaviour is predicted or explained (Maibom 2003; Godfrey-Smith 2005). Models can be understood as idealized versions of some parts of the world, and they are constructed to facilitate the activities connected with this part of the world. When folk psychology is practiced, the crucial component of the construed models of the minds of the target persons – their psychological profiles – is rationality. This aspect of folk psychology has been recognized by many philosophers interested in folk psychology. For instance, Daniel Dennet claims that:

> However rational we are, it is the myth of our rational agenthood that structures and organizes our attributions of belief and desire to others and that regulates our own deliberations and investigations. We aspire to rationality, and without the myth of our rationality the concepts of belief and desire would be uprooted. Folk psychology, then, is *idealized* in that it produces its predictions and explanations by calculating in a normative system; it predicts what we will believe, desire, and do, by determining what we ought to believe, desire, and do (Dennett 1987: 52).

To explicate the normativity of folk psychology in more detail it is useful to distinguish between three layers of folk psychology: linguistic, conceptual and cognitive. The linguistic layer pertains to linguistic expressions used in the folk psychological explanation of behavior. The linguistic layer consists in all commonly accepted – at least by the members of a particular culture – expressions of this sort (Lillard 1998; Russell 1991; Morris and Peng 1994). In the literature on folk psychology, these expressions are sometimes described as "folk psychological platitudes", which can include the following: "People will believe in what straightforwardly follows from what they already believe", or "People will be surprised if what they believe in will turn out to be false". The ability to form such platitudes appears to be grounded in the second layer of folk psychology, namely our understanding of mindreading concepts such as the concept of belief. The concepts in question are interconnected by semantical relations and they are the building blocks of the mental model of the target person.

Finally, the third layer of folk psychology, the cognitive layer, pertains to cognitive processes which underlie our ability to conceptualize the mind in everyday contexts. The processes in question may operate in a conscious and controlled manner, for instance when the behavior is explained in the court of law. In this situation – as it will be argued in more detail in the next part of this chapter – the folk psychological model of mind of the target person is construed in a somewhat elaborate manner, explicitly encapsulating her mental states. In other contexts, the cognitive processes operate unconsciously and automatically, for instance when we drive a car and predict the behavior of other drivers. Here the mental model of the person is austere, and, as psychological research suggests, it usually ignores her mental states, and instead takes into account such features as her situation, her traits, or stereotypes (Andrews 2012; Hutto 2008). The thesis that our ordinary psychology is normative may pertain to the second and to the third of the above mentioned layers, i.e. the conceptual and the cognitive. The linguistic layer can be understood as an expression of our folk psychological conceptual repertoire, so if the conceptual layer is normative the linguistic layer will inherit this property.

The examination of the normativity of both our folk psychological concepts and the cognitive mechanisms which utilize them exceeds the scope of this chapter. For the present purposes it will suffice to focus on the normative aspect of one of its building blocks – belief. Here, normativity may relate to the concept of belief or to the cognitive mechanisms which generate beliefs. Therefore, the slogan that "belief is normative" may mean either that there are rules of rationality which govern how we understand what belief is, or that there are cognitive mechanisms designed to follow these rules. Some examples of the rules of rationality governing belief attribution have been already proposed, e.g. "a person ought to believe that the ball is in the box if the ball is in the box" which may be generalized to "X ought to believe that Y is in Z if Y is in Z". The latter can be generalized even further, to "For any *S*, *p*: *S* ought to believe that *p* if and only if *p* is true." Because our everyday understanding of belief emphasizes the connection between belief and truth, the last rule has been usually taken as a starting point in the formulation of numerous accounts of the normativity of belief (McHugh and Whiting 2014). Due to the fact that there are important difficulties connected with this rule – e.g. it implicates an unsatisfiable requirement on believers – more recent accounts of the normativity of belief propose different candidates for the general rule governing belief attribution (Bykvist and Hattiangadi 2007). Due to the facts that belief appears to "aim at truth", and that only evidence appears to influence belief attribution, let us assume that an evidential rule would a good candidate for such a rule. Such an evidential rule states that "For every *S*, *p*: *S* ought to believe that *p* if and only if *S* has an adequate evidence for *p*." The evidential rule for belief may operate at two levels. At the conceptual level, it may be constitutive of our concept of belief, i.e. we cannot "recognize ourselves as believing *p* while believing that our reasons or evidence are not adequate to its truth and conversely" (Adler 2002: 32). At the psychological level, the rule may influence the operation of the cognitive mechanisms generating beliefs.

To illustrate how the evidential rule for belief works, it can be noted that in most cases when the person infers a mental state of another person to explain or predict behavior, she is faced with the problem of many possible results of such an inference. Take, for example, the scenario in which person A puts her ball into the round box, leaves the scene, and in her absence, person B moves the ball into the square box (Wimmer and Perner 1983). It seem obvious that if the observer of this scene understands how belief works, then when he is asked where person A will look for her ball, he will answer that she will look for it in the round box. However, why should we think that person A will look for her ball in the round box? There are multiple scenarios possible which change the correctness of the answer. Perhaps both protagonists know each other and person A can predict that person B will move the ball. Or perhaps person A informed person B that she will move the ball. So how do we arrive at the correct answer? It is implausible to suppose that we do this only after taking into account all possible scenarios. The plausible explanation appears to be that we understand that belief is governed by the evidential rule. This rule is a shortcut to arriving at the correct answer and it implies that a person usually ought to look for a thing where she believes she left it because her leaving it is an adequate evidence for this belief. Or that she has no reason to believe it is somewhere else if she did not see anyone moving it because her not seeing anyone moving it is an adequate evidence for her belief. What is more, folk psychological rules governing belief ascription seem to describe, at least to a certain extent, how beliefs actually work: a person will usually do look for a thing where she believes she left it, and she will not change her belief if she did not see anyone moving it.

The above considerations lead to a worry about the possible incommensurability between folk psychology and scientific psychology. Some philosophers claimed that because rules of rationality play such a prominent role in common sense psychology, and they have no counterpart in the scientific explanation of the mind, the folk psychological and the scientific explanation of the mind are radically incommensurable. According to John McDowell:

> The concepts of the propositional attitudes have their proper home in explanations of a special sort: explanations in which things are made intelligible by being revealed to be, or to approximate to being, as they rationally ought to be. This is to be contrasted with a style of explanation in which one makes things intelligible by representing their coming into being as a particular instance of how things generally tend to happen (McDowell 1985: 389).

However, even the proponents of the anomalousness of the mental view acknowledge that the mental is somehow dependent on the physical. Indeed, it was Donald Davidson, one of the advocates of both the normativity of folk psychology and the incommensurability between folk psychology and scientific psychology, who played the key role in bringing to general attention the most prominent idea of how to understand this dependence, namely the supervenience relation Davidson 1970).

Supervenience comes in many flavors, but the crucial component of this idea is that A properties supervene on B properties if a difference in B properties entails a difference in A properties (McLaughlin and Bennett 2014). In the discussed context, the properties of the mind understood from the folk psychological perspective are supervenient on the properties of the mind understood from the scientific perspective. Supervenience relation is attractive for the proponents of the normativity of folk psychology because it seems compatible not only with the claim that folk psychology in not superfluous – it has something to say about the architecture of the mind – but also with the claim that folk psychology is irreducible to scientific psychology. The former claim rests on the assumption that folk psychological explanation, despite its normativity, is causal on par with causal explanations in scientific explanation. To explain and to predict behavior, both folk psychologists and experimental psychologists construct hypothetical structures – models – the goal of which is to resemble the same object, i.e. the mind. There should be only some general pattern of similarity between these two types of models, for instance it seems that they both allow for such objects as beliefs or intentions.

In connection to the above mentioned distinction between the normativity of the conceptual and the cognitive layers of folk psychology, two notions of supervenience appear to be especially interesting: constitutive and causal (Searle 2002). Constitutive supervenience pertains to the conceptual layer of folk psychology. It means that our everyday mental concepts are constituted by our understanding of their semantical relations with other mental concepts. In the case of the normativity of the concept of belief, the semantical relations in question involve an understanding of what counts as adequate evidence and understanding that belief is subject to the evidential norm and that generating beliefs excludes other, non-evidential considerations. Causal supervenience pertains to the cognitive layer of folk psychology. It means that our folk psychological mental states are caused by the cognitive mechanisms designed to take into account only adequate evidence. These mechanisms may misfire, but their nature explains why beliefs are normative.

3 Legal Folk-Psychology

To a large extent law adopts the folk psychological view of the mind and legal folk psychology is normative in the above discussed manner. However, connecting the considerations pertaining to folk psychology and its normativity with legal considerations requires a proposal of a particular model of the psychology of the person assumed in legal contexts. As it was already mentioned, our everyday explanation of behavior is context-dependent and the idealizations we construct to describe the psychology of the target person will vary across situations. It appears that the model in question – which can be viewed as a conceptual bridge between law, philosophy and folk psychology – is the model according to which people are reason-responsive. For instance, referring to criminal Stephen Morse claims that:

> Criminal law presupposes a "folk psychological" view of the person and behavior. This psychological theory explains behavior in part by mental states such as desires, beliefs, intentions, willings, and plans. Biological, other psychological and sociological variables also play a causal role, but folk psychology considers mental states as fundamental to a full causal explanation and understanding of human action. Lawyers, philosophers and scientists argue about the definitions of mental states and theories of action, but that does not undermine the general claim that mental states are fundamental. Indeed, the arguments and evidence disputants use to convince others presuppose folk psychological view of the person. (...) Brief reflection should indicate that the law's psychology must be a folk psychological theory, a view of the person as a conscious (and potentially self-conscious) creature who forms and acts on intentions that are the product of the person's other mental states. We are the sort of creatures that can act for and respond to reasons. The law treats persons generally as intentional creatures and not simply as mechanistic forces of nature (Morse 2001: 115–116).

Reason-responsiveness is a philosophical construct, aimed to express the folk psychological assumptions concerning the conditions under which people can be held morally responsible. The basic idea is that people who are reason-responsive are sensitive to rational considerations in the appropriate way (Fischer and Ravizza 1998). To explicate the normativity of reason-responsiveness, it will be useful to break it down into two more specific abilities:

(1) The ability to recognize reasons and.
(2) The ability to follow reasons.

Both of these abilities are necessary for reason-responsiveness. When a person recognizes a reason she is aware of her beliefs and desires which form the reason in question, she reflects on these beliefs and desires and regards some of them as persuasive. For example, if a person bought a computer because it had the best price/performance ratio, she was aware that the computer had the best price/performance ratio and came to conclusion that this the appropriate reason to buy it. On the other hand, reacting to reasons consists in being motivated by reasons. Referring to the previous example, if a person bought a computer *because* it had the best price/performance ratio her action was motivated by the fact that the computer had the best price/performance ratio. On this account, when we are talking about reasons we are talking about the components of the person's decision-making process which resulted in the action in question, and we assume that this process really occurred.

The distinction between recognizing reasons and reacting to reasons is useful, because sometimes a person can lack the former but have the latter or she can lack both. Referring to the example of belief, these abilities may be described in the following way:

(1*) The ability to recognize adequate evidential reasons when generating beliefs and.
(2*) The ability to react to adequate evidential reasons when generating beliefs.

It is worth noting that both abilities should be understood dispositionally, as tendencies to recognize and to follow evidential reasons. If they would be understood as necessary conditions for belief formation, it would obviously be a too strong requirement. It can be illustrated on the following examples. In the case of the lack of the ability to recognize adequate evidential reasons, we can refer to the phenomenon of self-deception, which consists in believing that *p* even in the face of strong evidential reasons which undermine this belief. Self-deceivers are unable to recognize these evidential reasons, i.e. they have the tendency to not to recognize them. It seems that such beliefs are usually not the products of conscious deliberation because beliefs which are generated in such a manner tend to follow the evidential rule of belief. This does not entail that self-deceivers are completely unable to recognize evidential reasons. It only points to the fact that in certain situations they lack the ability to recognize evidential reasons, and as a consequence in these situations they lack reason-responsiveness.

In the case of the lack of the ability to react to adequate evidential reasons we can refer to the phenomenon of *akrasia* – weakness of will – which consists in an action which is inconsistent with the belief about what is the rational thing to do. Acratic behavior, however, leads to the satisfaction of a strong desire. On the one hand, the acratic person believes that a particular action is the correct action in the given circumstances, and this belief is generated by her recognizing evidential reasons. However, because the person is unable to react to the evidential reasons in the appropriate manner, she behaves acratically. Similarly to the case of self-deception, persons who act acratically should not be understood as unable to react to evidential reasons *tout court*. This ability is limited in the context of their acratic behavior.

In the legal context, the lack of the ability to recognize reasons can be observed in minors or people who suffer from certain mental disorders. Such people have the access to their beliefs and desires, they can be motivated by them, but they are unable to weigh them appropriately, and their motivation may be unintelligible for us. As a consequence, such people usually are not legally responsible for their actions. As for the lack of the ability to react to reasons, it can be observed in the case of the actions influenced by emotions. On the one hand, emotional influence does not exclude the ability to recognize reasons, but, on the other hand, acting on the basis of emotion often excludes the possibility of reacting to reasons appropriately. This is because reacting to reasons in an appropriate manner requires deliberation, a process of reflecting on the relevant beliefs and desires and regarding some of them as persuasive. As R. Jay Wallace remarks:

> It is important to our conception of persons as rational agents (...) that practical deliberation be correctly related to motivation. In particular, the motivation and actions of rational agents are guided by and responsive to their deliberative reflection about what they have reason to do. Unless this guidance condition (as we may call it) can be satisfied, we will not be able to make sense of the idea that persons are genuine agents, capable of determining what they shall do through the process of deliberation (Wallace 2006: 44).

Of course, people are held legally responsible for actions even if they were influenced by emotions and it seems that it is a justified practice. To explain how it is possible from the perspective of reason-responsiveness, it is worth reminding that reason-responsiveness should be understood dispositionally. It means that one may be morally responsible for an action independently of the actual reasons in the light of which and on the ground of which he acted. And even when one acts without deliberation it does not follow that he is not legally responsible for the action in question. What matters is whether – at the time of acting – he was able to recognize reasons and respond to them. For instance, it seems that when a person commits a crime because of her anger she still has the ability to recognize and to react to reasons even if she did not exercise this ability when she acted. If this is the case, such a person – in a similar situation – would be able to reflect about her reasons and override the "emotional" decision.

However, legal responsibility is sometimes ascribed even in situations when the person was unable to appropriately weigh her reasons. The simplest example is when a drunk driver runs someone over. At the moment of the action, the driver lacks the ability to recognize reasons but, nevertheless, we feel that he should be legally responsible. To allow for holding such a person legally responsible, in the legal context reason-responsiveness is coupled with a historical understanding of responsibility. On this account, when reflecting about legal responsibility for certain actions, one should look for reason-responsiveness at various places along the way to the action. For instance, when the action is "produced" directly by the cognitive mechanism which is not reason-responsive, and the lack of reason-responsiveness is caused by alcohol, it is possible to find a moment before the driver got himself into reason-unresponsive state when he could foresee – because he was reason-responsive at that moment – that alcohol will cause his reason-unresponsiveness.

Legal folk psychology grounded in reason-responsiveness is normative at the conceptual level and at the cognitive level. At the conceptual level, reason-responsiveness is constitutively supervenient on our understanding of, *inter alia*, reasons, and the abilities to recognize and to react to reasons. It may be argued that the reason-responsiveness model is not, strictly speaking, a folk psychological model of the person, because it is not used in everyday situations to explain behaviour. But it is worth remembering that the model required in legal contexts should be refined enough to allow for a conceptual linkage between behavioral sciences and legal practice. For instance, in some criminal cases it will be the behavioral scientists who will determine the state of the mind of the defendant at the moment of his action and the legal decision concerning his responsibility will be heavily influenced by their opinion. On the other hand, what law requires should be understandable for the lay person. To make it understandable in such a way, legal folk psychology appears to inherit the folk psychological assumption of the normativity of the mental.

At the cognitive level, reason-responsiveness is causally supervenient on the cognitive mechanisms which generate reasons and underlie our abilities to recognize and to react to reasons. In legal contexts it is not only necessary that we understand people as reason-responsive to treat them as agents. The second requirement is that people should actually be reason-responsive, although in a limited, dispositional manner. When ascriptions of responsibility refer to mental states which constitute reasons – which people are able to recognize and react to – the mental states are understood as the causes of the behavior. If in reality people would not be reason-responsive – because there would be no actual mechanisms designed to enable reason-responsiveness – but only appeared this way through folk psychological lenses, then the foundational facts for legal responsibility ascriptions would be mistaken (Morse 2001).

4 Empirical Challenges to Reason-Responsiveness

It has come to the attention of some philosophers that empirical evidence from different areas of cognitive sciences seems to challenge common sense understanding of the mind. The evidence in question can be divided into two types. The first type of challenges are aimed against the very possibility, both conceptual and causal, of the existence of reason-responsiveness. Here, the empirical evidence suggests that it is an illusion that people recognize and react to reasons. The second category pertains to the fact that reason-responsiveness is conceptualized as a unified ability – an ability which is realized by cognitive processes of a single type. However, according to an influential, scientific understanding of cognition, it is realized by two types of cognitive processes, and only one of them appears to be manifestly compatible with reason-responsiveness.

The experimental evidence of the first type appears to support a view that people lack direct access to the causes of their actions and that folk psychological reason-based explanations are not genuine causal explanations, but only rationalizations, or instances of theorizing or self-interpretation. An interesting example is the study by Michael Storms and Richard Nisbett, who ran an experiment on insomniacs, the partial goal of which was to help their insomnia (Nisbett and Wilson 1977). They asked insomniac subjects to record the time they went to bed and the time they finally fell asleep. After several days, one group of subjects was given a placebo pill to take before going to bed. They were told that the pill would produce typical symptoms of insomnia, such as rapid heart rate, breathing irregularities, bodily warmth and alertness. The second group of subjects was told that the pills would produce the opposite symptoms and reduce their insomnia.

The counterintuitive result was that the subjects in the first group ended up getting to sleep quicker and easier than the group that was given the pill that was supposed to reduce arousal. The first group felt aroused before they went to sleep – because they are insomniacs – but then attributed this arousal to the pill and not to the sleeping situation, which reduced their sleep-based anxiety and allowed them to go to sleep quicker and easier. The subjects in the relaxation group had their insomnia deepened because they too felt aroused before sleep but since they took a pill which was supposed to reduce arousal they then "overattributed" their arousal to the sleep situation, unconsciously reasoning that since they should be feeling less arousal than normal and yet are still feeling aroused, sleeping must really be an anxiety inducing endeavor. Arousal group subjects got to sleep 28% faster on the nights they took the pill, while relaxation subjects took 42% longer to get to sleep. What is perhaps even more interesting, however, is the second part of the study. After the completion of the initial insomnia experiments, the members of the arousal group were informed that they had gotten to sleep more quickly after taking the pill, and the members of the relaxation group were informed that they had taken longer to fall asleep. Subject in both groups were asked why this happened, and the experimenters report the following pattern of responses:

> Arousal subjects typically replied that they usually found it easier to get to sleep later in the week, or that they had taken an exam that had worried them but had done well on it and could now relax, or that problems with a roommate or girlfriend seemed on their way to resolution. Relaxation subjects were able to find similar sorts of reasons to explain their increased sleeplessness. When subjects were asked if they had thought about the pills at all before getting to sleep, they almost uniformly insisted that after taking the pills they had completely forgot about them. When asked if it had occurred to them that the pill might be producing (or counteracting) the arousal symptoms, they reiterated their insistence that they had not thought about the pills at all after taking them. Finally, the experimental hypothesis and the postulated attribution process were described in detail. Subjects showed no recognition of the hypothesized process and made little pretense of believing that any of the subjects could have gone through such processes (Nisbett and Wilson 1977: 238).

From the perspective of reason-responsiveness, it should be noted that experiments of this kind cannot show that people are generally reason-unresponsive, but only that there are cases when the reasons we think are the causes of our actions are not genuine causes of the actions in question. In the Storms-Nisbett experiment, it seems that the subjects lacked the ability to react to their reasons, because the cognitive mechanisms which were responsible for subjects' verbal responses in the second stage of the experiment were different from the cognitive mechanisms which actually operated and caused the reduction or the intensification of their insomnia. It also seems that they were unable to recognize reasons, because they did not believe the experimenters when they were told about the experimental hypothesis and the postulated attribution process. All of this suggests that their reason-responsiveness was limited only in context of the experimental situation. In their seminal paper on the cognitive impenetrability of higher cognitive processes, Richard Nisbett and Timothy Wilson claimed that the experimental evidence does not exclude the possibility that "people can sometimes accurately report on the stimuli that influenced particular cognitive process" (Nisbett and Wilson 1977: 253).

Furthermore, it should be noted that the explanation of the empirical evidence by Storms and Nisbett – why the subjects in the arousal group usually fell asleep quicker and why the subjects in the relaxation group usually fell asleep slower – works only when people are granted the ability to assess beliefs and reason unconsciously. This raises the issue of reason-responsiveness outside conscious deliberation. The explanation proposed by the attribution theory assumes that the subjects in question were able to respond to reasons but on the unconscious, automatic level. Although reason-responsiveness is usually understood as connected with conscious deliberation – in the case of which people are able to verbalize the weighted reasons – the naturalness of adopting the reason-responsiveness stance in connection to the operation of the unconscious mind suggests that constitutive supervenience of reason responsiveness on our folk psychological conceptual framework remains intact. The interesting issue is how rules of rationality may play a role also at the level of automatic mental system, which mediates behavior but which may be cognitively inaccessible. Some of the mechanisms operating at this level may be designed in such a way as to recognize and react to reasons – at least in a limited manner – which may support causal supervenience of reason-responsiveness on underlying cognitive mechanisms.

The second category of empirical challenges to reason-responsiveness is connected with the so-called dual system theory of cognition. In philosophy, it has been common to assume that reason-responsiveness is of one piece – i.e. that there is a single mechanism or faculty of practical reason that is responsive to reasons for action. In particular, it has been common to assume that one and the same mechanism is operative during both reflective deliberation and decision-making.

In contrast, cognitive sciences have developed a different understanding of cognition, according to which cognition is realized by two types of processes (Evans and Stanovich 2013). According to this influential view of the architecture of the mind, there are cognitive processes which belong to system 1 – the intuitive system – which operate in a fast, automatic manner, they do not require working memory and usually only their results are accessible in introspection. The intuitive system is the default system for cognition. System 2 – the analytical system – includes processes which are usually slow and controlled, which heavily burden working memory. Also, their operation is – at least to some extent – available to consciousness. The analytical system is activated rarely, because it is cognitively demanding. It intervenes when the situation is new, difficult, and the person is sufficiently motivated to devote her limited cognitive resources to override the intuitive judgment.

The role of system 1 in the context of reason-responsiveness can be illustrated by referring to the phenomenon of implicit bias which consists in evaluations of social groups that are largely outside of conscious awareness (Brownstein and Saul 2016). For instance, some research suggests that most people, often in spite of their conscious beliefs, values and attitudes, have implicit biases and that those biases impact social behavior in many ways. Implicit racial biases are thought to cause people to give more favourable evaluations of otherwise identical resumes if those resumes belong to participants with stereotypically white names than if they belong to participants with stereotypically black names (Bertrand and Mullainathan 2004; Fryer and Levitt 2004). It appears then that some people may have two conflicting mental states which guide their actions. One is consciously accessible, unbiased and generated by the controlled cognitive processes and the other is consciously inaccessible, biased, and generated by the automatic processes. What is interesting is that the mental concepts referring to the latter states are not constitutively supervenient on our other everyday mental concepts. Their semantical relations seem arbitrary from the folk psychological perspective. For instance, biased beliefs do not seem to be governed by the evidential rule. Furthermore, mental states generated by system 1 are not causally supervenient on the mechanisms which are designed to respond to the appropriate rules of rationality. There is a large body of research which suggests that cognitive processes forming the intuitive system are responsible for many biases in reasoning and decision making (Evans 2008).

Also, biased responses may heavily influence the analytical system, which can be unable to override the normatively incorrect judgment or decision. This is because slow, analytical thinking requires considerable amount of mental effort (Kahneman 2011).

Given the ubiquitous nature of system 1, the challenge against legal folk psychology presented by the dual system theory of cognition is a serious one. Despite the fact that system 2 looks like consisting of processes which support reason-responsiveness – they are supposed to be at work during conscious deliberation – it is not obvious whether system 1 also has this feature, and if so, to what extent. The difficulties pertaining to the claim that system 1 is reason-responsive are connected with the abilities to recognize reasons and to react to reasons (Brożek 2013). For instance, how could it be possible to weigh the beliefs and desires in an unconscious and automatic manner? Or how it could be possible for system 1 to react to the appropriate reasons when it appears that it can be relatively easily influenced by unconscious, "inappropriate" reasons? Such questions are difficult to answer because nonconscious cognition and influences are often viewed as "alien to the agent" (Churchland and Suhler 2014). One of the solutions for legal folk psychology to stay in touch with the behavioural sciences is to explain how, in the light of the above discussed empirical findings, reason-responsiveness could be both causally and constitutively supervenient on the mind as it is viewed from the scientific perspective.

5 Conclusion

In this chapter it was argued that folk psychology – conceived as our everyday understanding of other minds – is normative at the conceptual and at the cognitive level. At the conceptual level, our everyday mental concepts constitutively supervene on our understanding of their semantical relations with other mental concepts. This gives rise to normativity because when one understands at least some of these mental concepts – such as the concept of belief – one necessarily conceives of the corresponding attitudes as governed by rules of rationality. At the cognitive level, our folk psychological mental states causally supervene on cognitive mechanisms which enable us to follow the rules of rationality. Legal folk psychology, which can be reconstructed as the view according to which people are reason-responsive, adopts the normative understanding of the mind. Reason-responsiveness consists in being able to recognize reasons and to appropriately react to them which are – in essence – normative abilities, i.e. their assessment depends on what one ought to think or do in a particular situation. In the last part of the chapter, selected empirical challenges to reason-responsiveness were examined. It was argued that there is empirical evidence suggesting that our legal folk psychology should be amended to take into account the action-guiding mental states which is are inaccessible from the folk psychological perspective.

References

Adler, Jonathan. 2002. Belief's Own Ethics. Cambridge, MA: MIT Press.
Andrews, Kristen. 2012. Do Apes Read Minds? Toward a New Folk Psychology. Cambridge, MA: MIT Press.
Bertrand, Marianne, Sendhil Mullainathan. 2004. Are Emily and Greg More Employable than Lakisha and Jamal? A Field Experiment on Labor Market Discrimination. American Economic Review 94: 991–1013.
Brownstein, Michael, Jenifer Saul eds. 2016. Implicit Bias and Philosophy. Volume I: Metaphysics and Epistemology, Oxford: Oxford University Press.
Brożek, Bartosz. 2013. Rule-Following. From Imitation to the Normative Mind, Kraków: Copernicus Center Press.
Bykvist, Krister, Hattiangadi, Anandi. 2007. Does Thought Imply Ought?. Analysis 67: 277–285.
Churchland, Patricia Smith, Christopher Suhler. 2014. Agency and Control: The Subcortical Role in Good Decisions. In: *Moral Psychology. Volume 4: Free Will and Moral Responsibility*, ed. Walter Sinnott-Armstrong, Cambridge, 309–326. Cambridge, MA: MIT Press.
Davidson, Donald. 1970. Mental Events. In: *Experience and Theory*, eds. Lawrence Foster, Joe William Swanson, 207–227. Amherst, MA: University of Massachusetts Press.
Dennett, Daniel. 1987. The Intentional Stance. Cambridge, MA: MIT Press.
Evans, Jonathan. 2008. Dual-Processing Accounts of Reasoning, Judgment and Social Cognition. Annual Review of Psychology 59: 255–78.
Evans, Jonathan, Keith Stanovich. 2013. Dual-Process Theories of Higher Cognition: Advancing the Debate. Perspectives on Psychological Science 8: 223–241.
Fischer, John Martin, Mark Ravizza. 1998. Responsibility and Control: A Theory of Moral Responsibility. New York: Cambridge University Press.
Fryer, Roland, Steven Levitt. 2004. The Causes and Consequences of Distinctively Black Names. The Quarterly Journal of Economics 119: 767–805.
Godfrey-Smith, Peter. 2005. Folk Psychology as a Model. Philosophers' Imprint 5: 1–16.
Hutto, Daniel. 2008. Folk Psychological Narratives: The Sociocultural Basis of Understanding Reasons, Cambridge, MA: MIT Press.
Kahneman, Daniel. 2011. Thinking, fast and slow, New York: Farrar, Straus and Giroux.
Lillard, Angeline. 1998. Ethnopsychologies: Cultural Variations in Theories of Mind. Psychological Bulletin 123: 3–32.
Maibom, Heidi. 2003. The Mindreader and the Scientist. Mind and Language 18: 296–315.
McDowell, John. 1985. Functionalism and Anomalous Monism. In: *Action and Events*, eds. Ernest Lepore, Brian McLaughlin, 387–98. Oxford: Blackwell.
McHugh, Conor, Daniel Whiting. 2014. Recent Work on the Normativity of Belief. Analysis 74: 698–713.
McLaughlin, Brian, Karen Bennett. 2014. Supervenience. In: The Stanford Encyclopedia of Philosophy, ed. Edward N. .Zalta. http://plato.stanford.edu/archives/spr2014/entries/supervenience/. Accessed 10 July 2015.
Morris, Michael, Kaiping Peng. 1994. Culture and Cause: American and Chinese Attributions for Social and Physical Events. Journal of Personality and Social Psychology 67: 949–971.
Morse, Stephen. 2001. Neuroscience and the Future of Personhood and Responsibility. In: *Constitution 3.0: Freedom and Technical Change,* eds. Jeffrey Rosen, Benjamin Wittes, 113–129. Washington, D.C: Brookings Institution Press.
Nisbett, Richard, Timothy Wilson. 1977. Telling More Than We Can Know: Verbal Reports on Mental Processes. Psychological Review 84: 231–259.
Russell, James. 1991. Culture and the Categorization of Emotions. Psychological Bulletin 110: 426–450.

Searle, John. 2002. The Rediscovery of the Mind. Cambridge, MA: MIT Press.
Wallace, R. Jay. 2006. Normativity and the Will: Selected Essayson Moral Psychology and Practical Reason. Oxford: Clarendon Press.
Wimmer, Hans, Josef Perner. 1983. Beliefs about Beliefs: Representation and Constraining Function of Wrong Beliefs in Young Children Understanding of Deception. Cognition 13: 103–128.

MIX
Papier aus verantwortungsvollen Quellen
Paper from responsible sources
FSC® C105338

If you have any concerns about our products,
you can contact us on
ProductSafety@springernature.com

In case Publisher is established outside the EU,
the EU authorized representative is:
Springer Nature Customer Service Center GmbH
Europaplatz 3, 69115 Heidelberg, Germany

Printed by Libri Plureos GmbH
in Hamburg, Germany